WRITER: **JONATHAN HICKMAN**

ARTISTS: **JEROME OPEÑA** [ISSUES 1-3] & **ADAM KUBERT** [ISSUES 4-6]

COLOR ARTISTS: **DEAN WHITE** WITH **JUSTIN PONSOR, MORRY HOLLOWELL, FRANK MARTIN & RICHARD ISANOVE** [ISSUES 1-3]; **FRANK D'ARMATA** [ISSUE 4]; AND **FRANK MARTIN** [ISSUES 5-6]

LETTERER: **VC'S CORY PETIT**

COVER ART: **DUSTIN WEAVER & JUSTIN PONSOR**

ASSISTANT EDITOR: **JAKE THOMAS**

EDITORS: **TOM BREVOORT** WITH **LAUREN SANKOVITCH**

COLLECTION EDITOR: **JENNIFER GRÜNWALD**
ASSISTANT EDITORS: **ALEX STARBUCK & NELSON RIBEIRO**
EDITOR, SPECIAL PROJECTS: **MARK D. BEAZLEY**
SENIOR EDITOR, SPECIAL PROJECTS: **JEFF YOUNGQUIST**
SVP OF PRINT & DIGITAL PUBLISHING SALES: **DAVID GABRIEL**
BOOK DESIGN: **JEFF POWELL**

EDITOR IN CHIEF: **AXEL ALONSO**
CHIEF CREATIVE OFFICER: **JOE QUESADA**
PUBLISHER: **DAN BUCKLEY**
EXECUTIVE PRODUCER: **ALAN FINE**

AVENGERS VOL. 1: AVENGERS WORLD. Contains material originally published in magazine form as AVENGERS #1-6. First printing 2013. Hardcover ISBN# 978-0-7851-6823-2. Softcover ISBN# 978-0-7851-6652-8. Published by MARVEL WORLDWIDE, INC., a subsidiary of MARVEL ENTERTAINMENT, LLC. OFFICE OF PUBLICATION: 135 West 50th Street, New York, NY 10020. Copyright © 2012 and 2013 Marvel Characters, Inc. All rights reserved. All characters featured in this issue and the distinctive names and likenesses thereof, and all related indicia are trademarks of Marvel Characters, Inc. No similarity between any of the names, characters, persons, and/or institutions in this magazine with those of any living or dead person or institution is intended, and any such similarity which may exist is purely coincidental. **Printed in the U.S.A.** ALAN FINE, EVP - Office of the President, Marvel Worldwide, Inc. and EVP & CMO Marvel Characters B.V.; DAN BUCKLEY, Publisher & President - Print, Animation & Digital Divisions; JOE QUESADA, Chief Creative Officer; TOM BREVOORT, SVP of Publishing; DAVID BOGART, SVP of Operations & Procurement, Publishing; RUWAN JAYATILLEKE, SVP & Associate Publisher, Publishing; C.B. CEBULSKI, SVP of Creator & Content Development; DAVID GABRIEL, SVP of Print & Digital Publishing Sales; JIM O'KEEFE, VP of Operations & Logistics; DAN CARR, Executive Director of Publishing Technology; SUSAN CRESPI, Editorial Operations Manager; ALEX MORALES, Publishing Operations Manager; STAN LEE, Chairman Emeritus. For information regarding advertising in Marvel Comics or on Marvel.com, please contact Niza Disla, Director of Marvel Partnerships, at ndisla@marvel.com. For Marvel subscription inquiries, please call 800-217-9158. **Manufactured between 2/18/2013 and 3/22/2013 (hardcover), and 2/18/2013 and 11/22/2013 (softcover), by R.R. DONNELLEY, INC., SALEM, VA, USA.**

10 9 8 7 6 5 4 3 2 1

PREVIOUSLY IN AVENGERS

THERE WAS *NOTHING.*

FOLLOWED BY *EVERYTHING.*

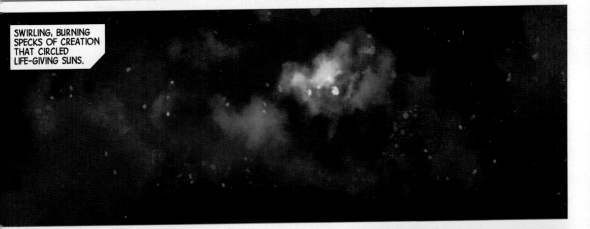

SWIRLING, BURNING SPECKS OF CREATION THAT CIRCLED LIFE-GIVING SUNS.

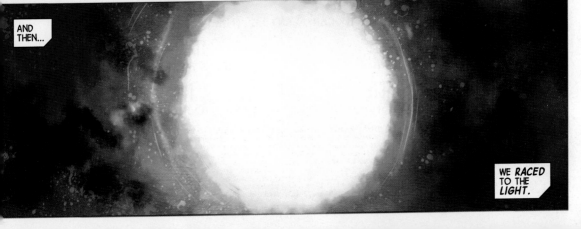

AND THEN...

WE *RACED* TO THE *LIGHT.*

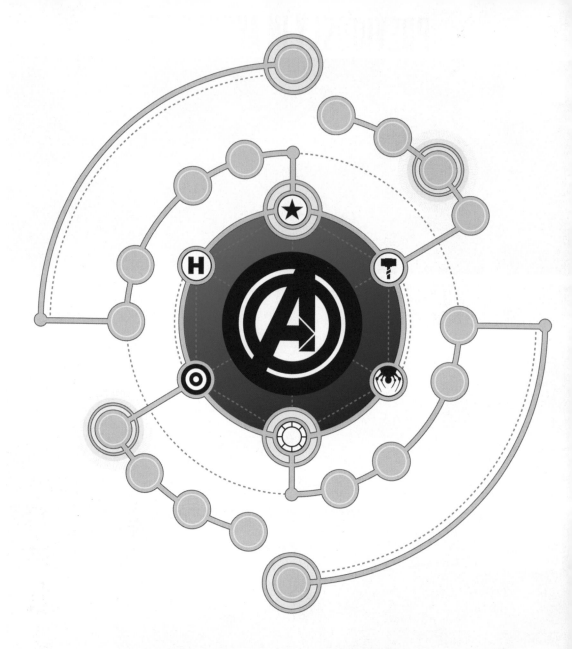

EARTH'S MIGHTIEST HEROES

CAPTAIN AMERICA
(Steve Rogers)

IRON MAN
(Tony Stark)

HAWKEYE
(Clint Barton)

BLACK WIDOW
(Natasha Romanova)

THE HULK
(Dr. Bruce Banner)

THOR
(Odinson)

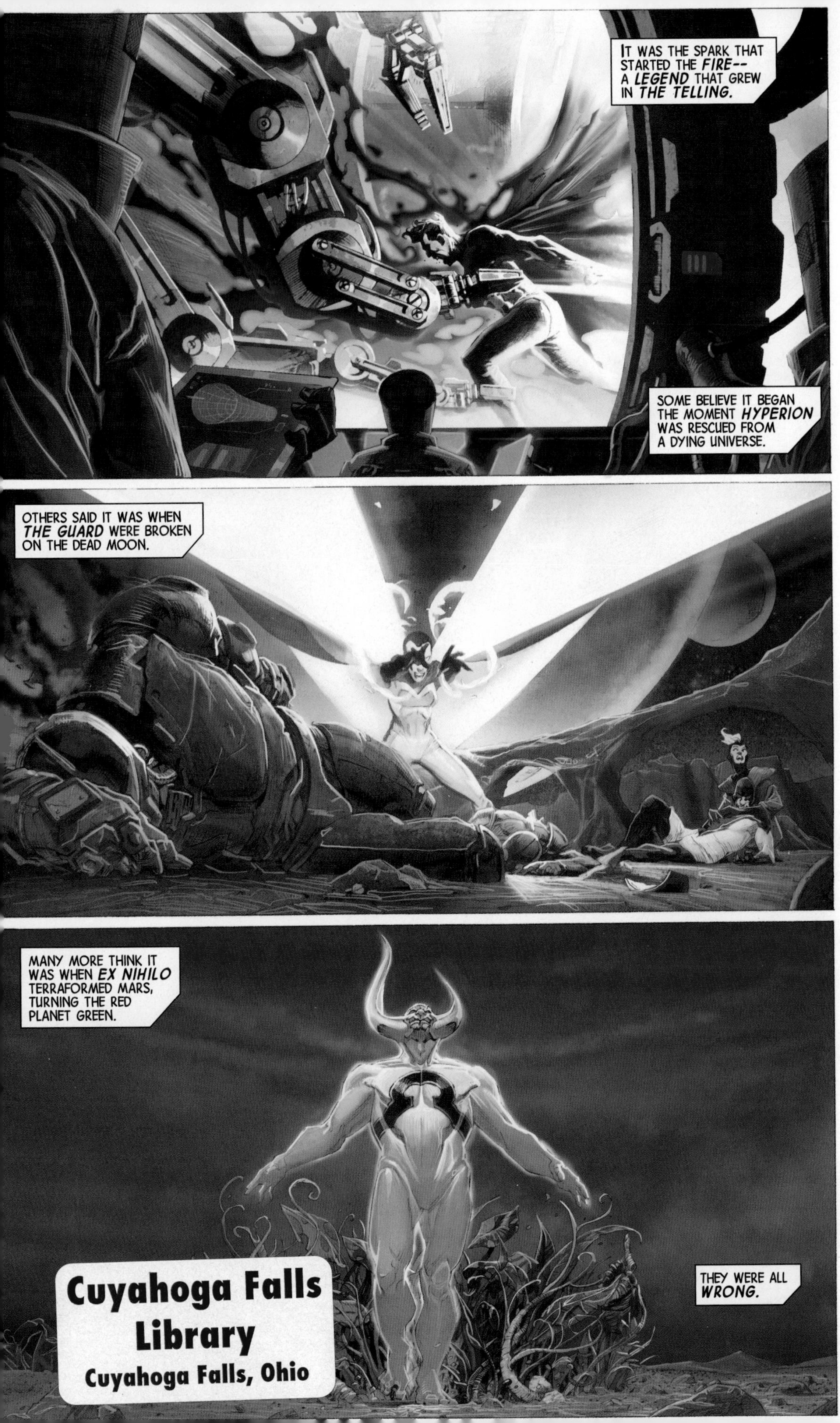
IT WAS THE SPARK THAT STARTED THE *FIRE--* A *LEGEND* THAT GREW IN *THE TELLING.*
SOME BELIEVE IT BEGAN THE MOMENT *HYPERION* WAS RESCUED FROM A DYING UNIVERSE.
OTHERS SAID IT WAS WHEN *THE GUARD* WERE BROKEN ON THE DEAD MOON.
MANY MORE THINK IT WAS WHEN *EX NIHILO* TERRAFORMED MARS, TURNING THE RED PLANET GREEN.
THEY WERE ALL *WRONG.*

AS IT HAPPENED BEFORE *THE LIGHT.*

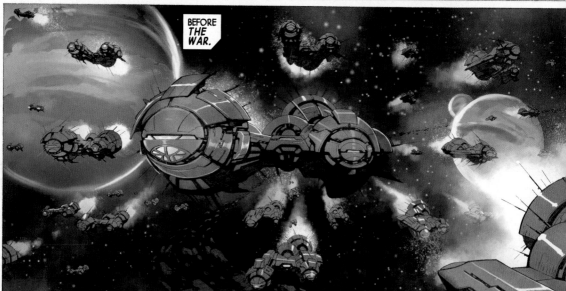

BEFORE *THE WAR.*

AND BEFORE *THE FALL.*

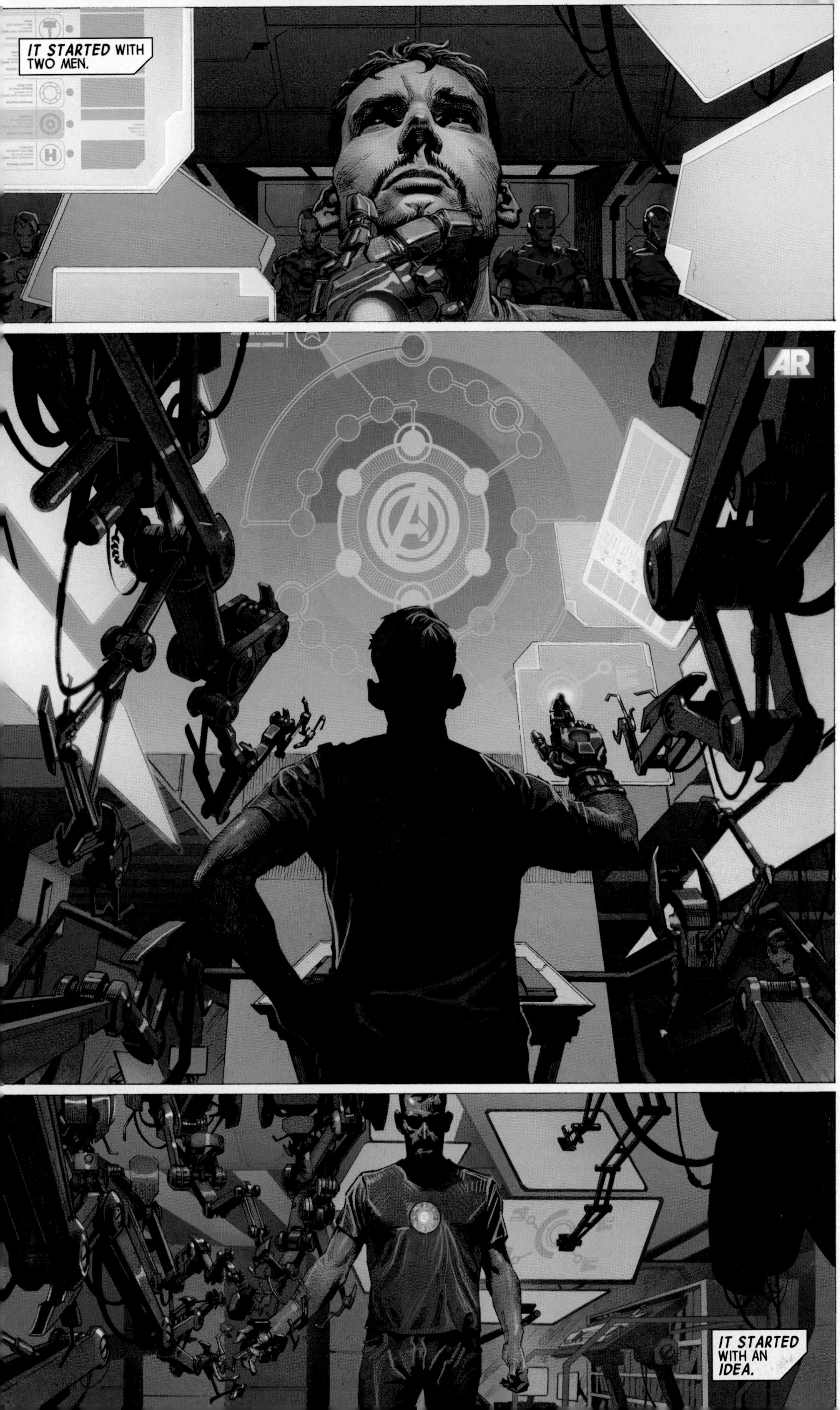
IT STARTED WITH TWO MEN.
AR
IT STARTED WITH AN IDEA.

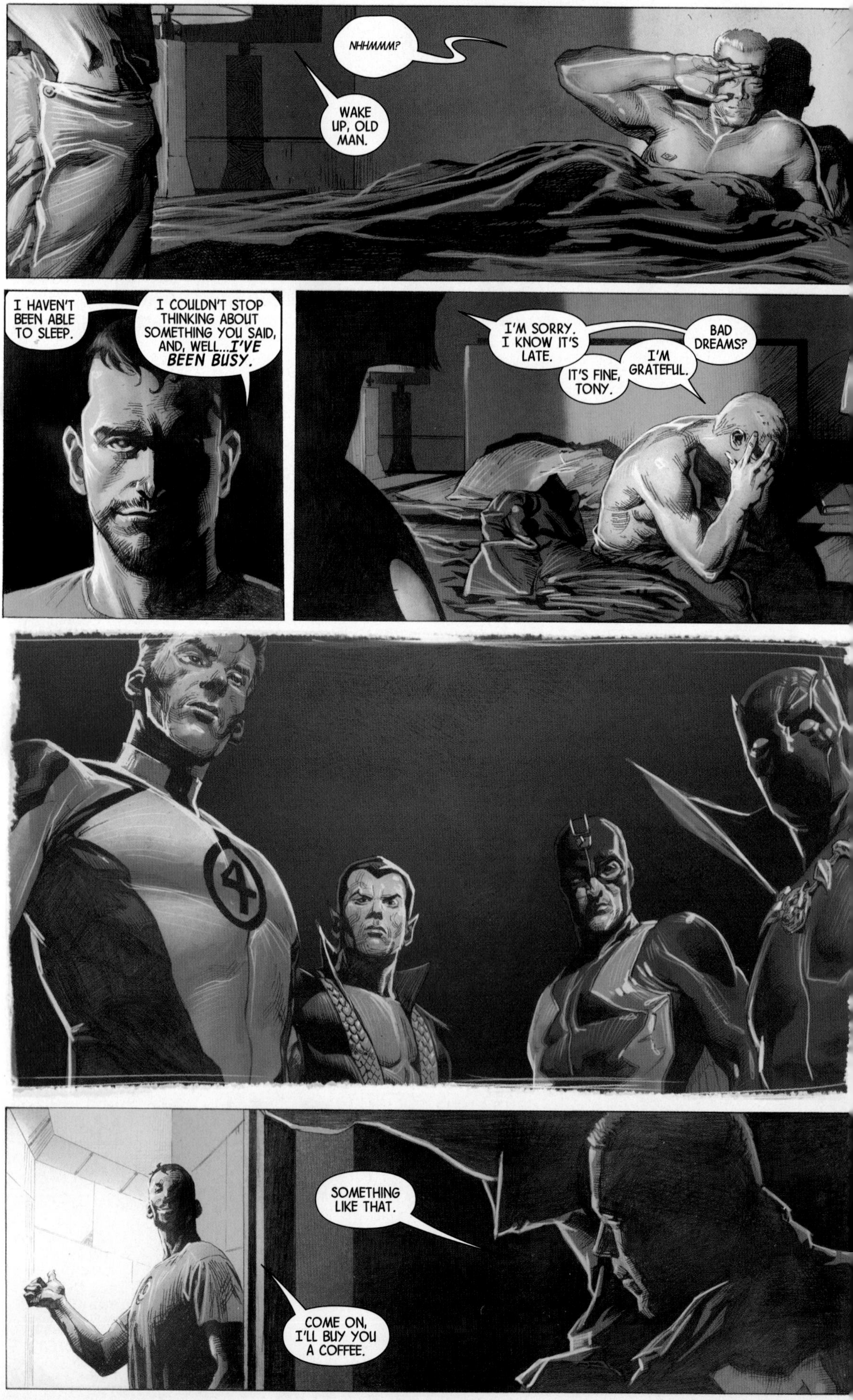
WAKE UP, OLD MAN.
NHHMMM?
I HAVEN'T BEEN ABLE TO SLEEP.
I COULDN'T STOP THINKING ABOUT SOMETHING YOU SAID, AND, WELL...*I'VE BEEN BUSY.*
I'M SORRY. I KNOW IT'S LATE.
BAD DREAMS?
IT'S FINE, TONY.
I'M GRATEFUL.
SOMETHING LIKE THAT.
COME ON, I'LL BUY YOU A COFFEE.

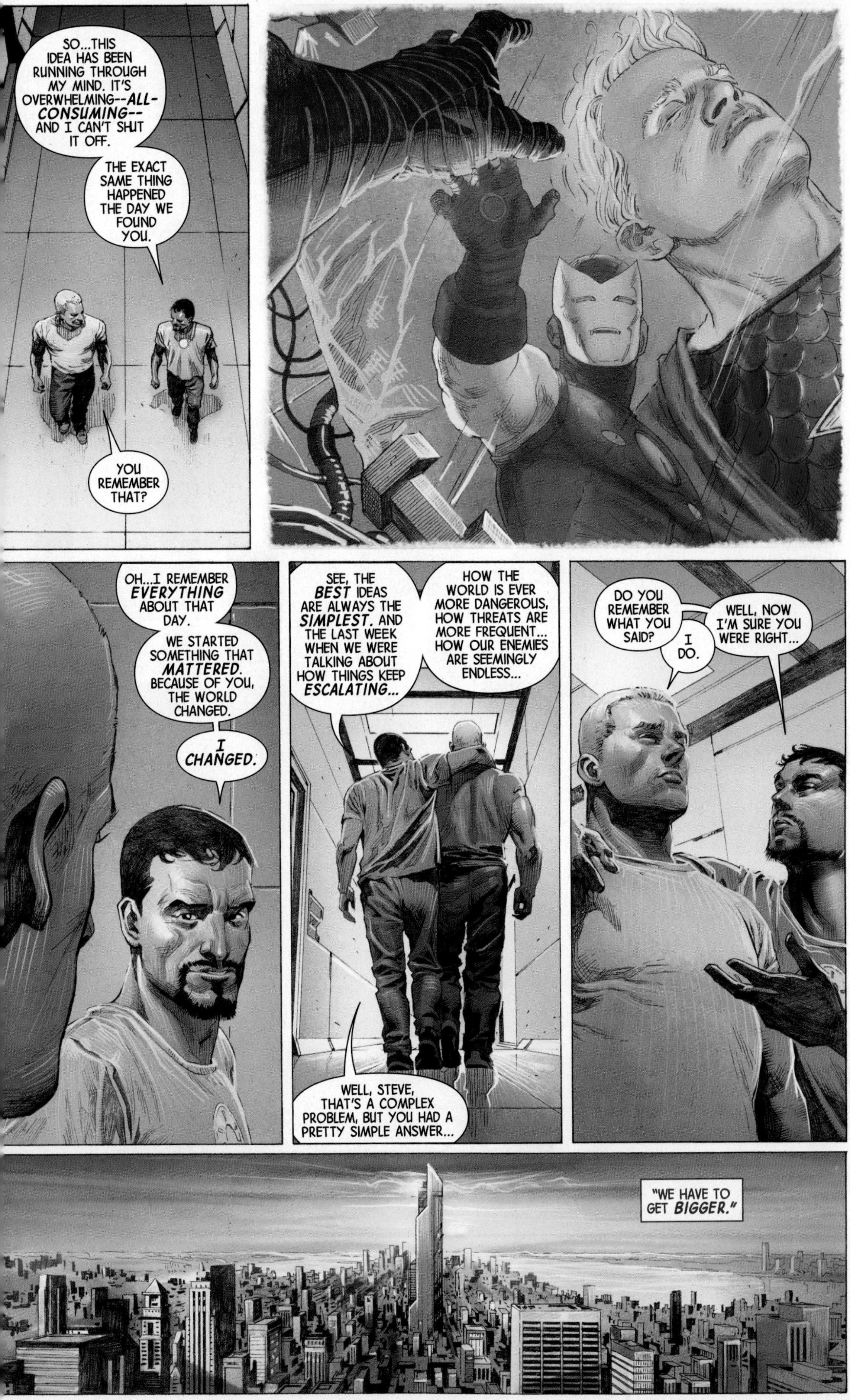
SO...THIS IDEA HAS BEEN RUNNING THROUGH MY MIND. IT'S OVERWHELMING--*ALL-CONSUMING*-- AND I CAN'T SHUT IT OFF.
THE EXACT SAME THING HAPPENED THE DAY WE FOUND YOU.
YOU REMEMBER THAT?
OH...I REMEMBER *EVERYTHING* ABOUT THAT DAY.
WE STARTED SOMETHING THAT *MATTERED*. BECAUSE OF YOU, THE WORLD CHANGED.
I CHANGED.
SEE, THE *BEST* IDEAS ARE ALWAYS THE *SIMPLEST.* AND THE LAST WEEK WHEN WE WERE TALKING ABOUT HOW THINGS KEEP *ESCALATING*...
HOW THE WORLD IS EVER MORE DANGEROUS, HOW THREATS ARE MORE FREQUENT... HOW OUR ENEMIES ARE SEEMINGLY ENDLESS...
WELL, STEVE, THAT'S A COMPLEX PROBLEM, BUT YOU HAD A PRETTY SIMPLE ANSWER...
DO YOU REMEMBER WHAT YOU SAID?
I DO.
WELL, NOW I'M SURE YOU WERE RIGHT...
"WE HAVE TO GET *BIGGER.*"

THE AVENGERS:

AVENGER

S WORLD

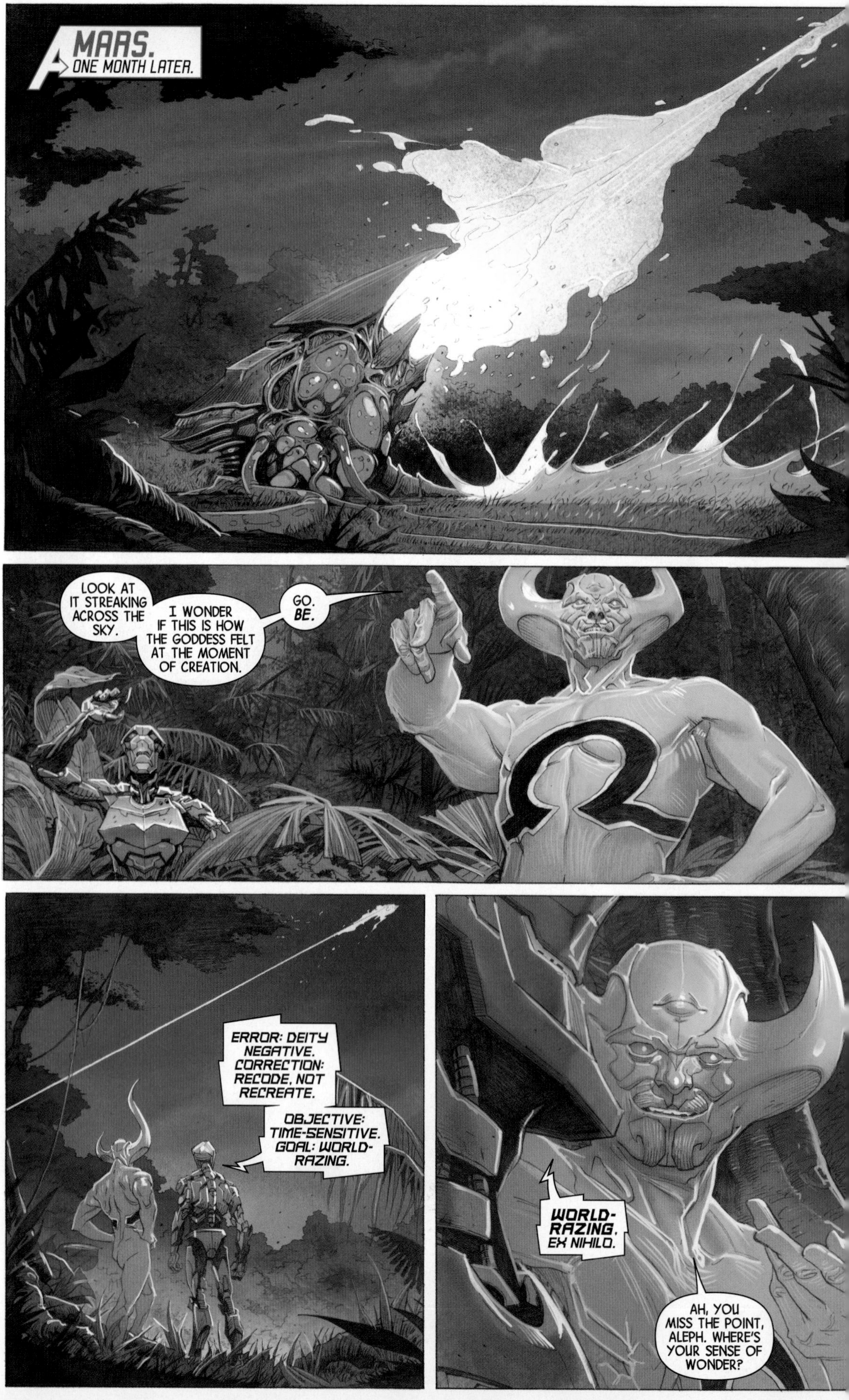
MARS.
ONE MONTH LATER.
LOOK AT IT STREAKING ACROSS THE SKY.
I WONDER IF THIS IS HOW THE GODDESS FELT AT THE MOMENT OF CREATION.
GO. BE.
ERROR: DEITY NEGATIVE. CORRECTION: RECODE, NOT RECREATE.
OBJECTIVE: TIME-SENSITIVE. GOAL: WORLD-RAZING.
WORLD-RAZING, EX NIHILO.
AH, YOU MISS THE POINT, ALEPH. WHERE'S YOUR SENSE OF WONDER?

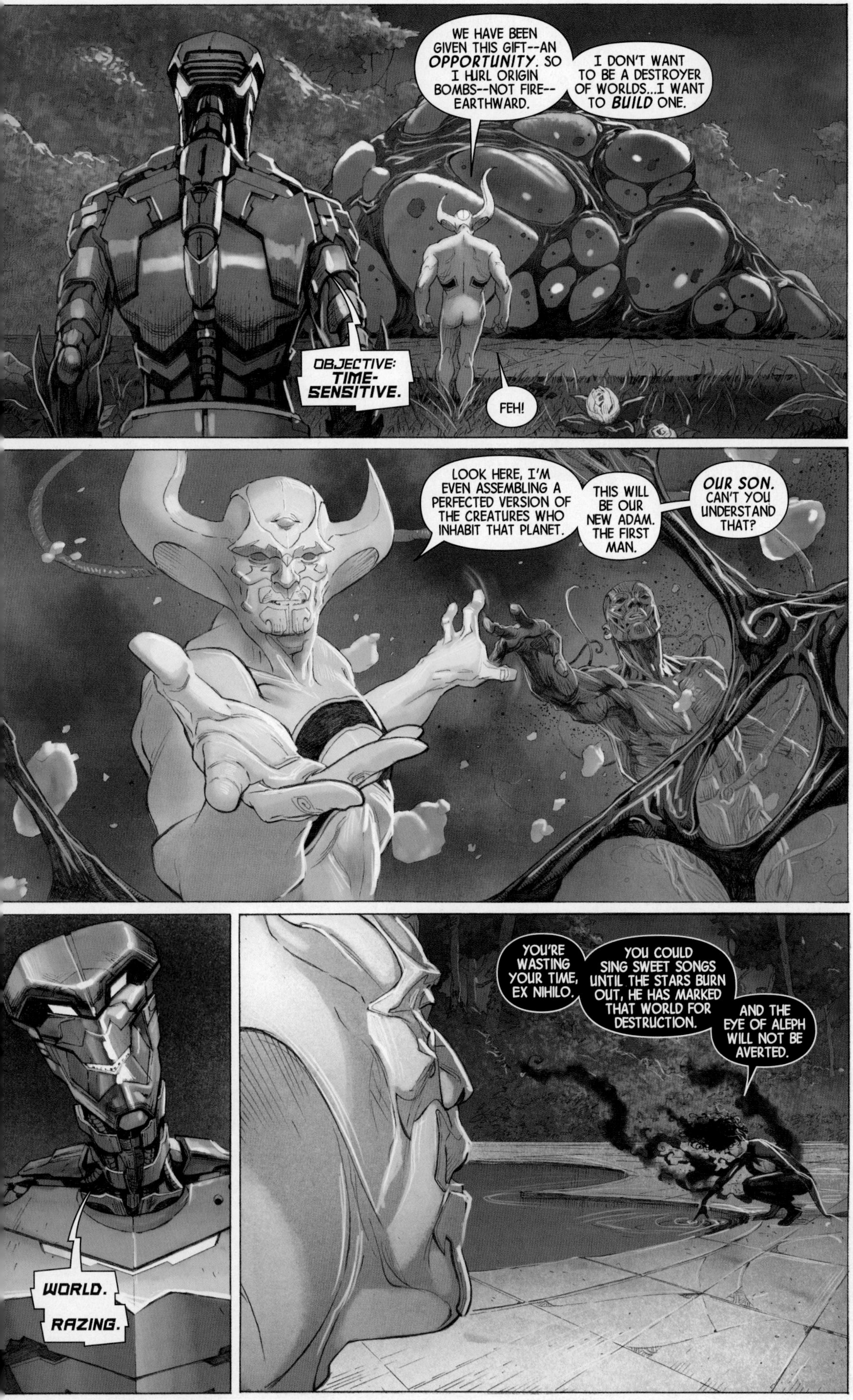

WE HAVE BEEN GIVEN THIS GIFT--AN OPPORTUNITY. SO I HURL ORIGIN BOMBS--NOT FIRE--EARTHWARD.
I DON'T WANT TO BE A DESTROYER OF WORLDS...I WANT TO BUILD ONE.
OBJECTIVE: TIME-SENSITIVE.
FEH!
LOOK HERE, I'M EVEN ASSEMBLING A PERFECTED VERSION OF THE CREATURES WHO INHABIT THAT PLANET.
THIS WILL BE OUR NEW ADAM. THE FIRST MAN.
OUR SON. CAN'T YOU UNDERSTAND THAT?
WORLD.
RAZING.
YOU'RE WASTING YOUR TIME, EX NIHILO.
YOU COULD SING SWEET SONGS UNTIL THE STARS BURN OUT, HE HAS MARKED THAT WORLD FOR DESTRUCTION.
AND THE EYE OF ALEPH WILL NOT BE AVERTED.

AND WHAT ABOUT YOU, ABYSS?

WHAT DO YOU SEE?

OH, I SEE THINGS FOR WHAT THEY ARE.

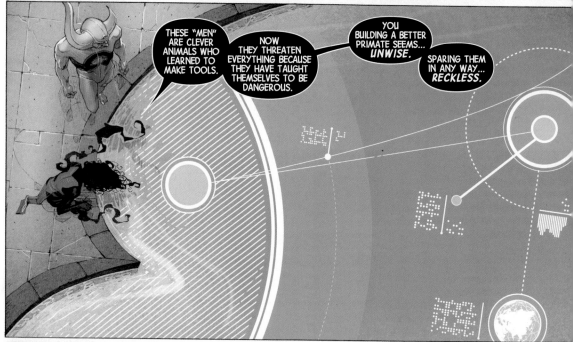

THESE "MEN" ARE CLEVER ANIMALS WHO LEARNED TO MAKE TOOLS.

NOW THEY THREATEN EVERYTHING BECAUSE THEY HAVE TAUGHT THEMSELVES TO BE DANGEROUS.

YOU BUILDING A BETTER PRIMATE SEEMS... *UNWISE.*

SPARING THEM IN ANY WAY... *RECKLESS.*

LOOK! SEE HOW AGGRESSIVE THEY ARE?

THEY'VE SENT HEROES TO STOP US, EX NIHILO. *THEIR VERY BEST.*

ACQUIRING...

APES.

INCOMING.

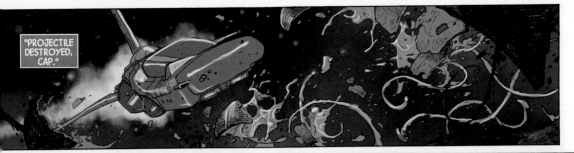

"PROJECTILE DESTROYED, CAP."

NICELY DONE, CLINT.

I MARKED, AND RECORDED, THE TRAJECTORY. BLACK WIDOW SHOULD BE ABLE TO FOLLOW--

GOT IT. PLOTTED, AND WE'RE LOCKED ON. SETTING A COURSE TO SLIP US IN ALONG THE HORIZON.

THEY WON'T SEE US COMING.

VEGETATION? IS THAT EVEN POSSIBLE.

I DON'T KNOW WHY IT WOULDN'T BE...

THERE IT IS!

PREPARE FOR LANDING.

IT'S...IT'S GREEN.

"THE FIRST TWO BOMBS THAT HIT EARTH COMPLETELY CHANGED THE BIOSPHERES OF THE IMPACT ZONES.

"WHOEVER THESE PEOPLE ARE, THEY'VE ALTERED BILLIONS OF YEARS OF EVOLUTION IN MINUTES."

AND THEY DID IT BY REMOTE, FROM OVER TWO HUNDRED MILLION KILOMETERS AWAY. AN IMPRESSIVE FEAT...

GODLIKE EVEN.

PFFT!

BRUCE, YOU'RE BETTER AT THIS STUFF THAN I AM. ANYTHING ELSE THAT NEEDS TO BE SAID?

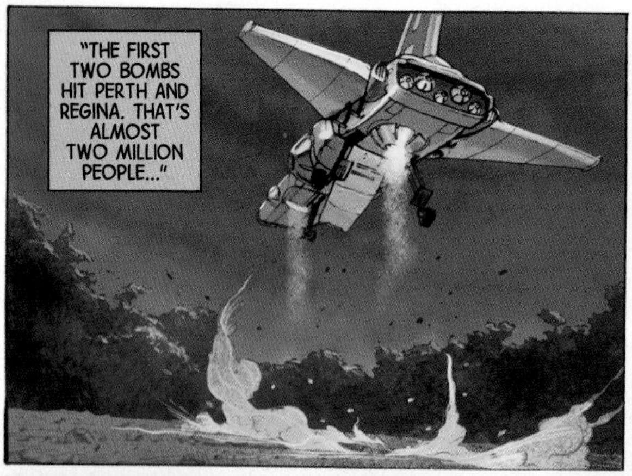
"THE FIRST TWO BOMBS HIT PERTH AND REGINA. THAT'S ALMOST TWO MILLION PEOPLE..."

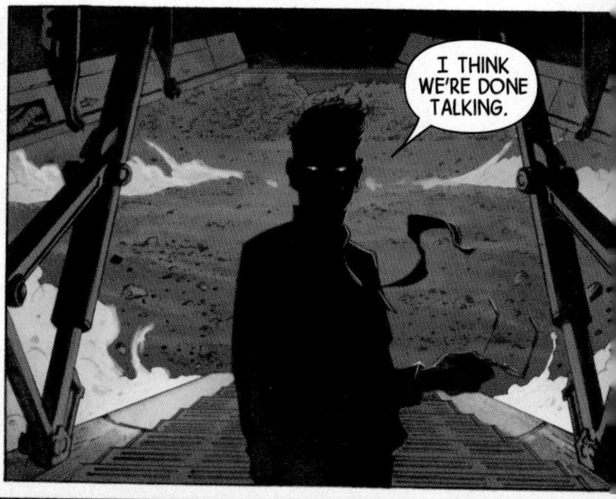
I THINK WE'RE DONE TALKING.

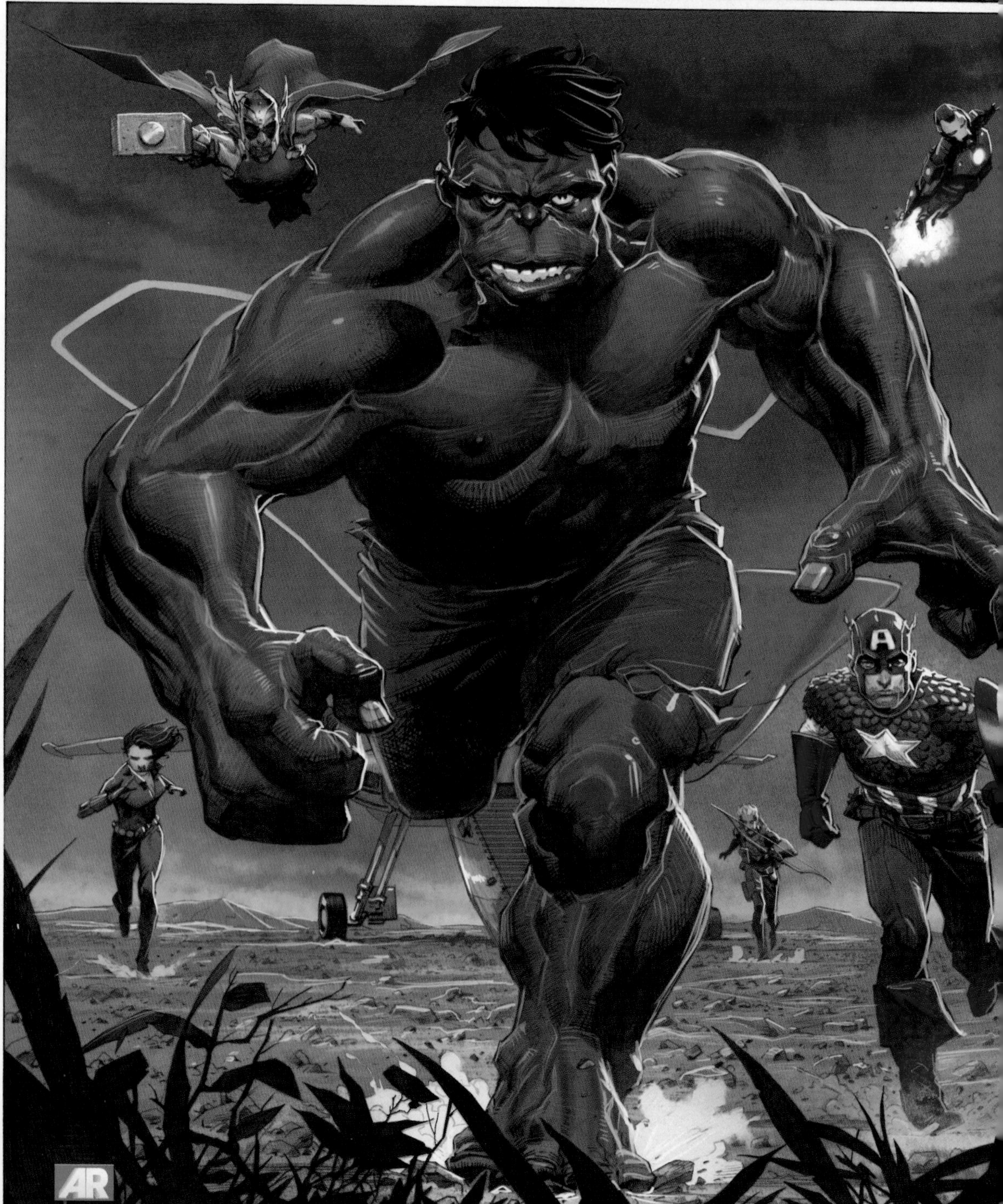

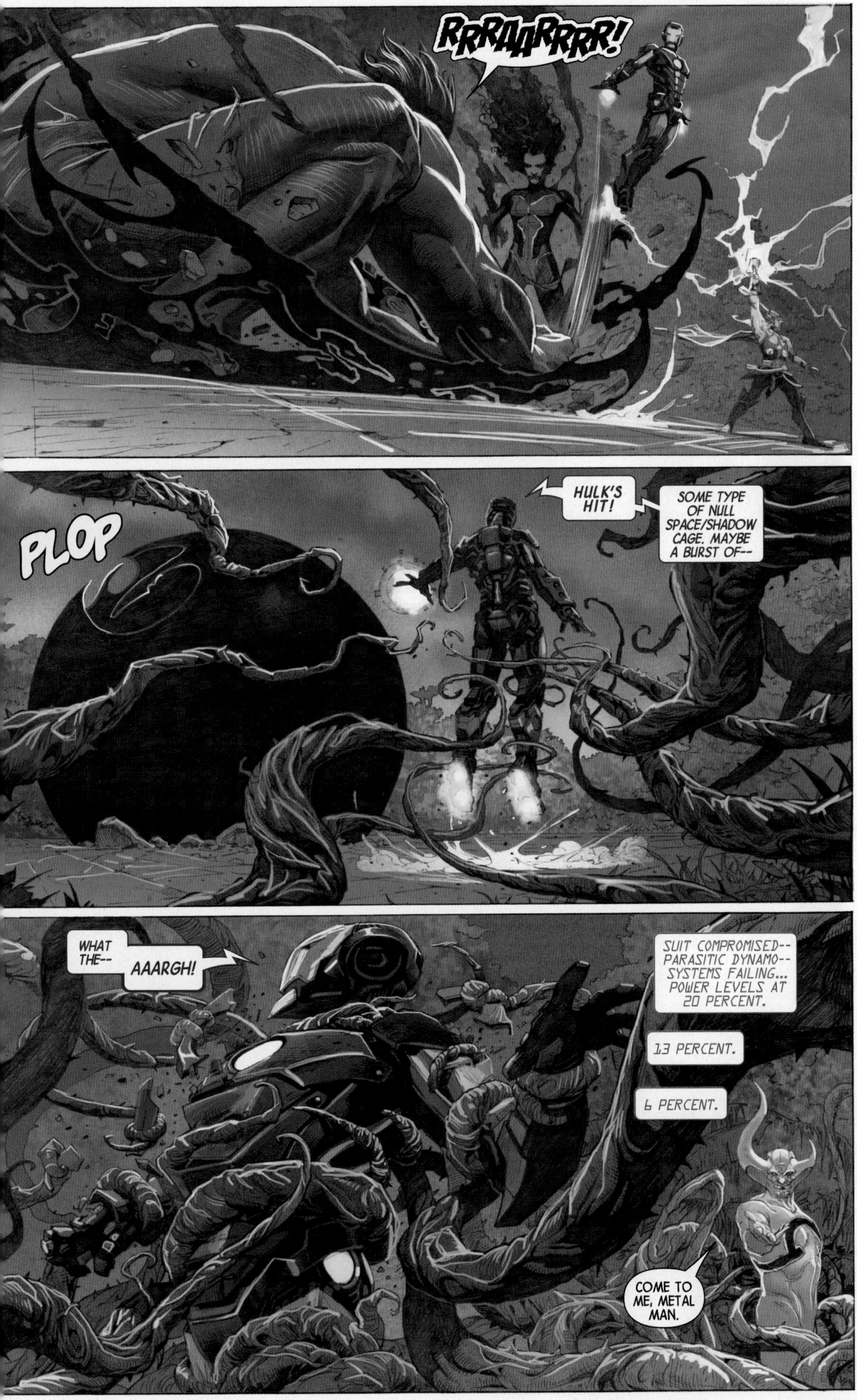
RRRAAARRRR!
PLOP
HULK'S HIT!
SOME TYPE OF NULL SPACE/SHADOW CAGE. MAYBE A BURST OF--
WHAT THE--
AAARGH!
SUIT COMPROMISED-- PARASITIC DYNAMO-- SYSTEMS FAILING... POWER LEVELS AT 20 PERCENT.
13 PERCENT.
6 PERCENT.
COME TO ME, METAL MAN.

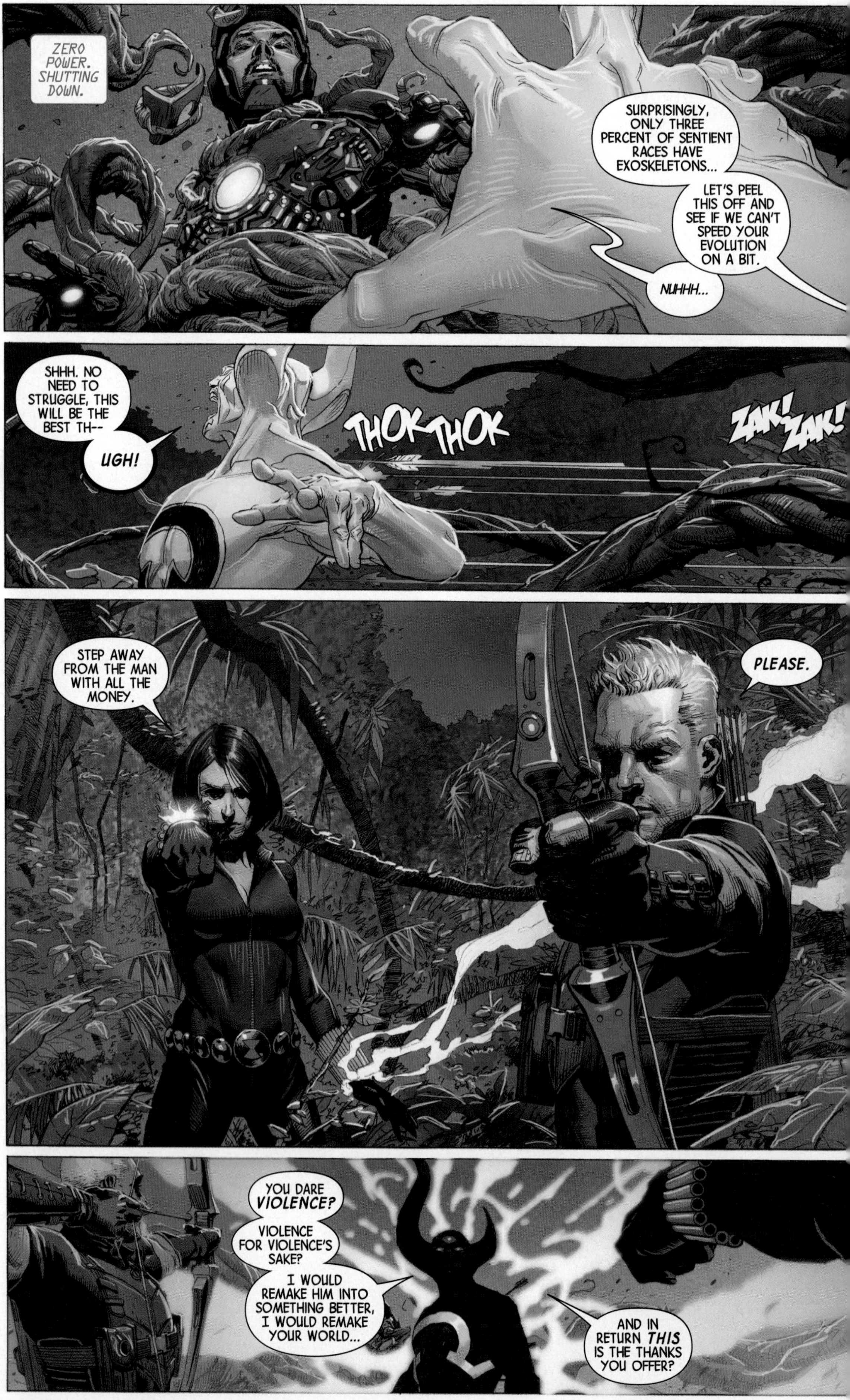
ZERO POWER. SHUTTING DOWN.
SURPRISINGLY, ONLY THREE PERCENT OF SENTIENT RACES HAVE EXOSKELETONS...
LET'S PEEL THIS OFF AND SEE IF WE CAN'T SPEED YOUR EVOLUTION ON A BIT.
NUHHH...
SHHH. NO NEED TO STRUGGLE, THIS WILL BE THE BEST TH--
UGH!
THOK THOK
ZAK! ZAK!
STEP AWAY FROM THE MAN WITH ALL THE MONEY.
PLEASE.
YOU DARE VIOLENCE?
VIOLENCE FOR VIOLENCE'S SAKE?
I WOULD REMAKE HIM INTO SOMETHING BETTER, I WOULD REMAKE YOUR WORLD...
AND IN RETURN THIS IS THE THANKS YOU OFFER?

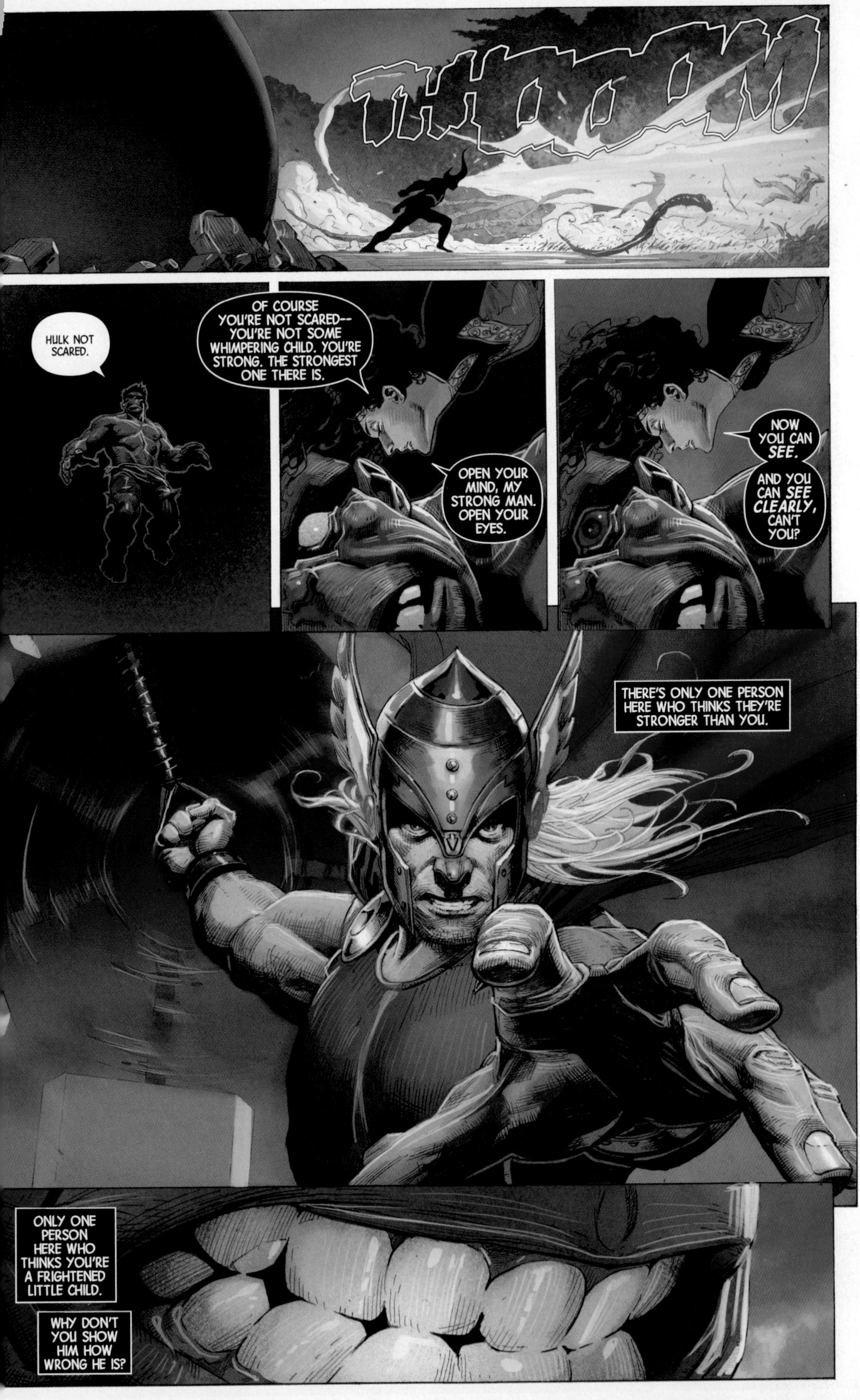
THOOOOM
HULK NOT SCARED.
OF COURSE YOU'RE NOT SCARED-- YOU'RE NOT SOME WHIMPERING CHILD. YOU'RE STRONG. THE STRONGEST ONE THERE IS.
OPEN YOUR MIND, MY STRONG MAN. OPEN YOUR EYES.
NOW YOU CAN SEE.
AND YOU CAN SEE CLEARLY, CAN'T YOU?
THERE'S ONLY ONE PERSON HERE WHO THINKS THEY'RE STRONGER THAN YOU.
ONLY ONE PERSON HERE WHO THINKS YOU'RE A FRIGHTENED LITTLE CHILD.
WHY DON'T YOU SHOW HIM HOW WRONG HE IS?

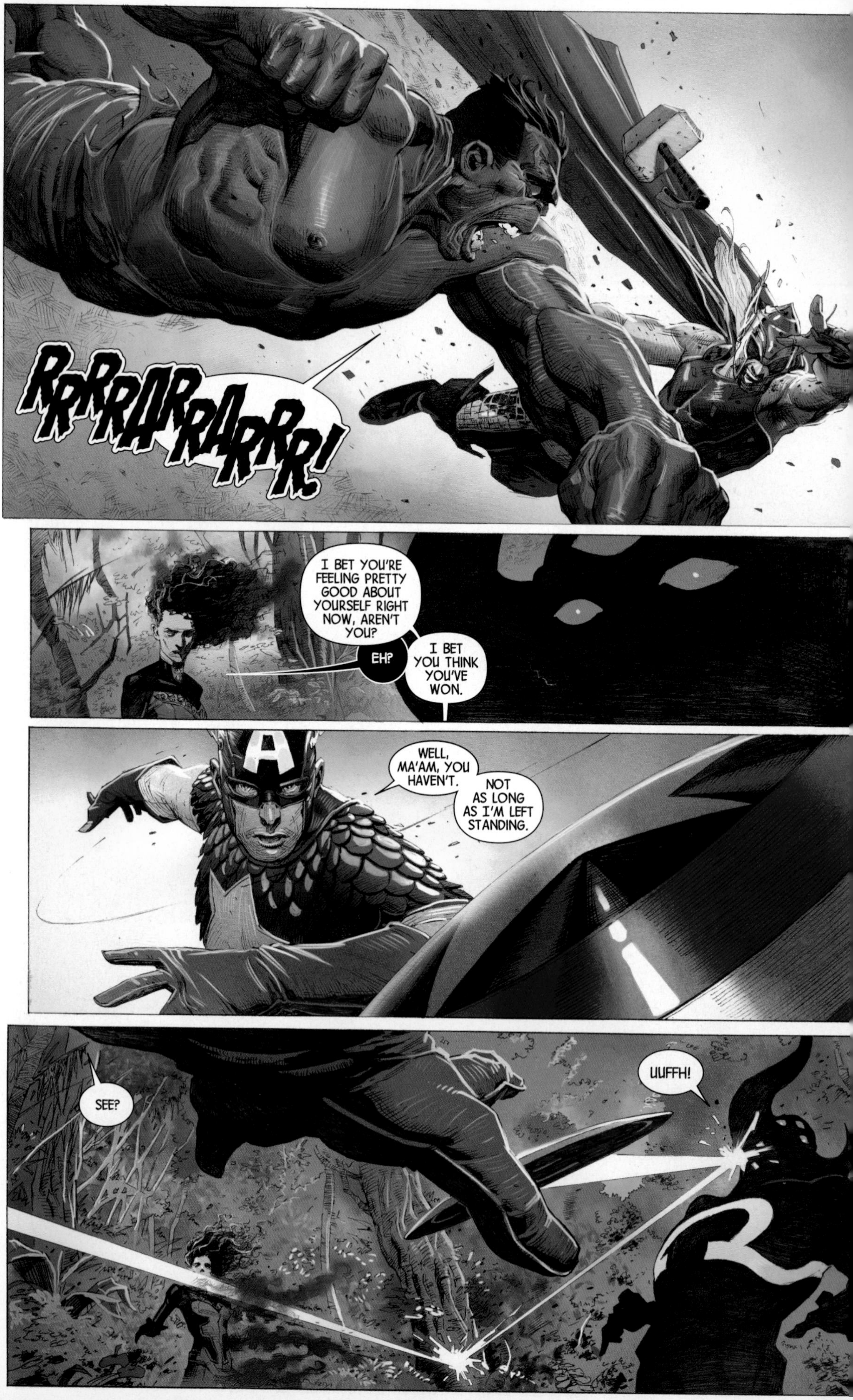
RRRRRARRRARRRR!
I BET YOU'RE FEELING PRETTY GOOD ABOUT YOURSELF RIGHT NOW, AREN'T YOU?
EH?
I BET YOU THINK YOU'VE WON.
WELL, MA'AM, YOU HAVEN'T.
NOT AS LONG AS I'M LEFT STANDING.
SEE?
UUFFH!

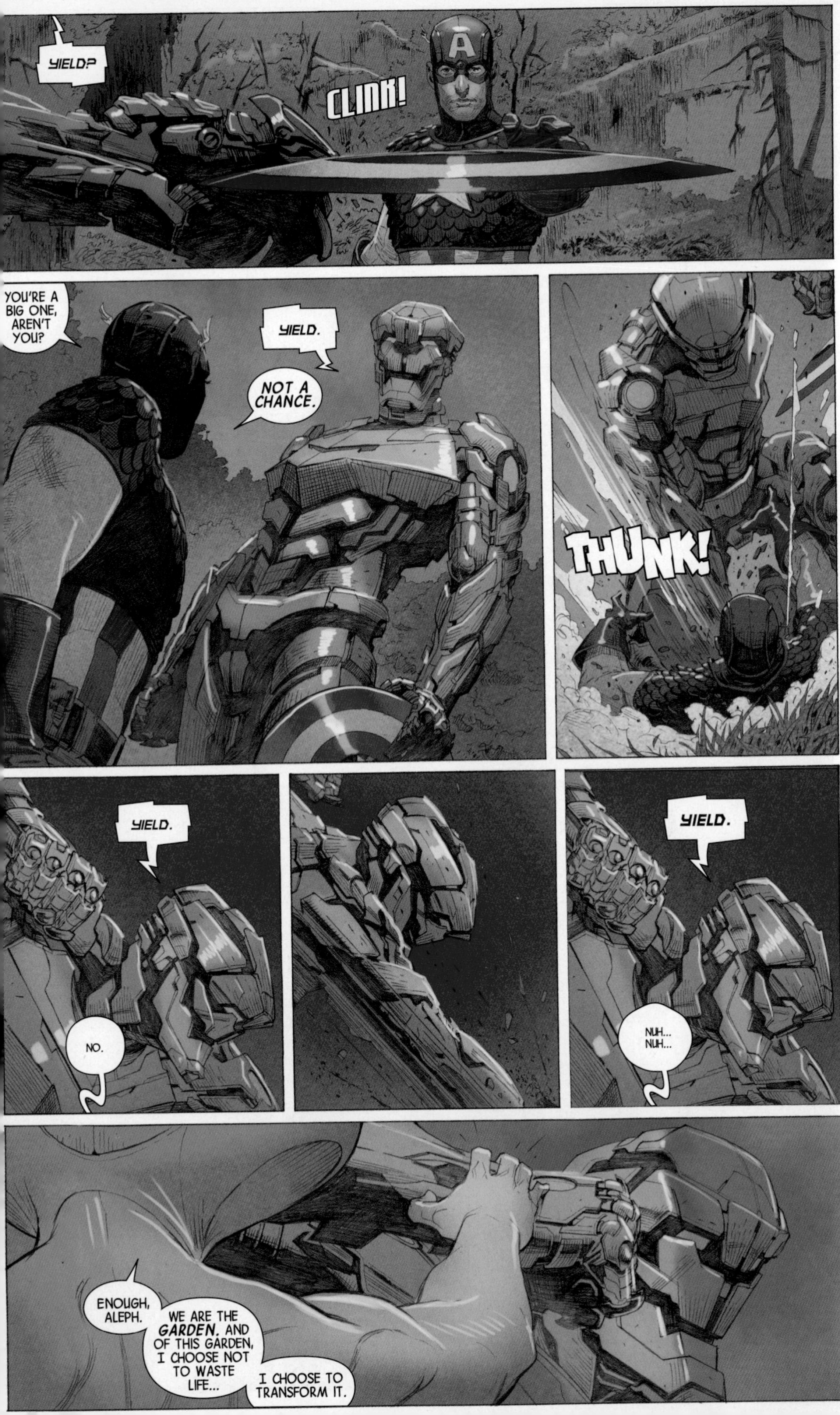
YIELD?
CLINK!
YOU'RE A BIG ONE, AREN'T YOU?
YIELD.
NOT A CHANCE.
THUNK!
YIELD.
NO.
YIELD.
NUH... NUH...
ENOUGH, ALEPH.
WE ARE THE GARDEN. AND OF THIS GARDEN, I CHOOSE NOT TO WASTE LIFE...
I CHOOSE TO TRANSFORM IT.

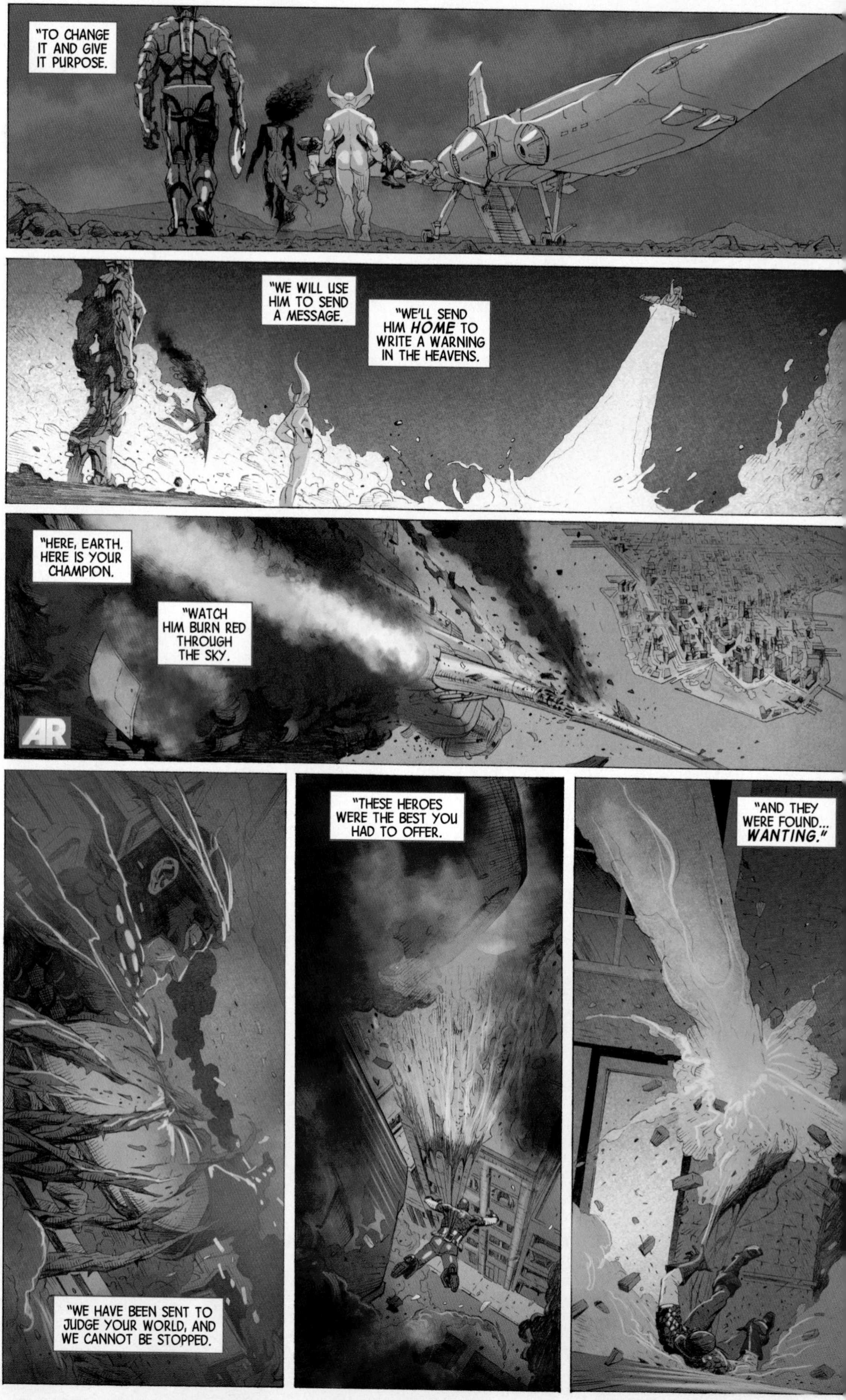
"TO CHANGE IT AND GIVE IT PURPOSE.
"WE WILL USE HIM TO SEND A MESSAGE.
"WE'LL SEND HIM *HOME* TO WRITE A WARNING IN THE HEAVENS.
"HERE, EARTH. HERE IS YOUR CHAMPION.
"WATCH HIM BURN RED THROUGH THE SKY.
"WE HAVE BEEN SENT TO JUDGE YOUR WORLD, AND WE CANNOT BE STOPPED.
"THESE HEROES WERE THE BEST YOU HAD TO OFFER.
"AND THEY WERE FOUND... ***WANTING.***"

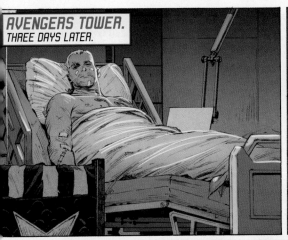

AVENGERS TOWER.
THREE DAYS LATER.

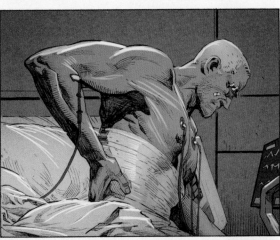

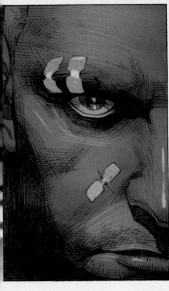

"WE HAVE TO GET BIGGER."

WE HAVE HELD FOR SO LONG, BUT THERE IS SOMETHING LOOMING JUST PAST THE HORIZON.

WE CAN'T SEE IT, BUT IT'S COMING. IT'S GOING TO BE TOO MUCH, AND TOO SOON--AND WE HAVE TO GET READY NOW.

WE'LL KEEP THIS QUIET UNTIL THEY'RE NEEDED-- YOU AND I WILL DO MOST OF THE RECRUITING. SPECIFIC PEOPLE FOR SPECIFIC NEEDS.

BUT THEY'LL BE OUT THERE. READY...

WAITING...

"AND THEN, WHEN THAT DAY COMES, ALL *YOU* HAVE TO DO IS *SAY THE WORDS.*"

WAKE THE WORLD

CLICK!

IT WAS A *SUMMONING.*

HE WAS THE FIRST-- *OUR VERY BEST.*

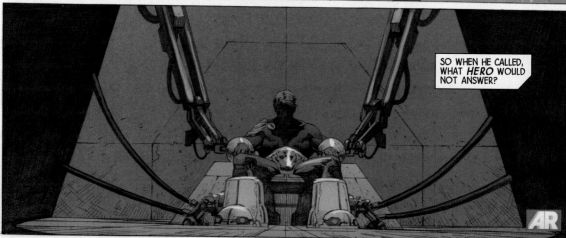

SO WHEN HE CALLED, WHAT *HERO* WOULD NOT ANSWER?

AR

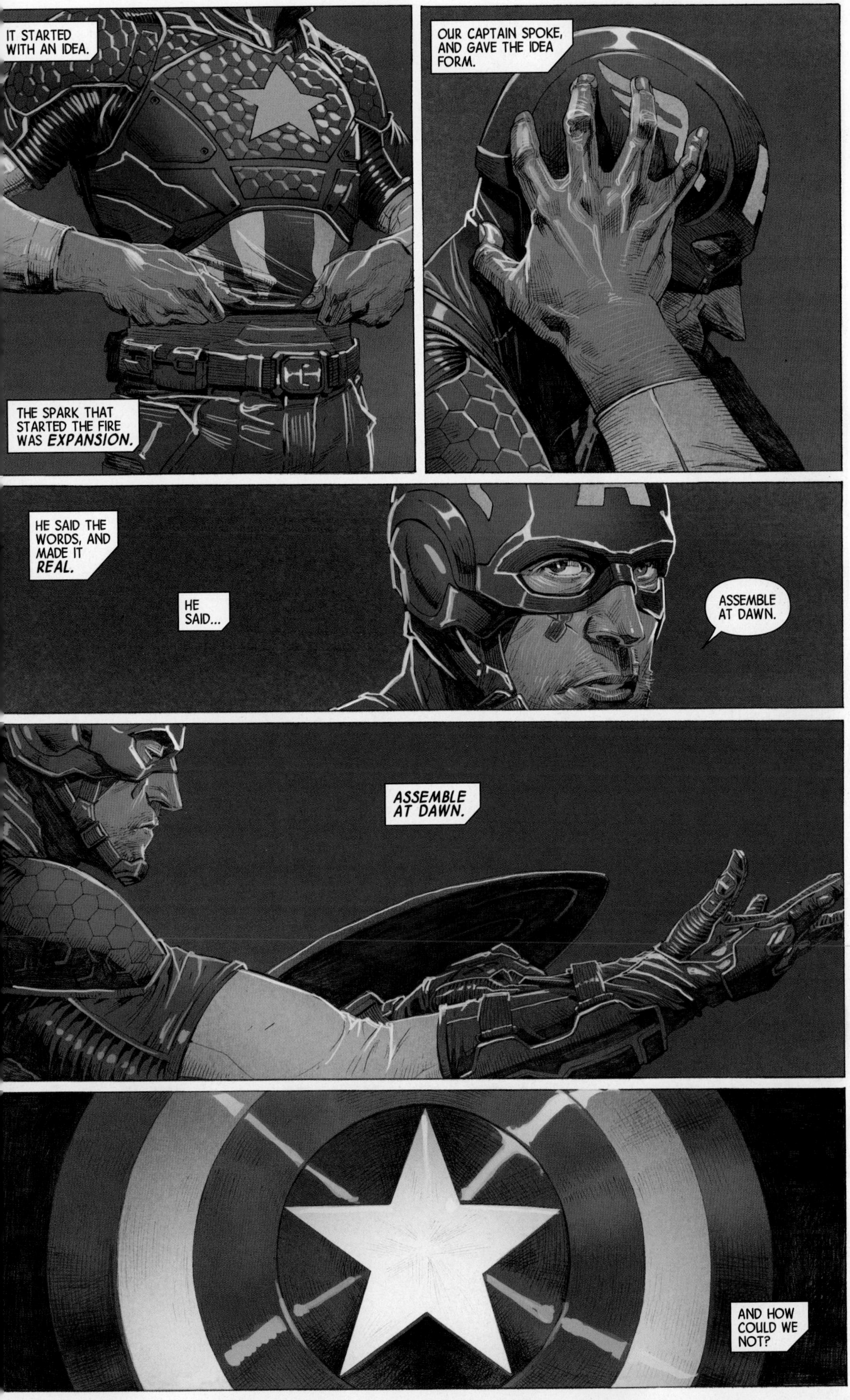
IT STARTED WITH AN IDEA.
THE SPARK THAT STARTED THE FIRE WAS *EXPANSION.*
OUR CAPTAIN SPOKE, AND GAVE THE IDEA FORM.
HE SAID THE WORDS, AND MADE IT *REAL.*
HE SAID...
ASSEMBLE AT DAWN.
ASSEMBLE AT DAWN.
AND HOW COULD WE NOT?

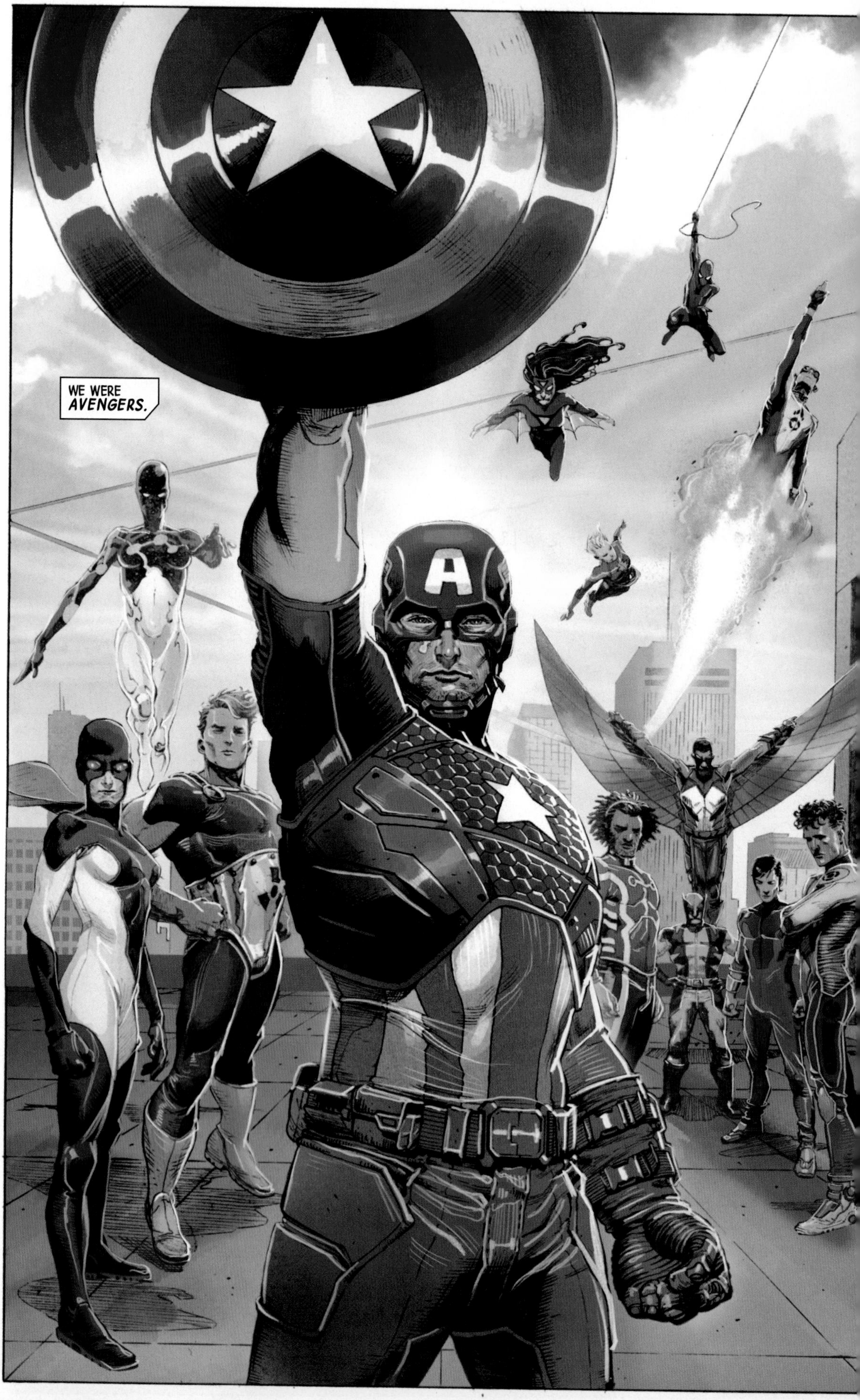
WE WERE
AVENGERS.

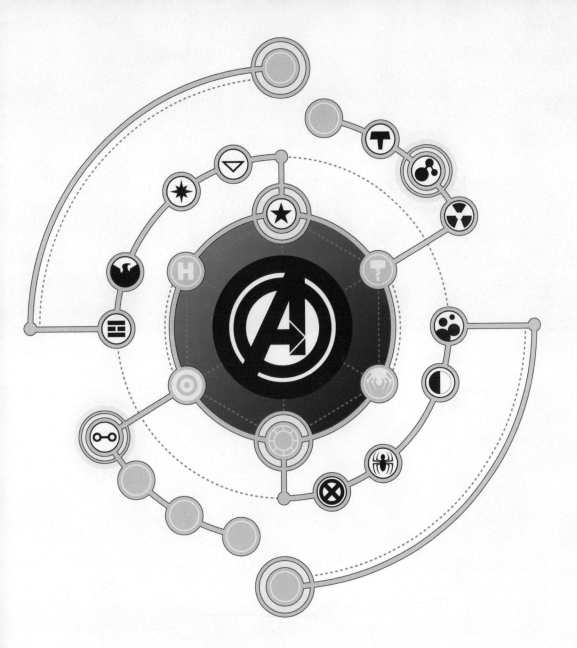

WAKE THE
WORLD

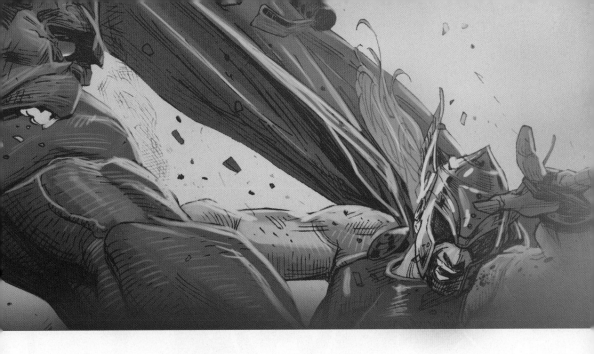

"WE WERE AVENGERS"

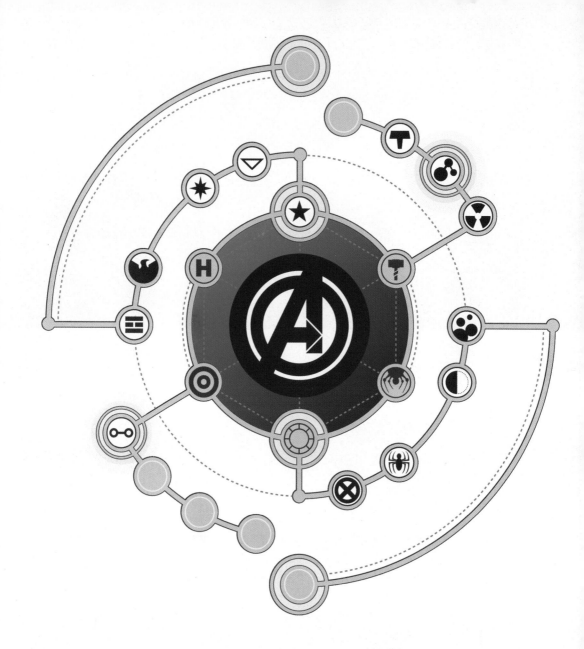

EARTH'S MIGHTIEST HEROES

CAPTAIN AMERICA · IRON MAN · THOR · HAWKEYE · BLACK WIDOW · HULK
WOLVERINE · SPIDER-MAN · CAPTAIN MARVEL · SPIDER-WOMAN
FALCON · SHANG-CHI · SUNSPOT · CANNONBALL · MANIFOLD
SMASHER · CAPTAIN UNIVERSE · HYPERION

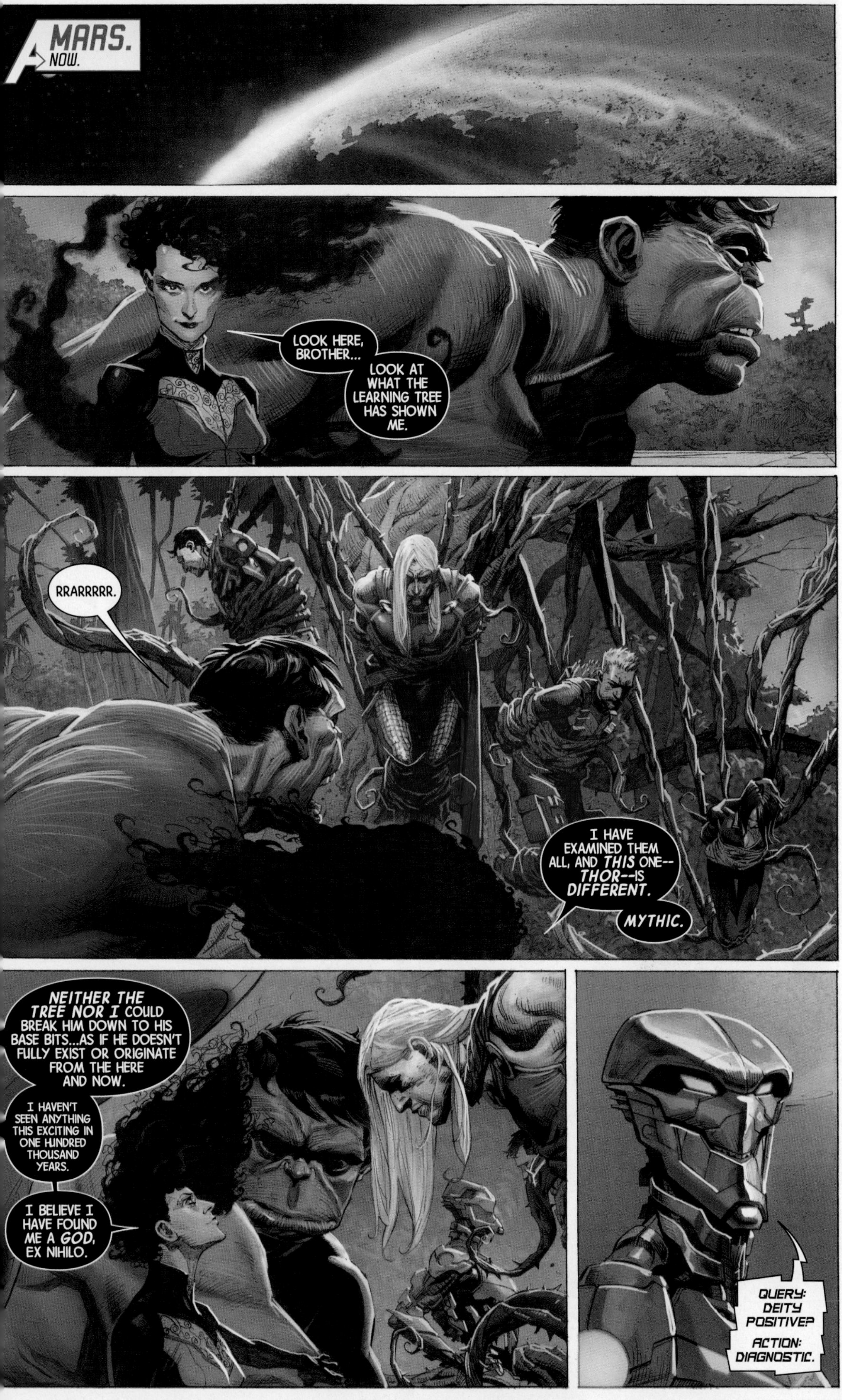
MARS.
NOW.
LOOK HERE, BROTHER...
LOOK AT WHAT THE LEARNING TREE HAS SHOWN ME.
RRARRRRR.
I HAVE EXAMINED THEM ALL, AND THIS ONE--THOR--IS DIFFERENT.
MYTHIC.
NEITHER THE TREE NOR I COULD BREAK HIM DOWN TO HIS BASE BITS...AS IF HE DOESN'T FULLY EXIST OR ORIGINATE FROM THE HERE AND NOW.
I HAVEN'T SEEN ANYTHING THIS EXCITING IN ONE HUNDRED THOUSAND YEARS.
I BELIEVE I HAVE FOUND ME A GOD, EX NIHILO.
QUERY: DEITY POSITIVE?
ACTION: DIAGNOSTIC.

URK!

SCANNING...

SCANNING...

WELL, IF YOU *ARE A GOD*, THEN--*LIKE MYSELF*--YOU KNOW SOMETHING ABOUT CREATION STORIES.

DON'T YOU?

YES.

IN THE SHADOW OF THE *WORLD TREE* LIES THE REALM *ASGARD*.

IT IS RULED BY THE *ALL-FATHER, ODIN.* WHO--

YES, YES... *THAT'S ALL VERY NICE*, BUT I'M INTERESTED IN WHAT CLOSES THE LOOP.

WHEN YOU GET TO THE END OF YOUR STORY...

DO YOU HAVE A *RESURRECTION MYTH*...OR IS THERE JUST AN *APOCALYPSE* WAITING FOR YOU?

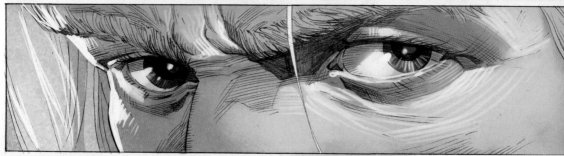

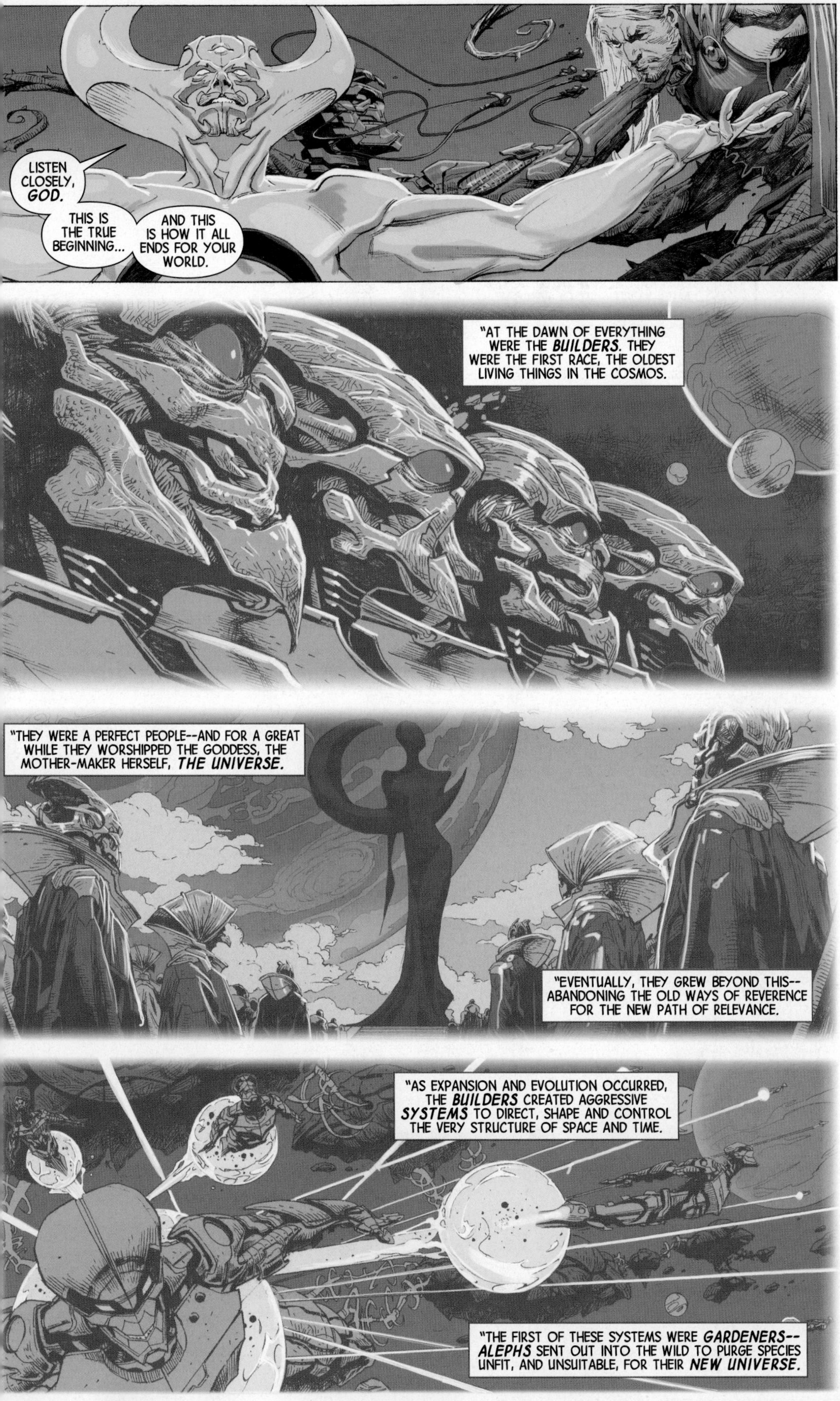

LISTEN CLOSELY, GOD.
THIS IS THE TRUE BEGINNING...
AND THIS IS HOW IT ALL ENDS FOR YOUR WORLD.
"AT THE DAWN OF EVERYTHING WERE THE BUILDERS. THEY WERE THE FIRST RACE, THE OLDEST LIVING THINGS IN THE COSMOS.
"THEY WERE A PERFECT PEOPLE--AND FOR A GREAT WHILE THEY WORSHIPPED THE GODDESS, THE MOTHER-MAKER HERSELF, THE UNIVERSE.
"EVENTUALLY, THEY GREW BEYOND THIS--ABANDONING THE OLD WAYS OF REVERENCE FOR THE NEW PATH OF RELEVANCE.
"AS EXPANSION AND EVOLUTION OCCURRED, THE BUILDERS CREATED AGGRESSIVE SYSTEMS TO DIRECT, SHAPE AND CONTROL THE VERY STRUCTURE OF SPACE AND TIME.
"THE FIRST OF THESE SYSTEMS WERE GARDENERS--ALEPHS SENT OUT INTO THE WILD TO PURGE SPECIES UNFIT, AND UNSUITABLE, FOR THEIR NEW UNIVERSE.

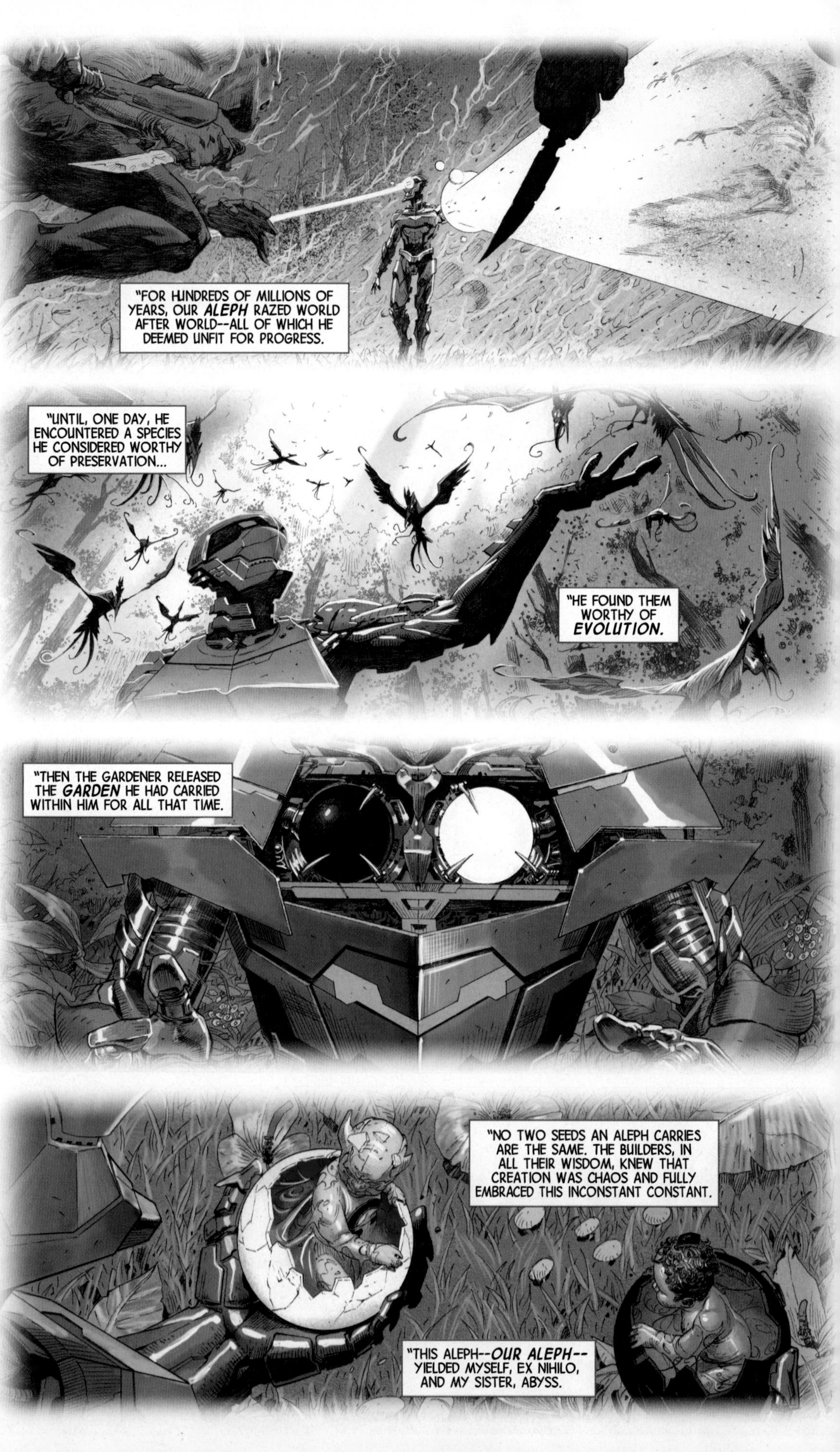
"FOR HUNDREDS OF MILLIONS OF YEARS, OUR ALEPH RAZED WORLD AFTER WORLD--ALL OF WHICH HE DEEMED UNFIT FOR PROGRESS.
"UNTIL, ONE DAY, HE ENCOUNTERED A SPECIES HE CONSIDERED WORTHY OF PRESERVATION...
"HE FOUND THEM WORTHY OF EVOLUTION.
"THEN THE GARDENER RELEASED THE GARDEN HE HAD CARRIED WITHIN HIM FOR ALL THAT TIME.
"NO TWO SEEDS AN ALEPH CARRIES ARE THE SAME. THE BUILDERS, IN ALL THEIR WISDOM, KNEW THAT CREATION WAS CHAOS AND FULLY EMBRACED THIS INCONSTANT CONSTANT.
"THIS ALEPH--OUR ALEPH--YIELDED MYSELF, EX NIHILO, AND MY SISTER, ABYSS.

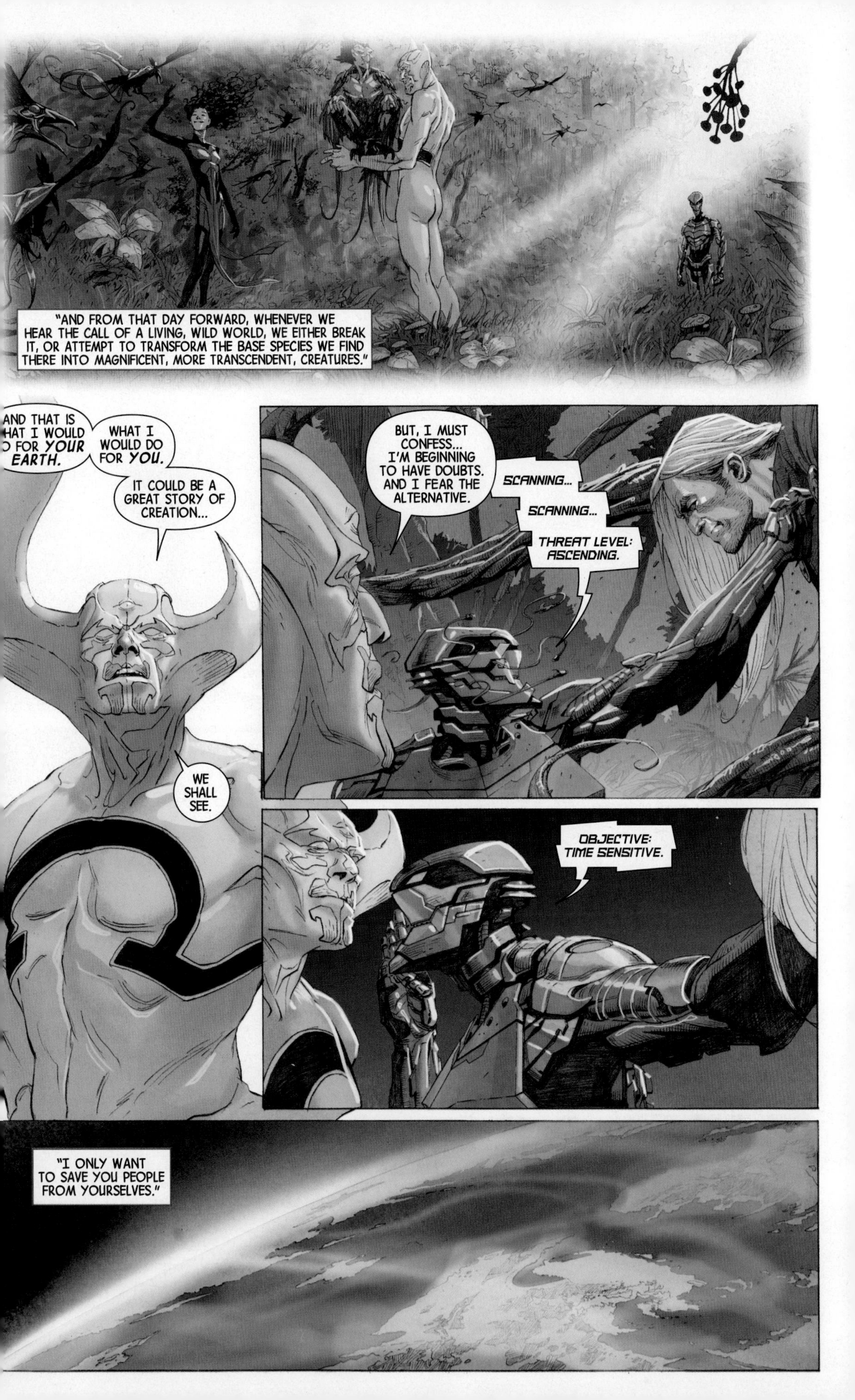
"AND FROM THAT DAY FORWARD, WHENEVER WE HEAR THE CALL OF A LIVING, WILD WORLD, WE EITHER BREAK IT, OR ATTEMPT TO TRANSFORM THE BASE SPECIES WE FIND THERE INTO MAGNIFICENT, MORE TRANSCENDENT, CREATURES."
AND THAT IS HAT I WOULD O FOR YOUR EARTH.
WHAT I WOULD DO FOR YOU.
IT COULD BE A GREAT STORY OF CREATION...
WE SHALL SEE.
BUT, I MUST CONFESS... I'M BEGINNING TO HAVE DOUBTS. AND I FEAR THE ALTERNATIVE.
SCANNING...
SCANNING...
THREAT LEVEL: ASCENDING.
OBJECTIVE: TIME SENSITIVE.
"I ONLY WANT TO SAVE YOU PEOPLE FROM YOURSELVES."

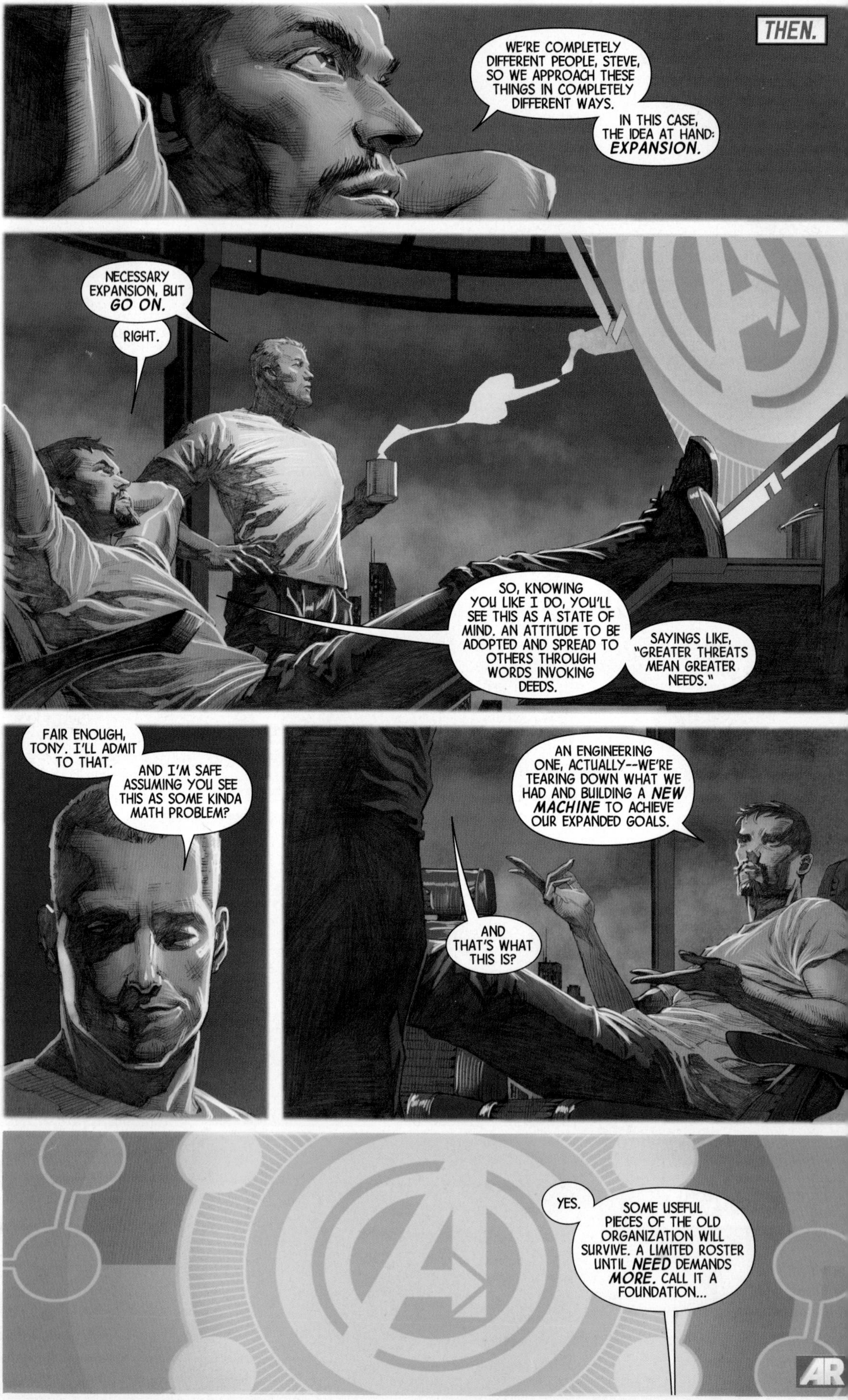
THEN.
WE'RE COMPLETELY DIFFERENT PEOPLE, STEVE, SO WE APPROACH THESE THINGS IN COMPLETELY DIFFERENT WAYS.
IN THIS CASE, THE IDEA AT HAND: EXPANSION.
NECESSARY EXPANSION, BUT GO ON.
RIGHT.
SO, KNOWING YOU LIKE I DO, YOU'LL SEE THIS AS A STATE OF MIND. AN ATTITUDE TO BE ADOPTED AND SPREAD TO OTHERS THROUGH WORDS INVOKING DEEDS.
SAYINGS LIKE, "GREATER THREATS MEAN GREATER NEEDS."
FAIR ENOUGH, TONY. I'LL ADMIT TO THAT.
AND I'M SAFE ASSUMING YOU SEE THIS AS SOME KINDA MATH PROBLEM?
AN ENGINEERING ONE, ACTUALLY--WE'RE TEARING DOWN WHAT WE HAD AND BUILDING A NEW MACHINE TO ACHIEVE OUR EXPANDED GOALS.
AND THAT'S WHAT THIS IS?
YES.
SOME USEFUL PIECES OF THE OLD ORGANIZATION WILL SURVIVE. A LIMITED ROSTER UNTIL NEED DEMANDS MORE. CALL IT A FOUNDATION...
AR

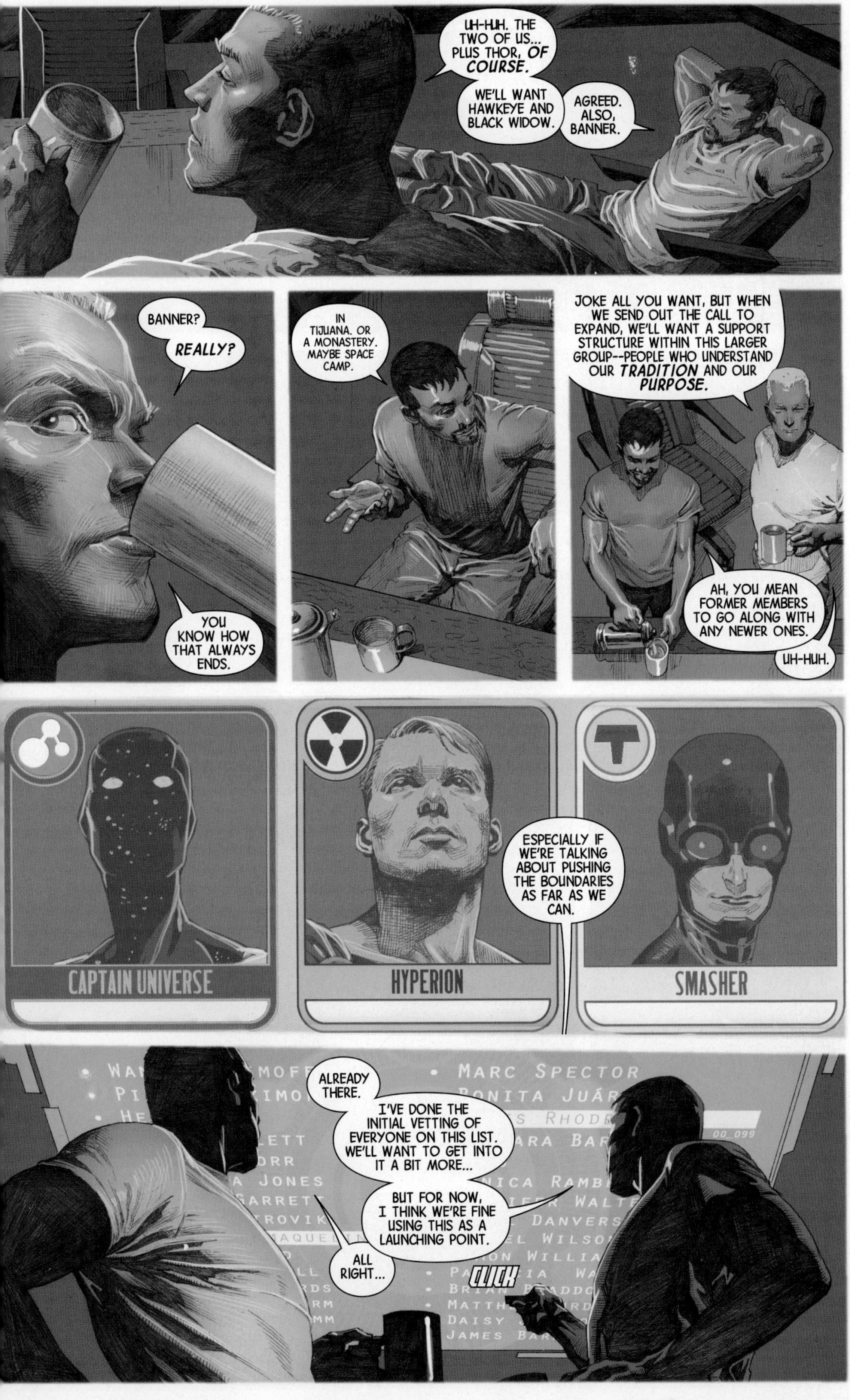
UH-HUH. THE TWO OF US... PLUS THOR, OF COURSE.
WE'LL WANT HAWKEYE AND BLACK WIDOW.
AGREED. ALSO, BANNER.
BANNER? REALLY?
YOU KNOW HOW THAT ALWAYS ENDS.
IN TIJUANA. OR A MONASTERY. MAYBE SPACE CAMP.
JOKE ALL YOU WANT, BUT WHEN WE SEND OUT THE CALL TO EXPAND, WE'LL WANT A SUPPORT STRUCTURE WITHIN THIS LARGER GROUP--PEOPLE WHO UNDERSTAND OUR TRADITION AND OUR PURPOSE.
AH, YOU MEAN FORMER MEMBERS TO GO ALONG WITH ANY NEWER ONES.
UH-HUH.
CAPTAIN UNIVERSE
HYPERION
SMASHER
ESPECIALLY IF WE'RE TALKING ABOUT PUSHING THE BOUNDARIES AS FAR AS WE CAN.
MARC SPECTOR
ALREADY THERE.
I'VE DONE THE INITIAL VETTING OF EVERYONE ON THIS LIST. WE'LL WANT TO GET INTO IT A BIT MORE...
BUT FOR NOW, I THINK WE'RE FINE USING THIS AS A LAUNCHING POINT.
ALL RIGHT...
CLICK

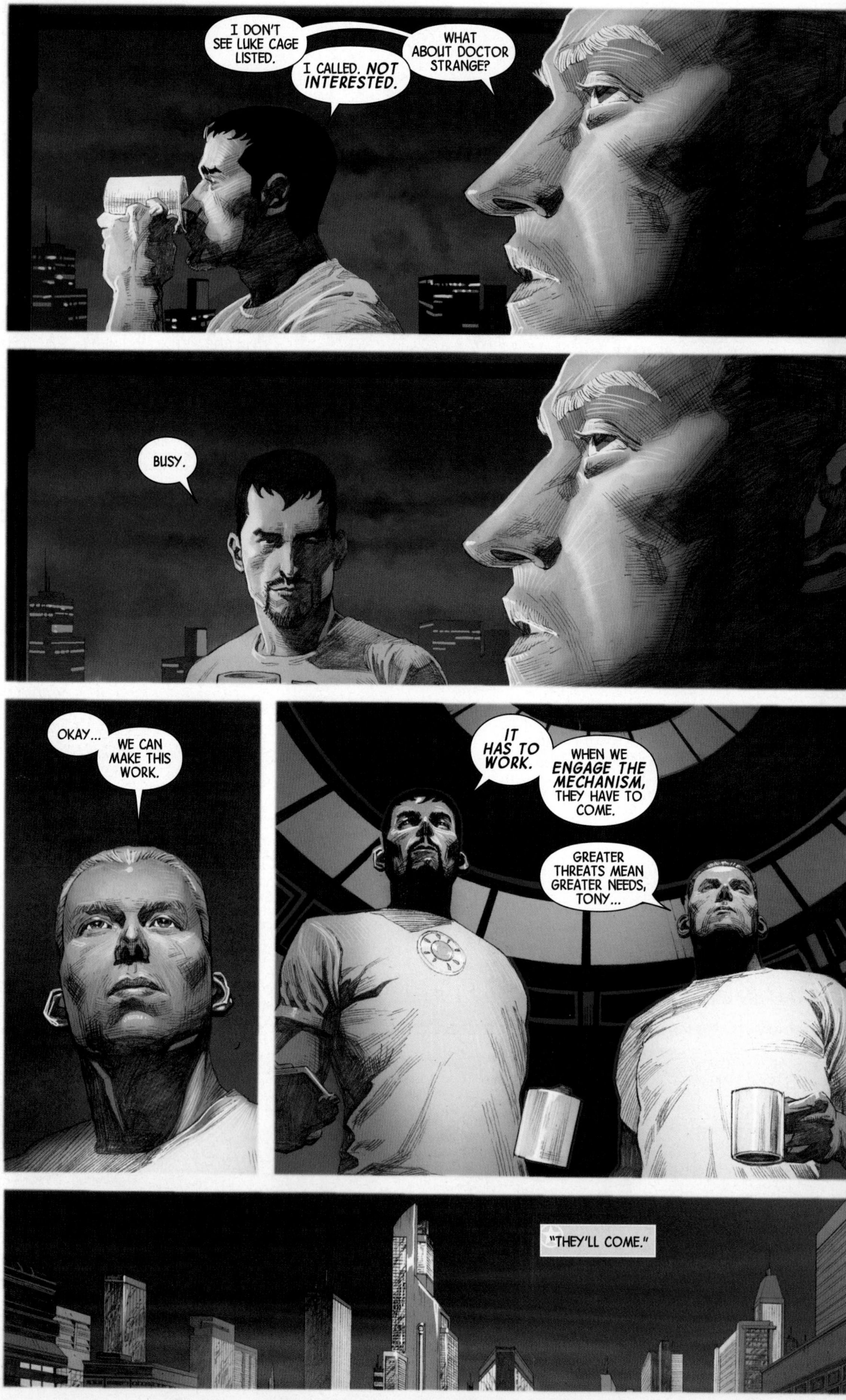
I DON'T SEE LUKE CAGE LISTED.
WHAT ABOUT DOCTOR STRANGE?
I CALLED. NOT INTERESTED.
BUSY.
OKAY...
WE CAN MAKE THIS WORK.
IT HAS TO WORK.
WHEN WE ENGAGE THE MECHANISM, THEY HAVE TO COME.
GREATER THREATS MEAN GREATER NEEDS, TONY...
"THEY'LL COME."

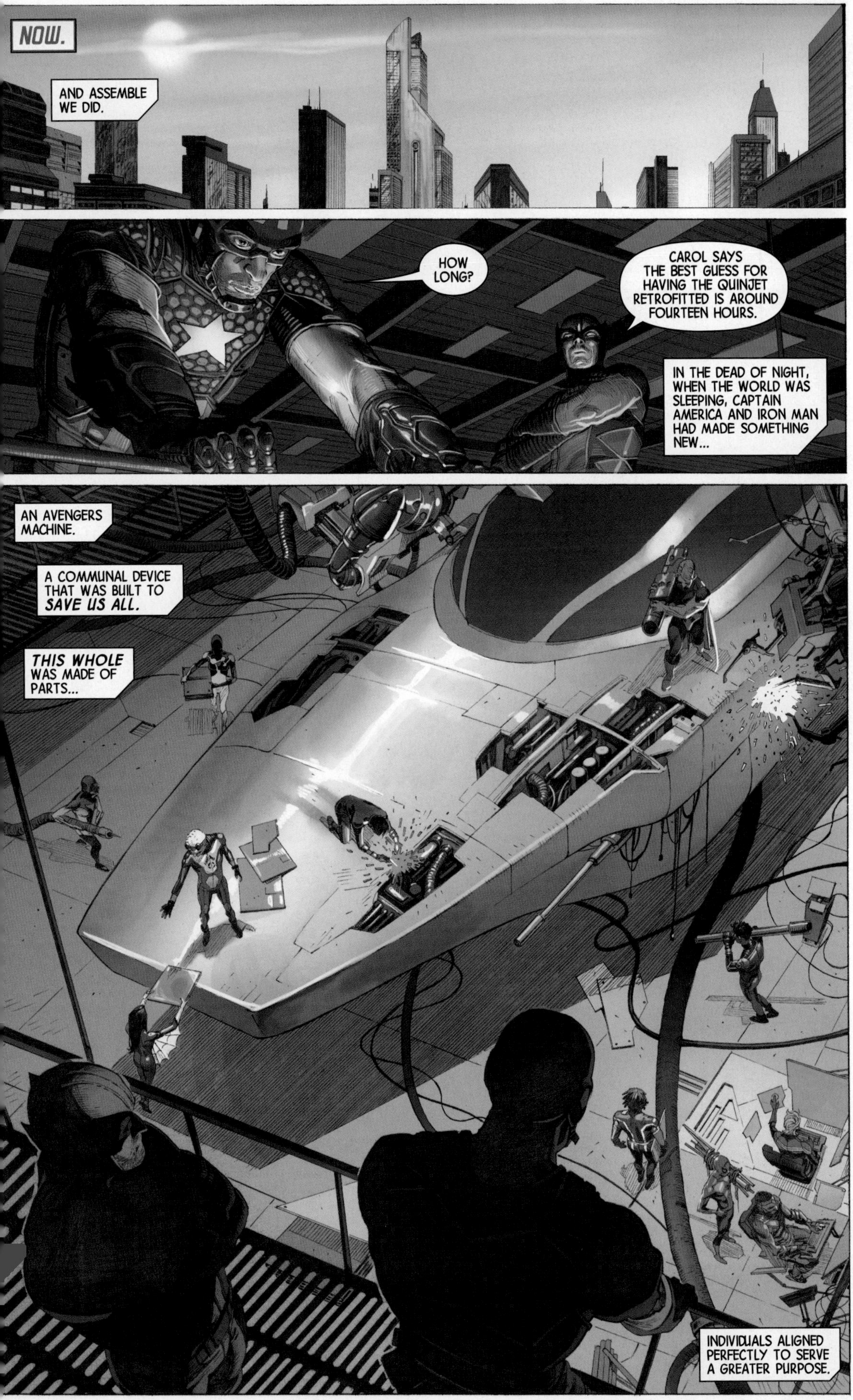
NOW.
AND ASSEMBLE WE DID.
HOW LONG?
CAROL SAYS THE BEST GUESS FOR HAVING THE QUINJET RETROFITTED IS AROUND FOURTEEN HOURS.
IN THE DEAD OF NIGHT, WHEN THE WORLD WAS SLEEPING, CAPTAIN AMERICA AND IRON MAN HAD MADE SOMETHING NEW...
AN AVENGERS MACHINE.
A COMMUNAL DEVICE THAT WAS BUILT TO *SAVE US ALL.*
THIS WHOLE WAS MADE OF PARTS...
INDIVIDUALS ALIGNED PERFECTLY TO SERVE A GREATER PURPOSE.

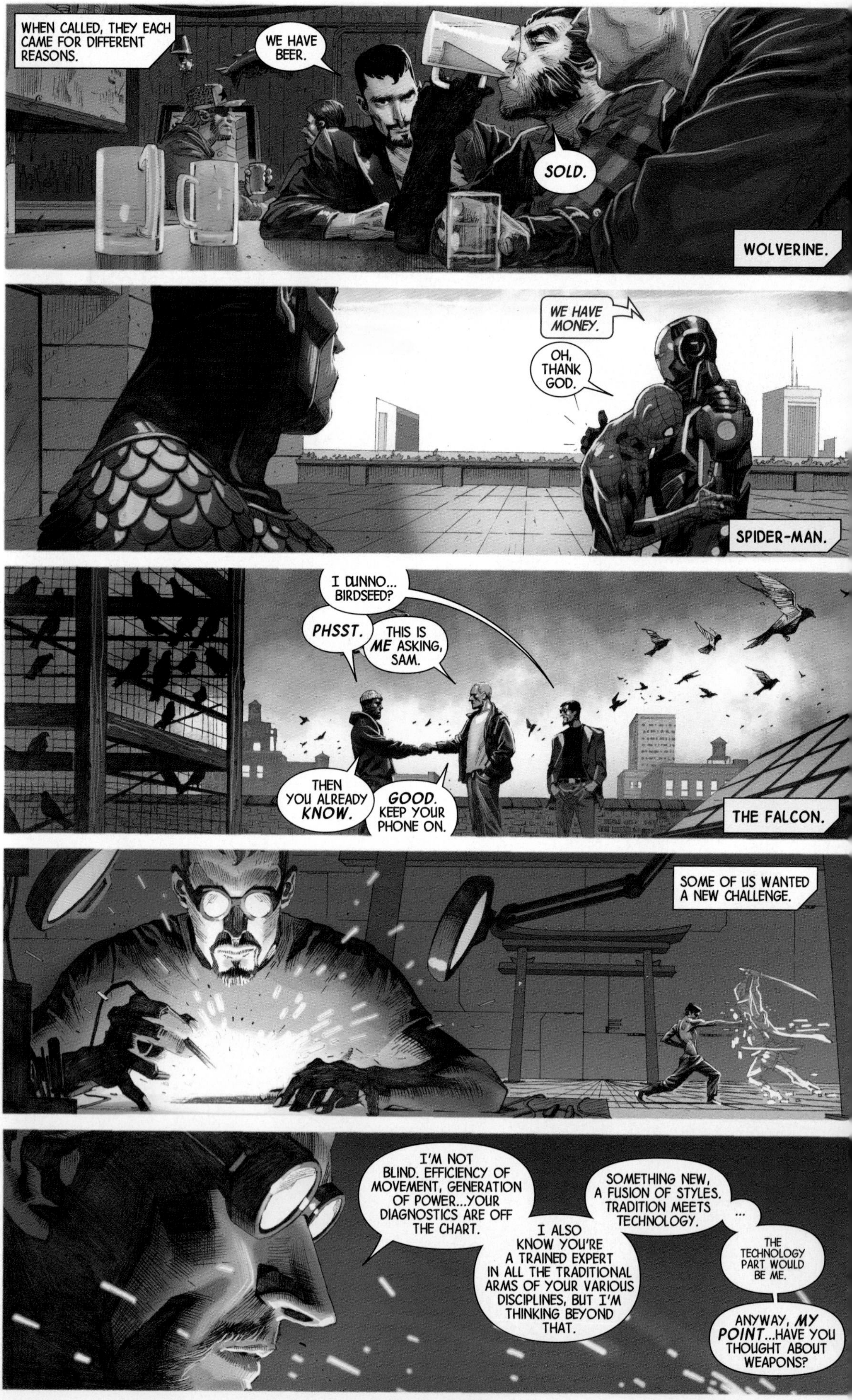
WHEN CALLED, THEY EACH CAME FOR DIFFERENT REASONS.
WE HAVE BEER.
SOLD.
WOLVERINE.
WE HAVE MONEY.
OH, THANK GOD.
SPIDER-MAN.
I DUNNO... BIRDSEED?
PHSST.
THIS IS ME ASKING, SAM.
THEN YOU ALREADY KNOW.
GOOD. KEEP YOUR PHONE ON.
THE FALCON.
SOME OF US WANTED A NEW CHALLENGE.
I'M NOT BLIND. EFFICIENCY OF MOVEMENT, GENERATION OF POWER...YOUR DIAGNOSTICS ARE OFF THE CHART.
I ALSO KNOW YOU'RE A TRAINED EXPERT IN ALL THE TRADITIONAL ARMS OF YOUR VARIOUS DISCIPLINES, BUT I'M THINKING BEYOND THAT.
SOMETHING NEW, A FUSION OF STYLES. TRADITION MEETS TECHNOLOGY.
...
THE TECHNOLOGY PART WOULD BE ME.
ANYWAY, MY POINT...HAVE YOU THOUGHT ABOUT WEAPONS?

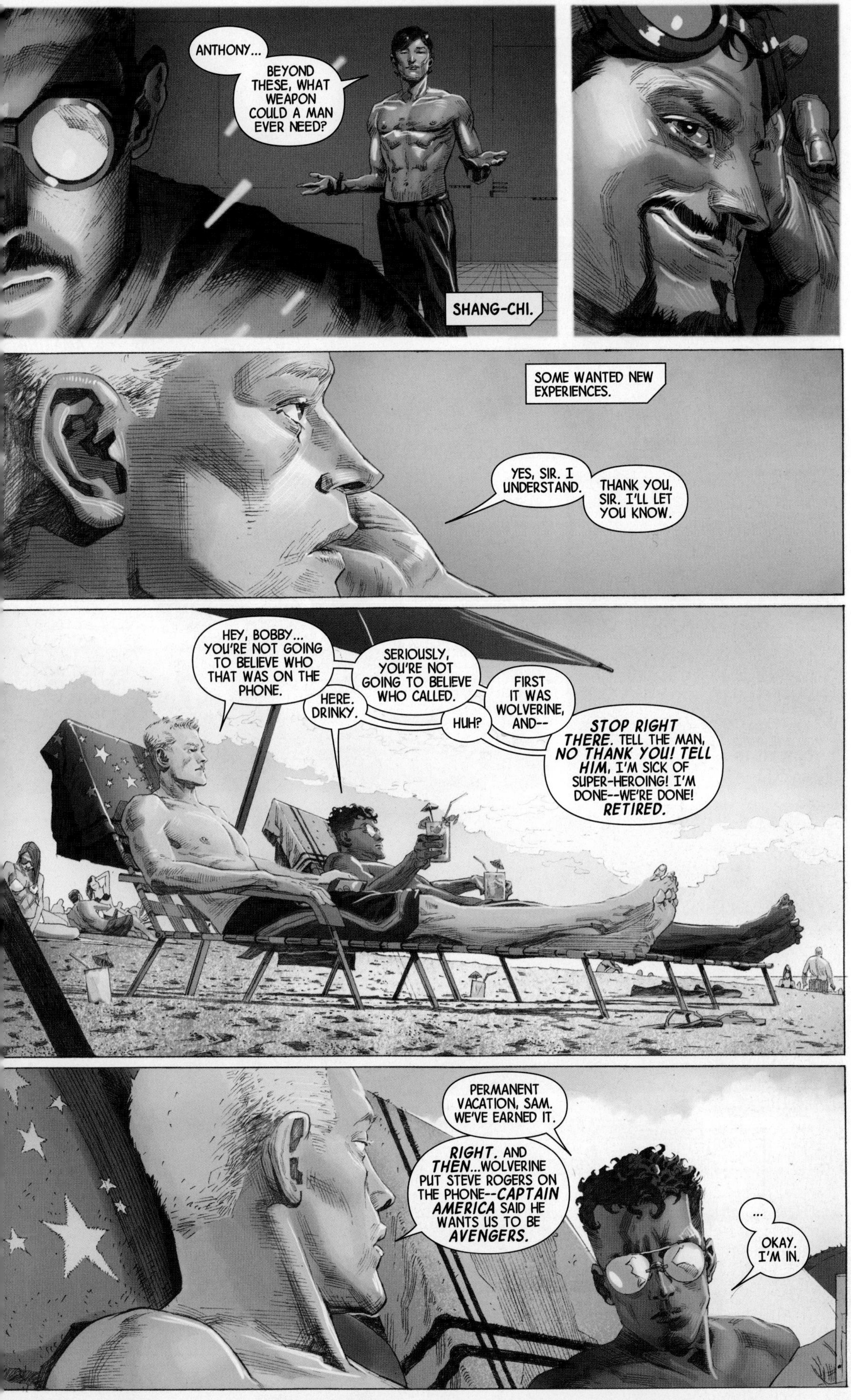

ANTHONY...
BEYOND THESE, WHAT WEAPON COULD A MAN EVER NEED?
SHANG-CHI.
SOME WANTED NEW EXPERIENCES.
YES, SIR. I UNDERSTAND.
THANK YOU, SIR. I'LL LET YOU KNOW.
HEY, BOBBY... YOU'RE NOT GOING TO BELIEVE WHO THAT WAS ON THE PHONE.
HERE. DRINKY.
SERIOUSLY, YOU'RE NOT GOING TO BELIEVE WHO CALLED.
HUH?
FIRST IT WAS WOLVERINE, AND--
STOP RIGHT THERE. TELL THE MAN, NO THANK YOU! TELL HIM, I'M SICK OF SUPER-HEROING! I'M DONE--WE'RE DONE! RETIRED.
PERMANENT VACATION, SAM. WE'VE EARNED IT.
RIGHT. AND THEN...WOLVERINE PUT STEVE ROGERS ON THE PHONE--CAPTAIN AMERICA SAID HE WANTS US TO BE AVENGERS.
...
OKAY. I'M IN.

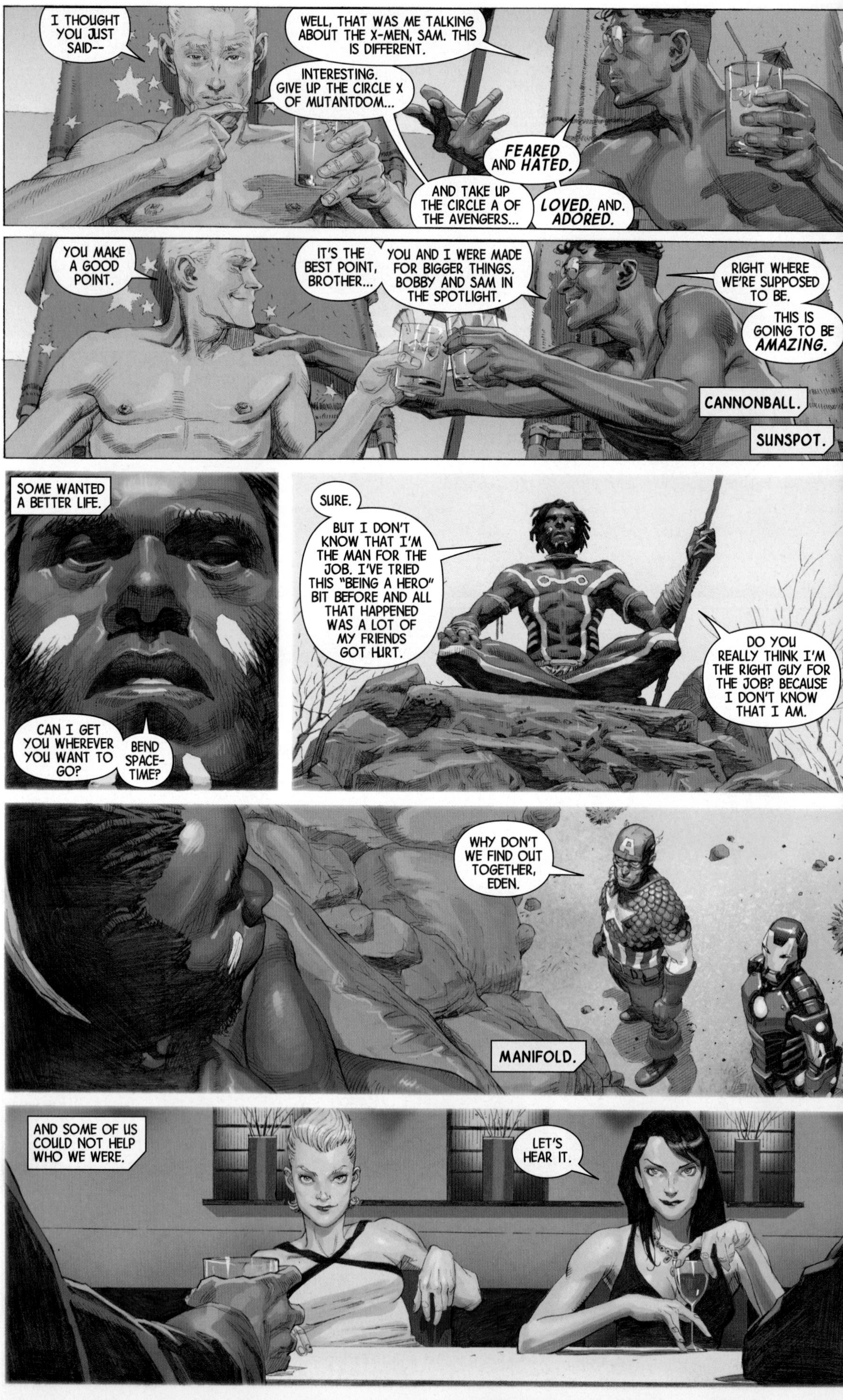

I THOUGHT YOU JUST SAID--
WELL, THAT WAS ME TALKING ABOUT THE X-MEN, SAM. THIS IS DIFFERENT.
INTERESTING. GIVE UP THE CIRCLE X OF MUTANTDOM...
FEARED AND HATED.
AND TAKE UP THE CIRCLE A OF THE AVENGERS...
LOVED. AND. ADORED.
YOU MAKE A GOOD POINT.
IT'S THE BEST POINT, BROTHER...
YOU AND I WERE MADE FOR BIGGER THINGS. BOBBY AND SAM IN THE SPOTLIGHT.
RIGHT WHERE WE'RE SUPPOSED TO BE.
THIS IS GOING TO BE AMAZING.
CANNONBALL.
SUNSPOT.
SOME WANTED A BETTER LIFE.
CAN I GET YOU WHEREVER YOU WANT TO GO?
BEND SPACE-TIME?
SURE.
BUT I DON'T KNOW THAT I'M THE MAN FOR THE JOB. I'VE TRIED THIS "BEING A HERO" BIT BEFORE AND ALL THAT HAPPENED WAS A LOT OF MY FRIENDS GOT HURT.
DO YOU REALLY THINK I'M THE RIGHT GUY FOR THE JOB? BECAUSE I DON'T KNOW THAT I AM.
WHY DON'T WE FIND OUT TOGETHER, EDEN.
MANIFOLD.
AND SOME OF US COULD NOT HELP WHO WE WERE.
LET'S HEAR IT.

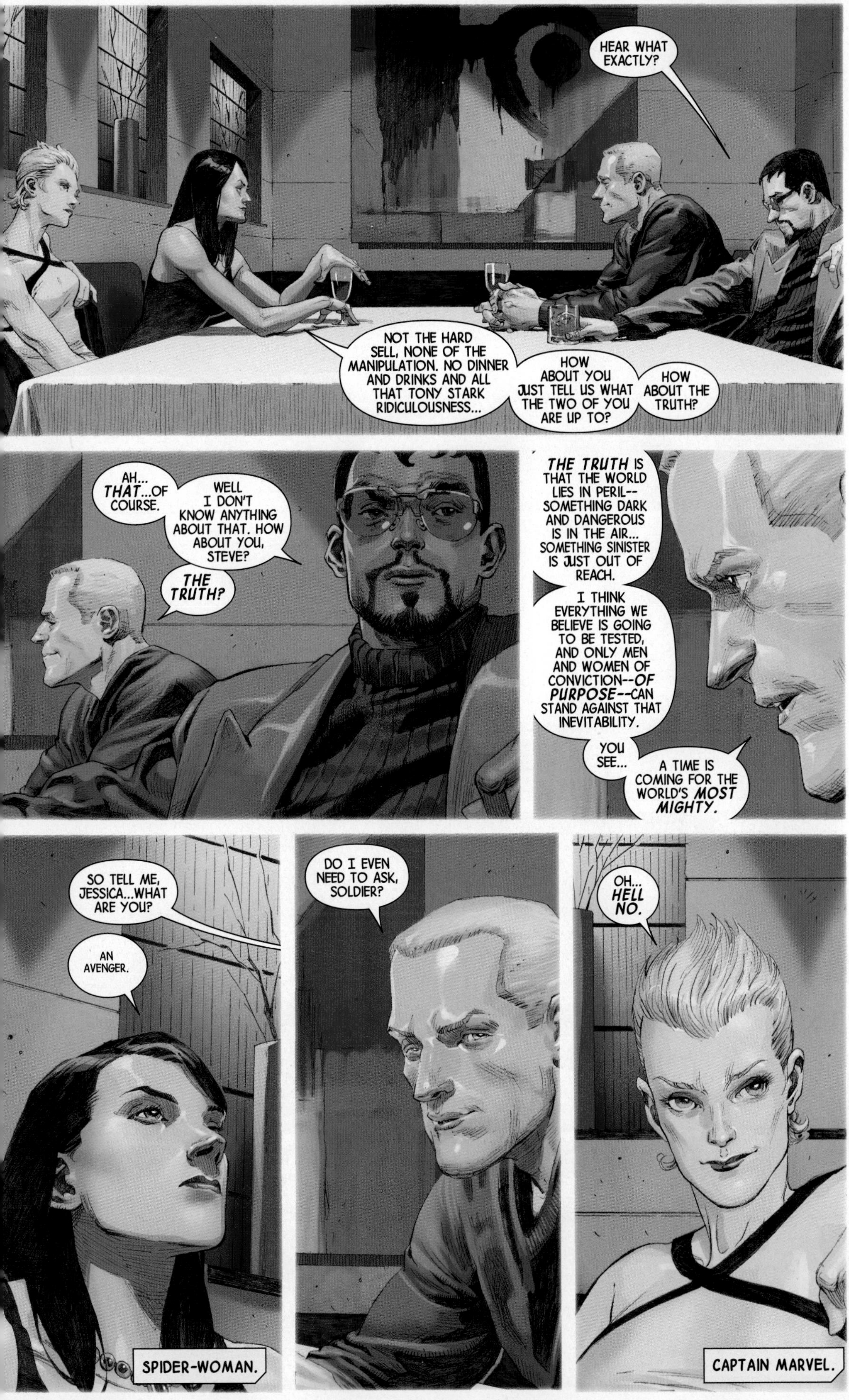
HEAR WHAT EXACTLY?
NOT THE HARD SELL, NONE OF THE MANIPULATION. NO DINNER AND DRINKS AND ALL THAT TONY STARK RIDICULOUSNESS...
HOW ABOUT YOU JUST TELL US WHAT THE TWO OF YOU ARE UP TO?
HOW ABOUT THE TRUTH?
AH... THAT...OF COURSE.
WELL I DON'T KNOW ANYTHING ABOUT THAT. HOW ABOUT YOU, STEVE?
THE TRUTH?
THE TRUTH IS THAT THE WORLD LIES IN PERIL--SOMETHING DARK AND DANGEROUS IS IN THE AIR... SOMETHING SINISTER IS JUST OUT OF REACH.
I THINK EVERYTHING WE BELIEVE IS GOING TO BE TESTED, AND ONLY MEN AND WOMEN OF CONVICTION--OF PURPOSE--CAN STAND AGAINST THAT INEVITABILITY.
YOU SEE...
A TIME IS COMING FOR THE WORLD'S MOST MIGHTY.
SO TELL ME, JESSICA...WHAT ARE YOU?
AN AVENGER.
SPIDER-WOMAN.
DO I EVEN NEED TO ASK, SOLDIER?
OH... HELL NO.
CAPTAIN MARVEL.

EARTH.
NOW.

CAP!

STARKCOMM SATELLITES PICKING UP MULTIPLE INCOMING TARGETS--TRAJECTORY MARKS THEM AS EXTRAPLANETARY...

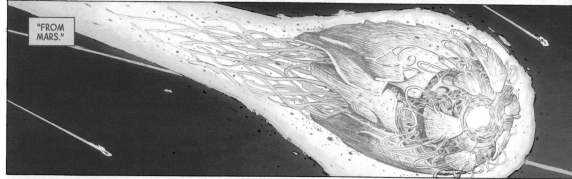

"FROM MARS."

KOBE, JAPAN.
POPULATION: 1,543,091.

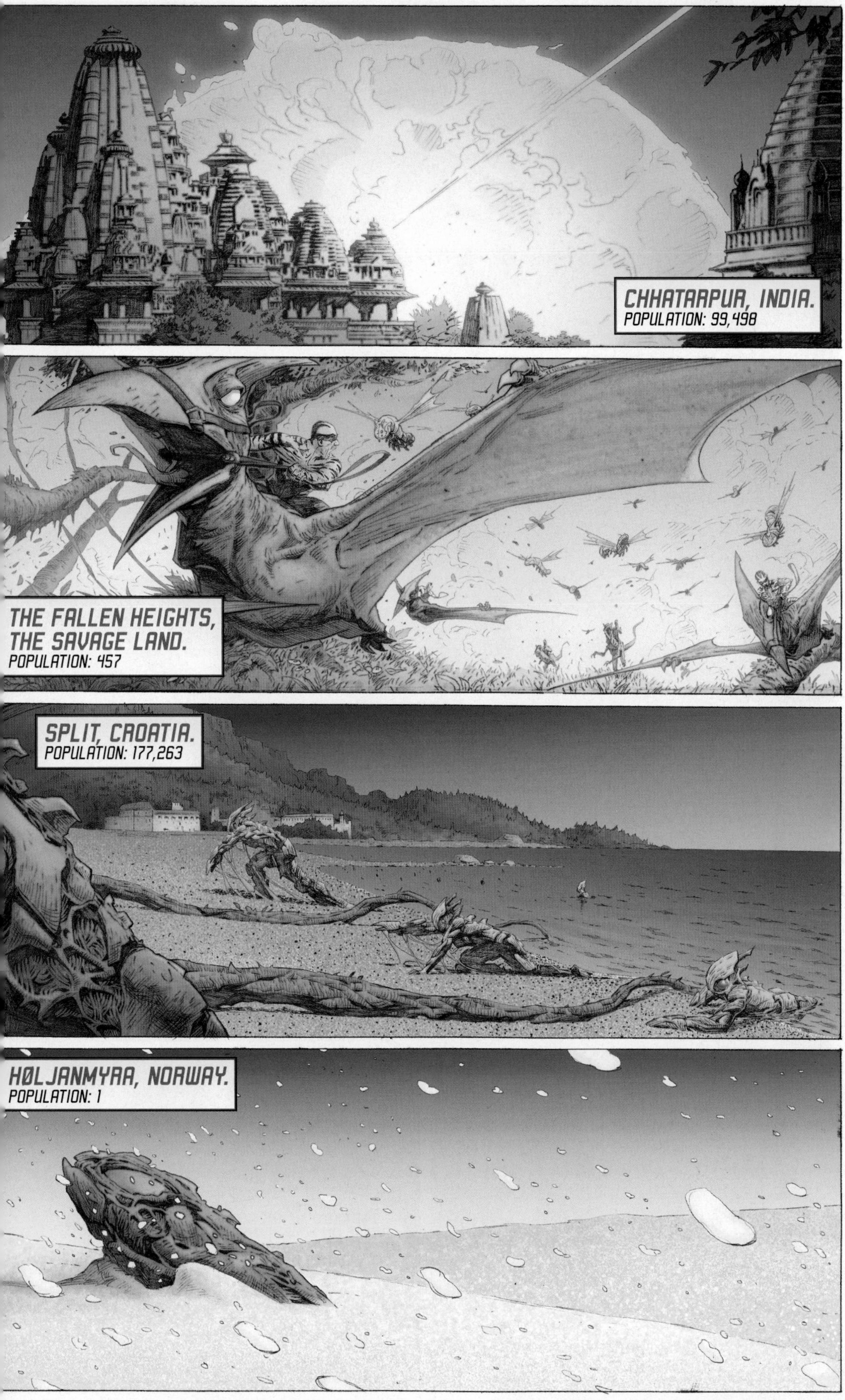
CHHATARPUR, INDIA.
POPULATION: 99,498
THE FALLEN HEIGHTS, THE SAVAGE LAND.
POPULATION: 457
SPLIT, CROATIA.
POPULATION: 177,263
HØLJANMYRA, NORWAY.
POPULATION: 1

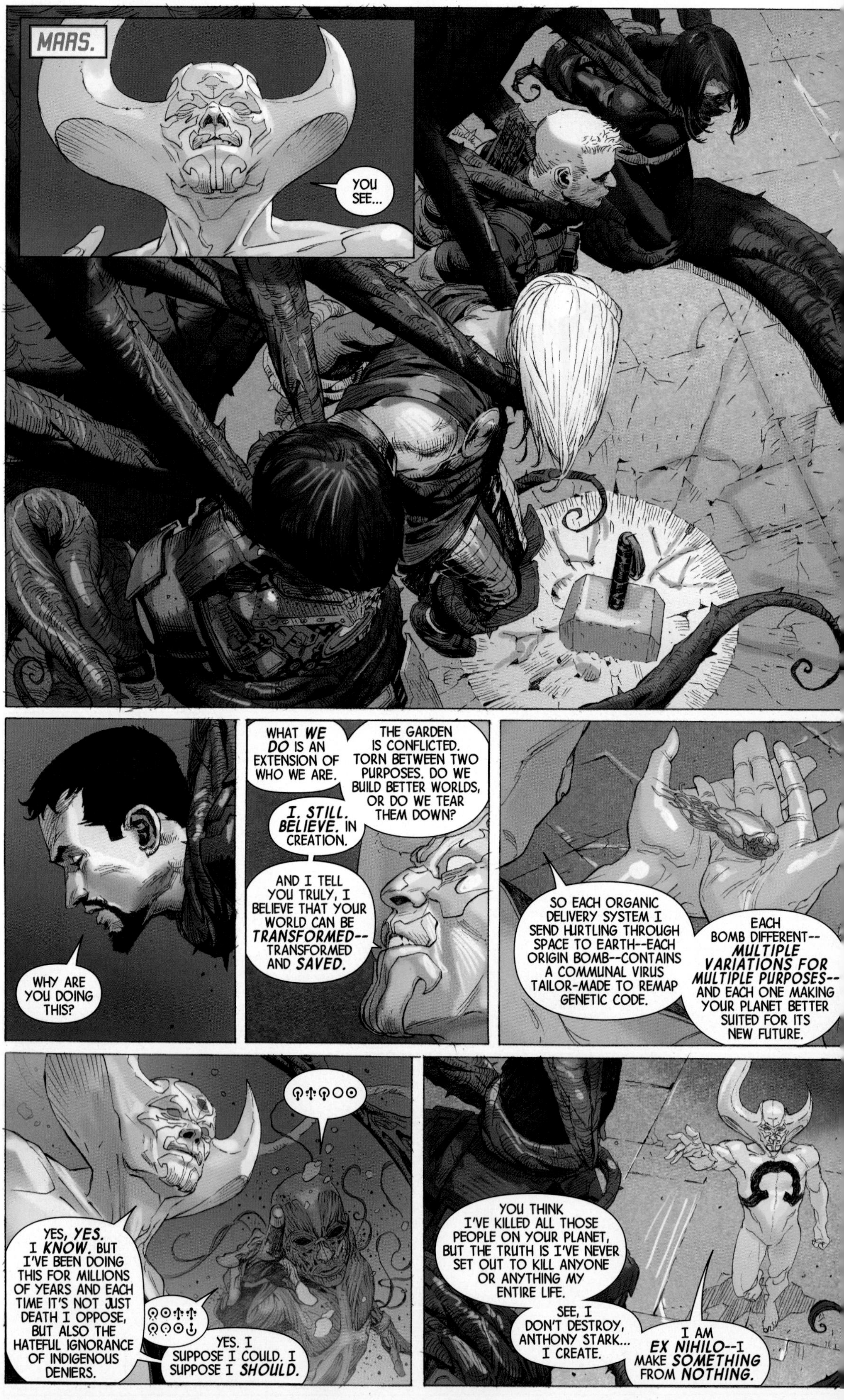
MARS.
YOU SEE...
WHY ARE YOU DOING THIS?
WHAT WE DO IS AN EXTENSION OF WHO WE ARE.
THE GARDEN IS CONFLICTED. TORN BETWEEN TWO PURPOSES. DO WE BUILD BETTER WORLDS, OR DO WE TEAR THEM DOWN?
I. STILL. BELIEVE. IN CREATION.
AND I TELL YOU TRULY, I BELIEVE THAT YOUR WORLD CAN BE TRANSFORMED-- TRANSFORMED AND SAVED.
SO EACH ORGANIC DELIVERY SYSTEM I SEND HURTLING THROUGH SPACE TO EARTH--EACH ORIGIN BOMB--CONTAINS A COMMUNAL VIRUS TAILOR-MADE TO REMAP GENETIC CODE.
EACH BOMB DIFFERENT-- MULTIPLE VARIATIONS FOR MULTIPLE PURPOSES-- AND EACH ONE MAKING YOUR PLANET BETTER SUITED FOR ITS NEW FUTURE.
YES, YES. I KNOW. BUT I'VE BEEN DOING THIS FOR MILLIONS OF YEARS AND EACH TIME IT'S NOT JUST DEATH I OPPOSE, BUT ALSO THE HATEFUL IGNORANCE OF INDIGENOUS DENIERS.
YES. I SUPPOSE I COULD. I SUPPOSE I SHOULD.
YOU THINK I'VE KILLED ALL THOSE PEOPLE ON YOUR PLANET, BUT THE TRUTH IS I'VE NEVER SET OUT TO KILL ANYONE OR ANYTHING MY ENTIRE LIFE.
SEE, I DON'T DESTROY, ANTHONY STARK... I CREATE.
I AM EX NIHILO--I MAKE SOMETHING FROM NOTHING.

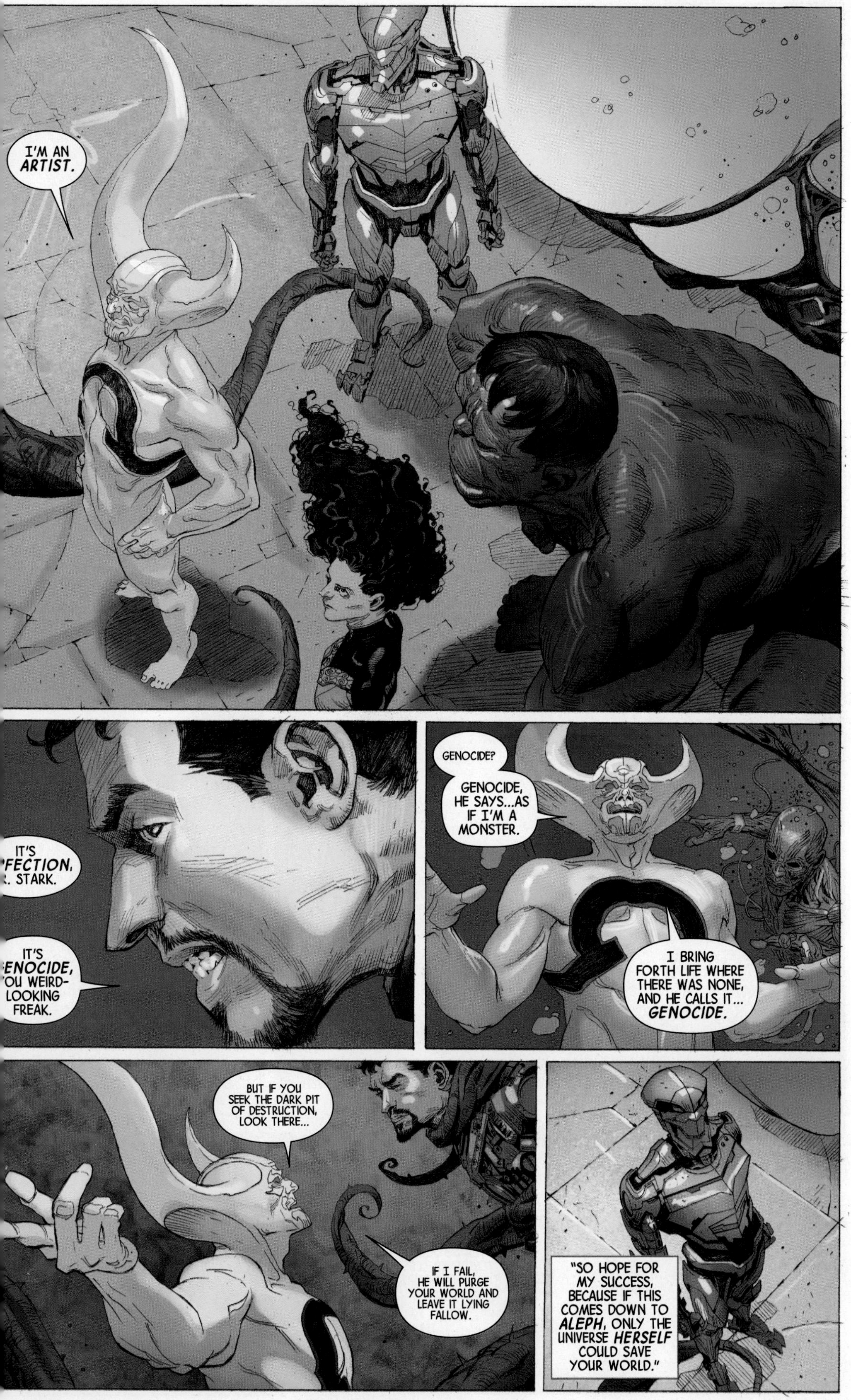
I'M AN *ARTIST.*
IT'S *FECTION,* STARK.
IT'S *ENOCIDE,* OU WEIRD-LOOKING FREAK.
GENOCIDE?
GENOCIDE, HE SAYS...AS IF I'M A MONSTER.
I BRING FORTH LIFE WHERE THERE WAS NONE, AND HE CALLS IT... *GENOCIDE.*
BUT IF YOU SEEK THE DARK PIT OF DESTRUCTION, LOOK THERE...
IF I FAIL, HE WILL PURGE YOUR WORLD AND LEAVE IT LYING FALLOW.
"SO HOPE FOR MY SUCCESS, BECAUSE IF THIS COMES DOWN TO *ALEPH*, ONLY THE UNIVERSE *HERSELF* COULD SAVE YOUR WORLD."

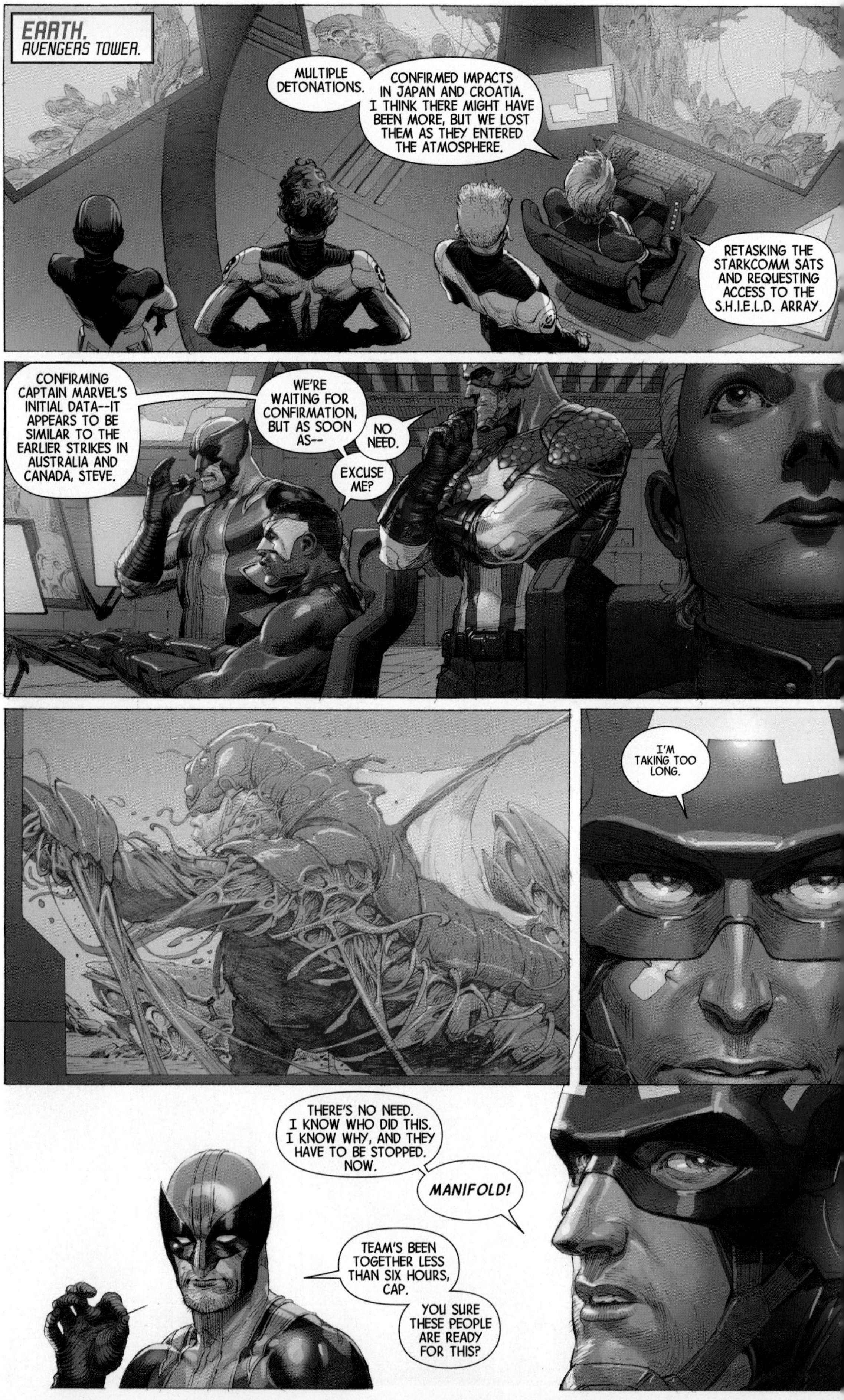

EARTH.
AVENGERS TOWER.
MULTIPLE DETONATIONS.
CONFIRMED IMPACTS IN JAPAN AND CROATIA. I THINK THERE MIGHT HAVE BEEN MORE, BUT WE LOST THEM AS THEY ENTERED THE ATMOSPHERE.
RETASKING THE STARKCOMM SATS AND REQUESTING ACCESS TO THE S.H.I.E.L.D. ARRAY.
CONFIRMING CAPTAIN MARVEL'S INITIAL DATA--IT APPEARS TO BE SIMILAR TO THE EARLIER STRIKES IN AUSTRALIA AND CANADA, STEVE.
WE'RE WAITING FOR CONFIRMATION, BUT AS SOON AS--
NO NEED.
EXCUSE ME?
I'M TAKING TOO LONG.
THERE'S NO NEED. I KNOW WHO DID THIS. I KNOW WHY, AND THEY HAVE TO BE STOPPED. NOW.
MANIFOLD!
TEAM'S BEEN TOGETHER LESS THAN SIX HOURS, CAP.
YOU SURE THESE PEOPLE ARE READY FOR THIS?

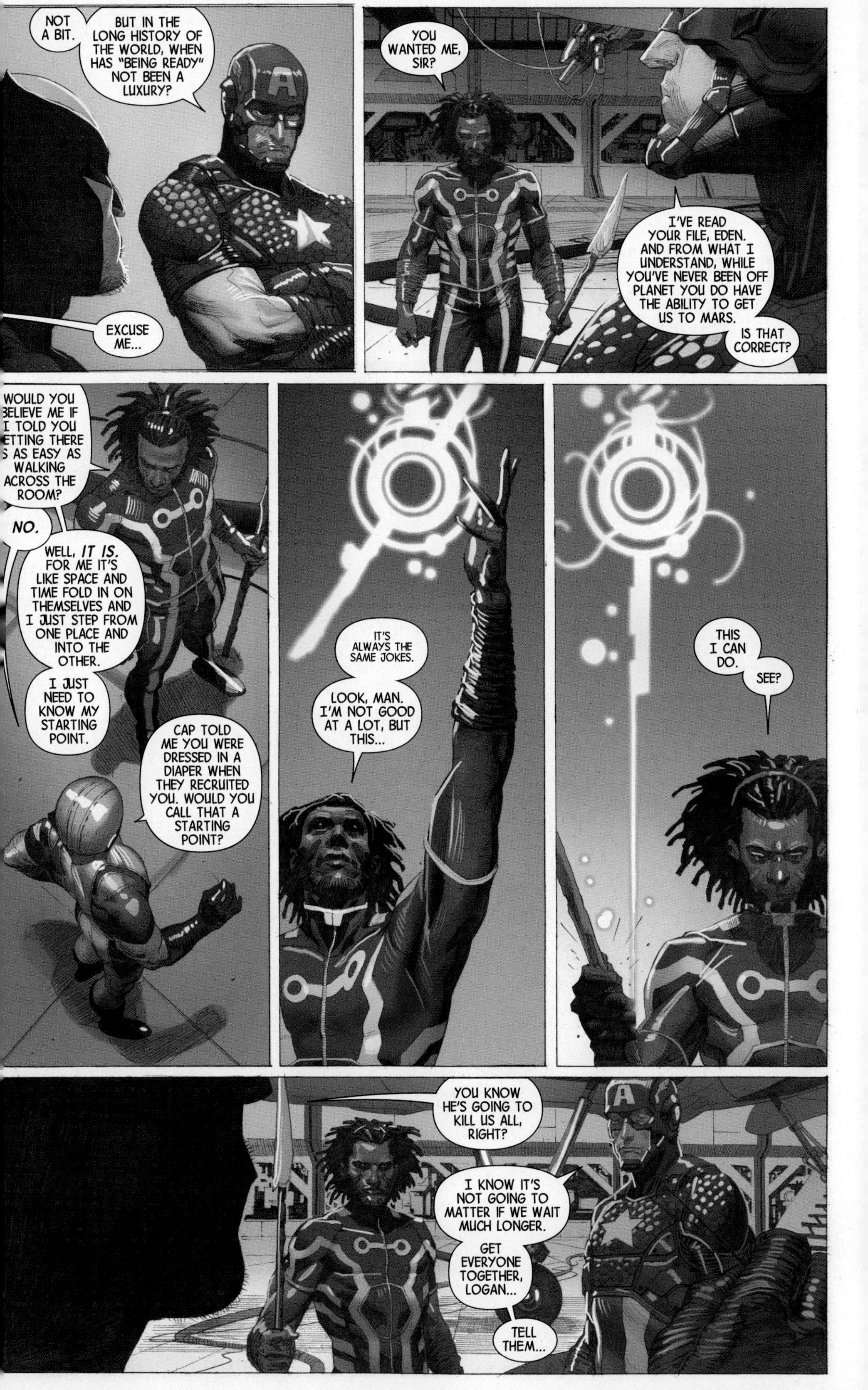
NOT A BIT.
BUT IN THE LONG HISTORY OF THE WORLD, WHEN HAS "BEING READY" NOT BEEN A LUXURY?
EXCUSE ME...
YOU WANTED ME, SIR?
I'VE READ YOUR FILE, EDEN. AND FROM WHAT I UNDERSTAND, WHILE YOU'VE NEVER BEEN OFF PLANET YOU DO HAVE THE ABILITY TO GET US TO MARS.
IS THAT CORRECT?
WOULD YOU BELIEVE ME IF I TOLD YOU ETTING THERE S AS EASY AS WALKING ACROSS THE ROOM?
NO.
WELL, IT IS. FOR ME IT'S LIKE SPACE AND TIME FOLD IN ON THEMSELVES AND I JUST STEP FROM ONE PLACE AND INTO THE OTHER.
I JUST NEED TO KNOW MY STARTING POINT.
CAP TOLD ME YOU WERE DRESSED IN A DIAPER WHEN THEY RECRUITED YOU. WOULD YOU CALL THAT A STARTING POINT?
IT'S ALWAYS THE SAME JOKES.
LOOK, MAN. I'M NOT GOOD AT A LOT, BUT THIS...
THIS I CAN DO.
SEE?
YOU KNOW HE'S GOING TO KILL US ALL, RIGHT?
I KNOW IT'S NOT GOING TO MATTER IF WE WAIT MUCH LONGER.
GET EVERYONE TOGETHER, LOGAN...
TELL THEM...

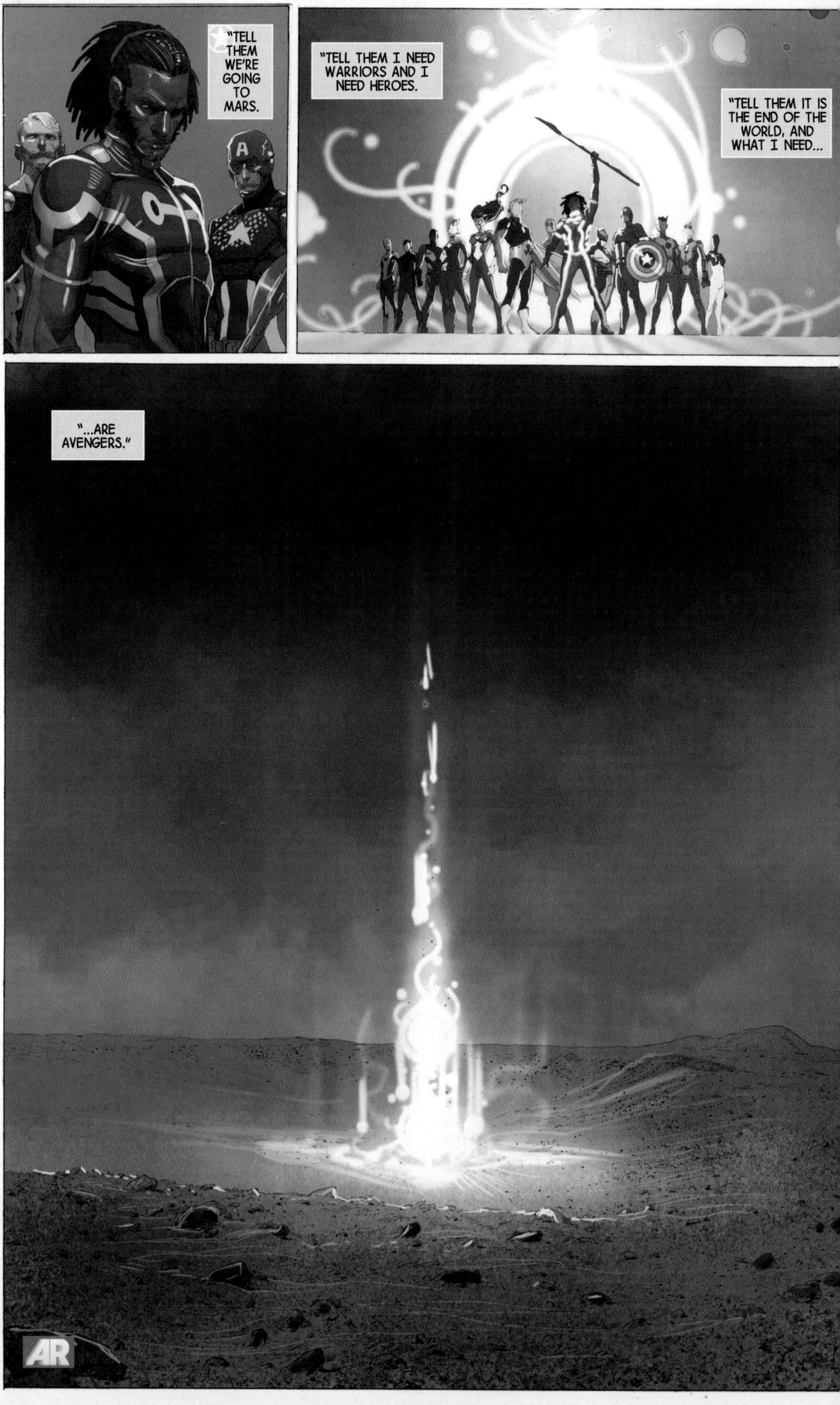
"TELL THEM WE'RE GOING TO MARS.
"TELL THEM I NEED WARRIORS AND I NEED HEROES.
"TELL THEM IT IS THE END OF THE WORLD, AND WHAT I NEED...
"...ARE AVENGERS."

"THE GARDEN"

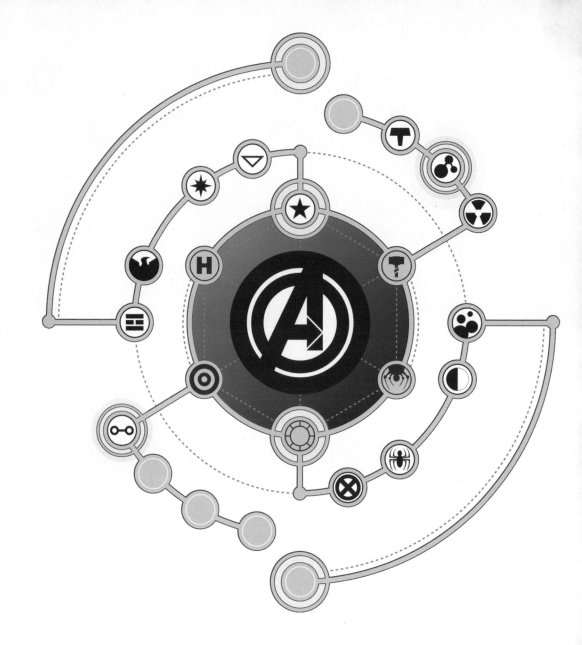

EARTH'S MIGHTIEST HEROES

CAPTAIN AMERICA · IRON MAN · THOR · HAWKEYE · BLACK WIDOW · HULK
WOLVERINE · SPIDER-MAN · CAPTAIN MARVEL · SPIDER-WOMAN
FALCON · SHANG-CHI · SUNSPOT · CANNONBALL · MANIFOLD
SMASHER · CAPTAIN UNIVERSE · HYPERION

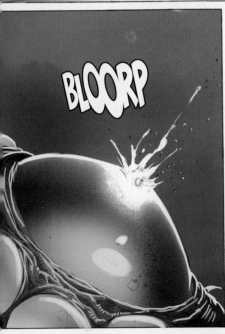
BLOORP

ALERT,
EX NIHILO: A
BREACH,
PRECEDING
DELIVERY.

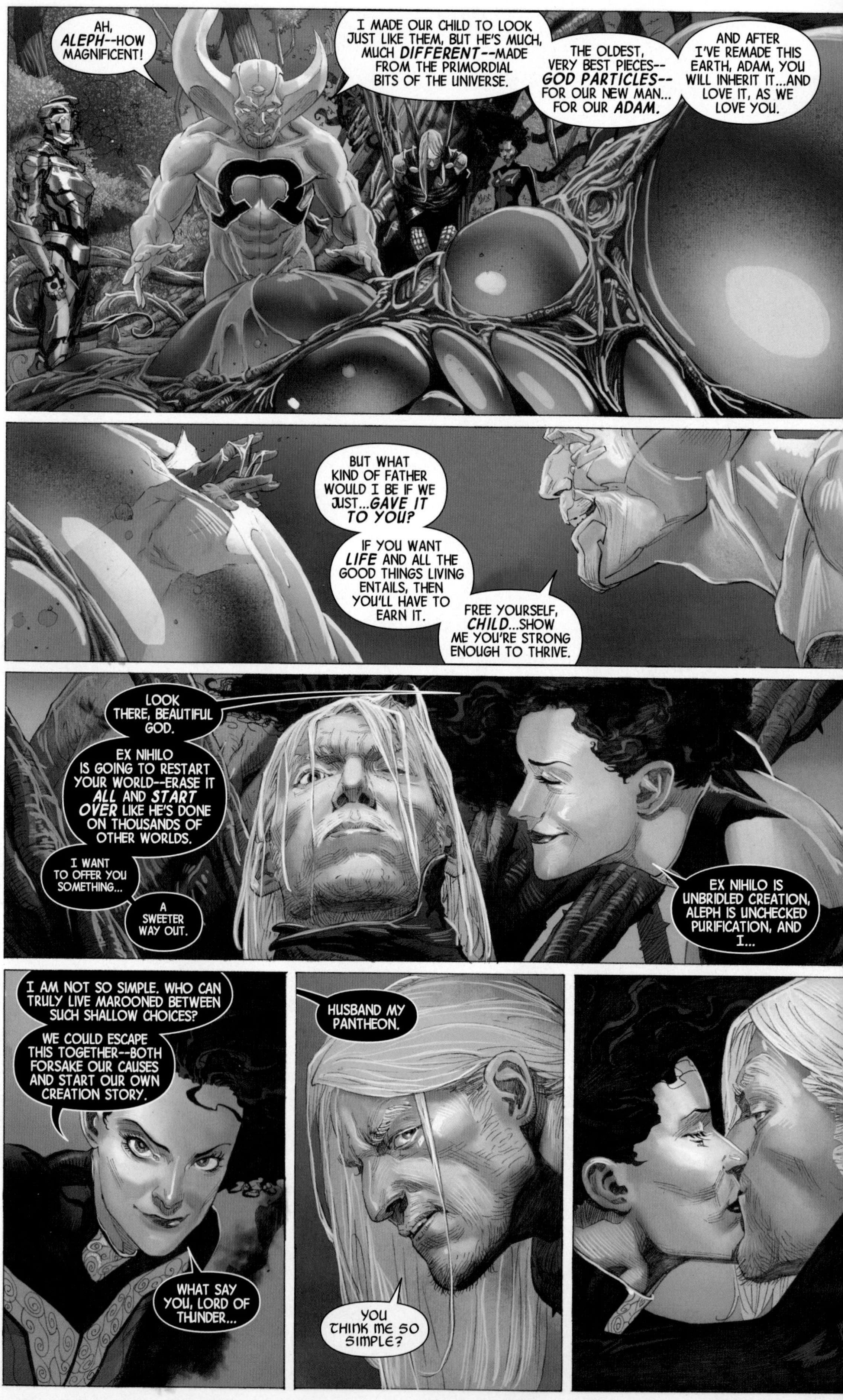
AH, ALEPH--HOW MAGNIFICENT!
I MADE OUR CHILD TO LOOK JUST LIKE THEM, BUT HE'S MUCH, MUCH DIFFERENT--MADE FROM THE PRIMORDIAL BITS OF THE UNIVERSE.
THE OLDEST, VERY BEST PIECES--GOD PARTICLES--FOR OUR NEW MAN... FOR OUR ADAM.
AND AFTER I'VE REMADE THIS EARTH, ADAM, YOU WILL INHERIT IT...AND LOVE IT, AS WE LOVE YOU.
BUT WHAT KIND OF FATHER WOULD I BE IF WE JUST...GAVE IT TO YOU?
IF YOU WANT LIFE AND ALL THE GOOD THINGS LIVING ENTAILS, THEN YOU'LL HAVE TO EARN IT.
FREE YOURSELF, CHILD...SHOW ME YOU'RE STRONG ENOUGH TO THRIVE.
LOOK THERE, BEAUTIFUL GOD.
EX NIHILO IS GOING TO RESTART YOUR WORLD--ERASE IT ALL AND START OVER LIKE HE'S DONE ON THOUSANDS OF OTHER WORLDS.
I WANT TO OFFER YOU SOMETHING...
A SWEETER WAY OUT.
EX NIHILO IS UNBRIDLED CREATION, ALEPH IS UNCHECKED PURIFICATION, AND I...
I AM NOT SO SIMPLE. WHO CAN TRULY LIVE MAROONED BETWEEN SUCH SHALLOW CHOICES?
WE COULD ESCAPE THIS TOGETHER--BOTH FORSAKE OUR CAUSES AND START OUR OWN CREATION STORY.
WHAT SAY YOU, LORD OF THUNDER...
HUSBAND MY PANTHEON.
YOU THINK ME SO SIMPLE?

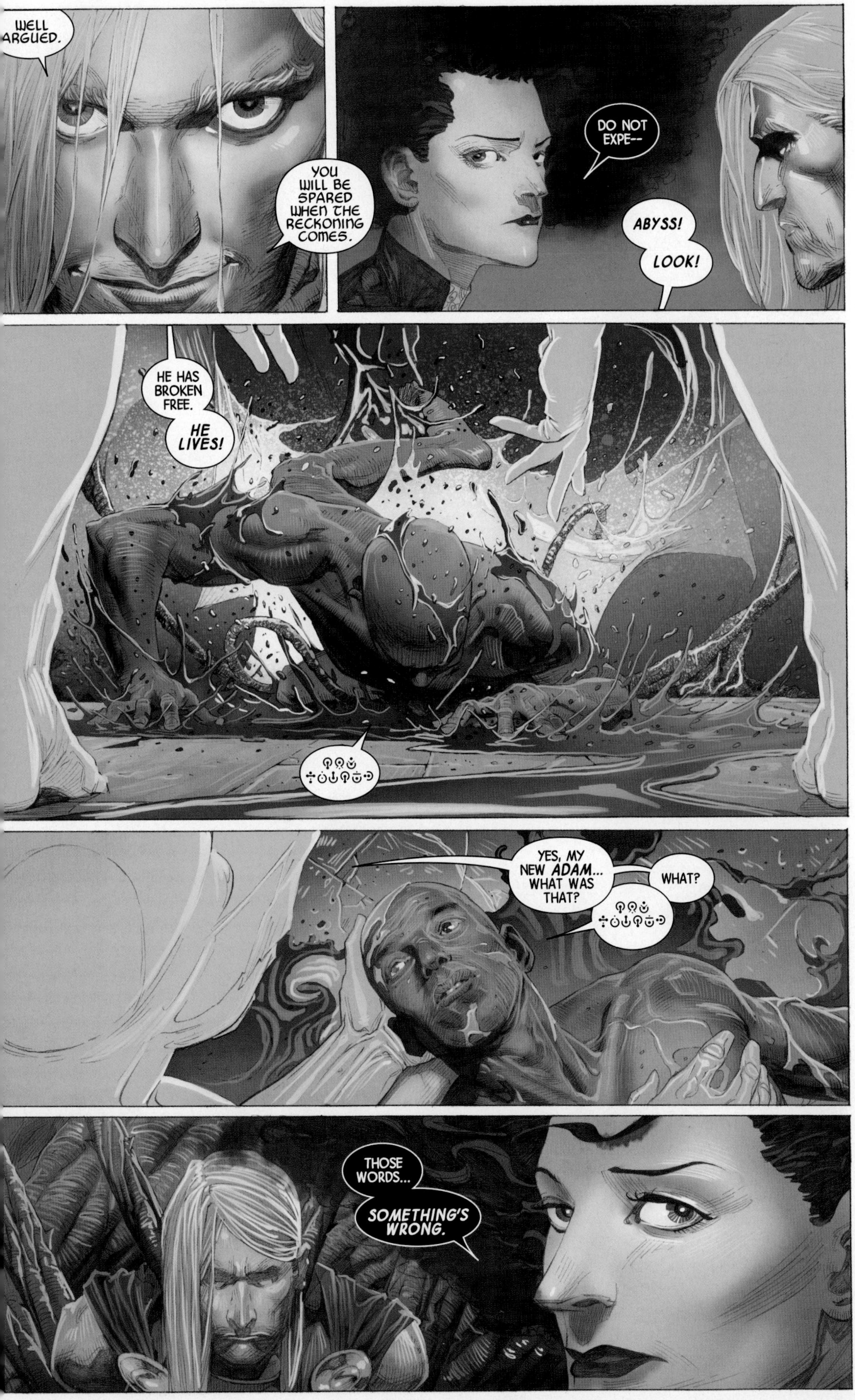
WELL ARGUED.
YOU WILL BE SPARED WHEN THE RECKONING COMES.
DO NOT EXPE--
ABYSS!
LOOK!
HE HAS BROKEN FREE.
HE LIVES!
YES, MY NEW ADAM... WHAT WAS THAT?
WHAT?
THOSE WORDS...
SOMETHING'S WRONG.

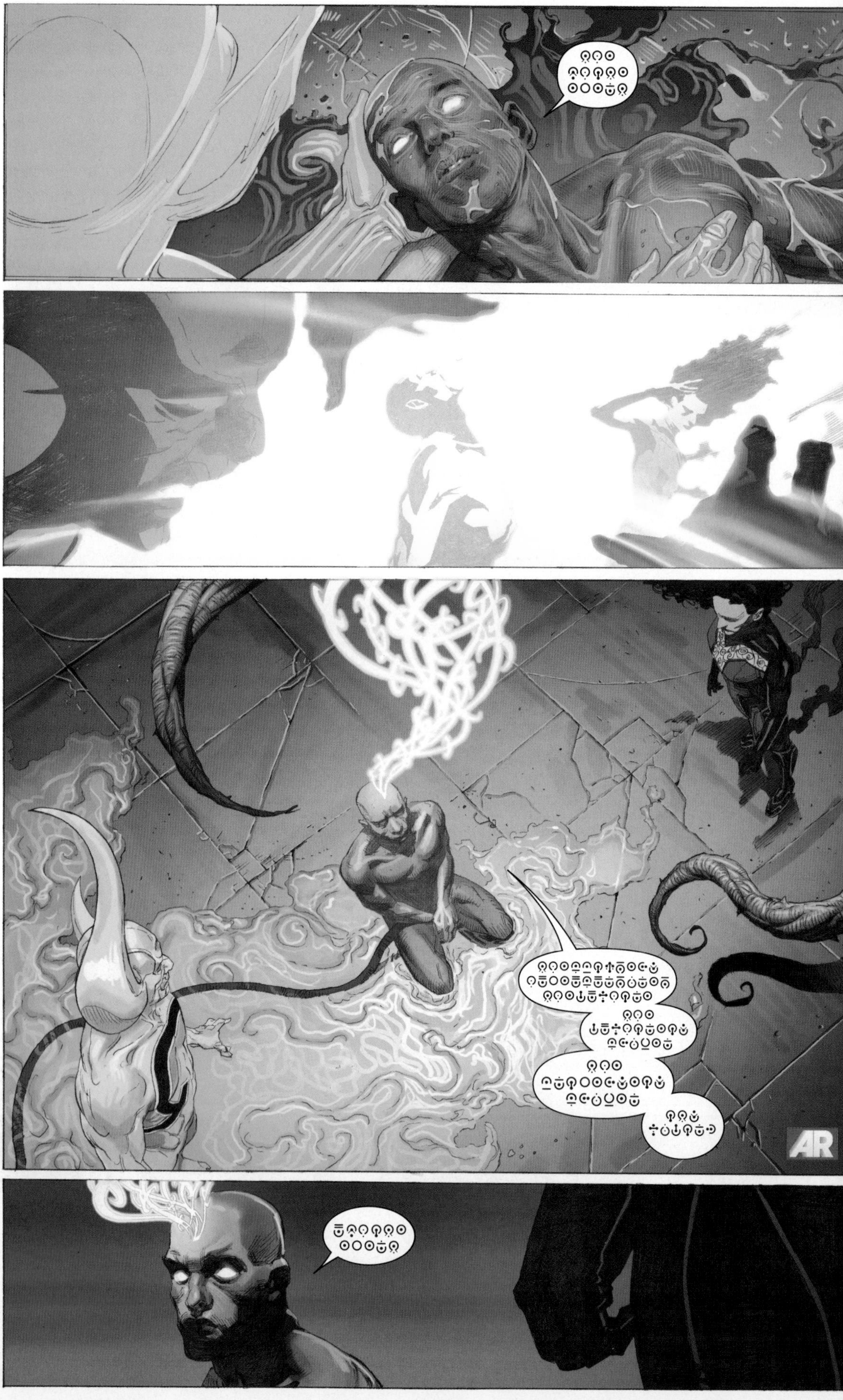

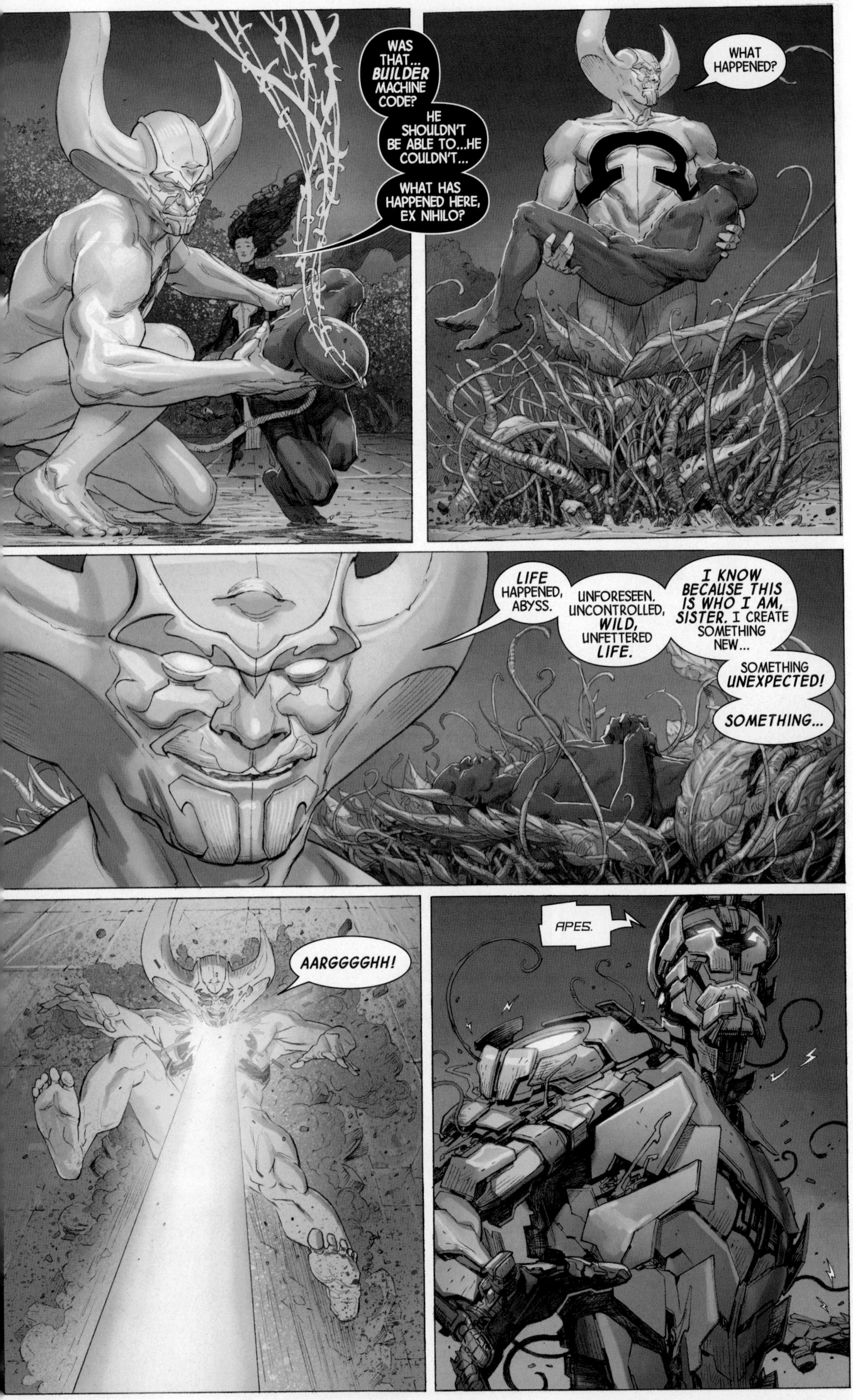
WAS THAT... BUILDER MACHINE CODE?
HE SHOULDN'T BE ABLE TO...HE COULDN'T...
WHAT HAS HAPPENED HERE, EX NIHILO?
WHAT HAPPENED?
LIFE HAPPENED, ABYSS.
UNFORESEEN. UNCONTROLLED, WILD, UNFETTERED LIFE.
I KNOW BECAUSE THIS IS WHO I AM, SISTER. I CREATE SOMETHING NEW...
SOMETHING UNEXPECTED!
SOMETHING...
AARGGGGHH!
APES.

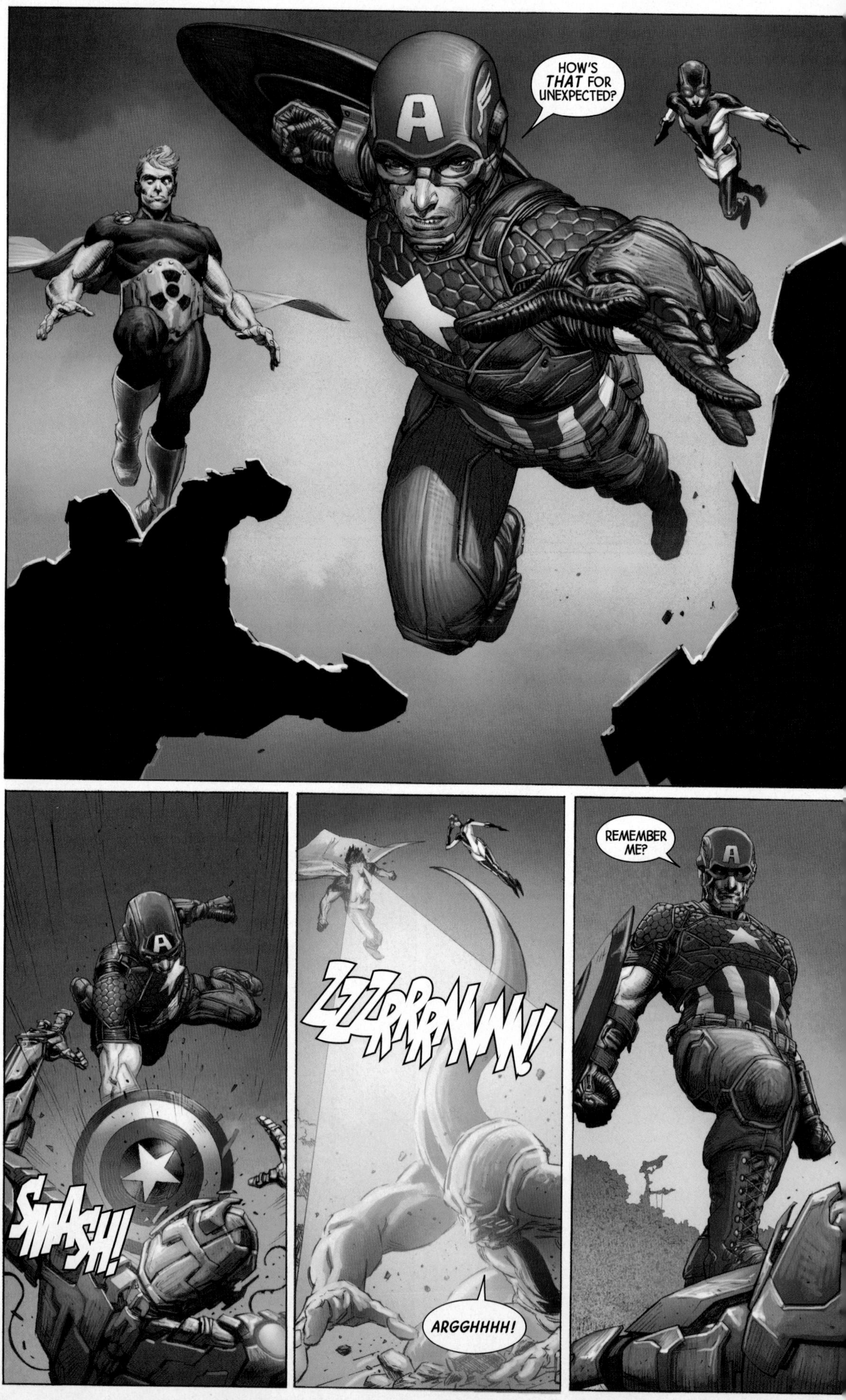
HOW'S THAT FOR UNEXPECTED?
SMASH!
ZZZRRRNNN!
ARGGHHHH!
REMEMBER ME?

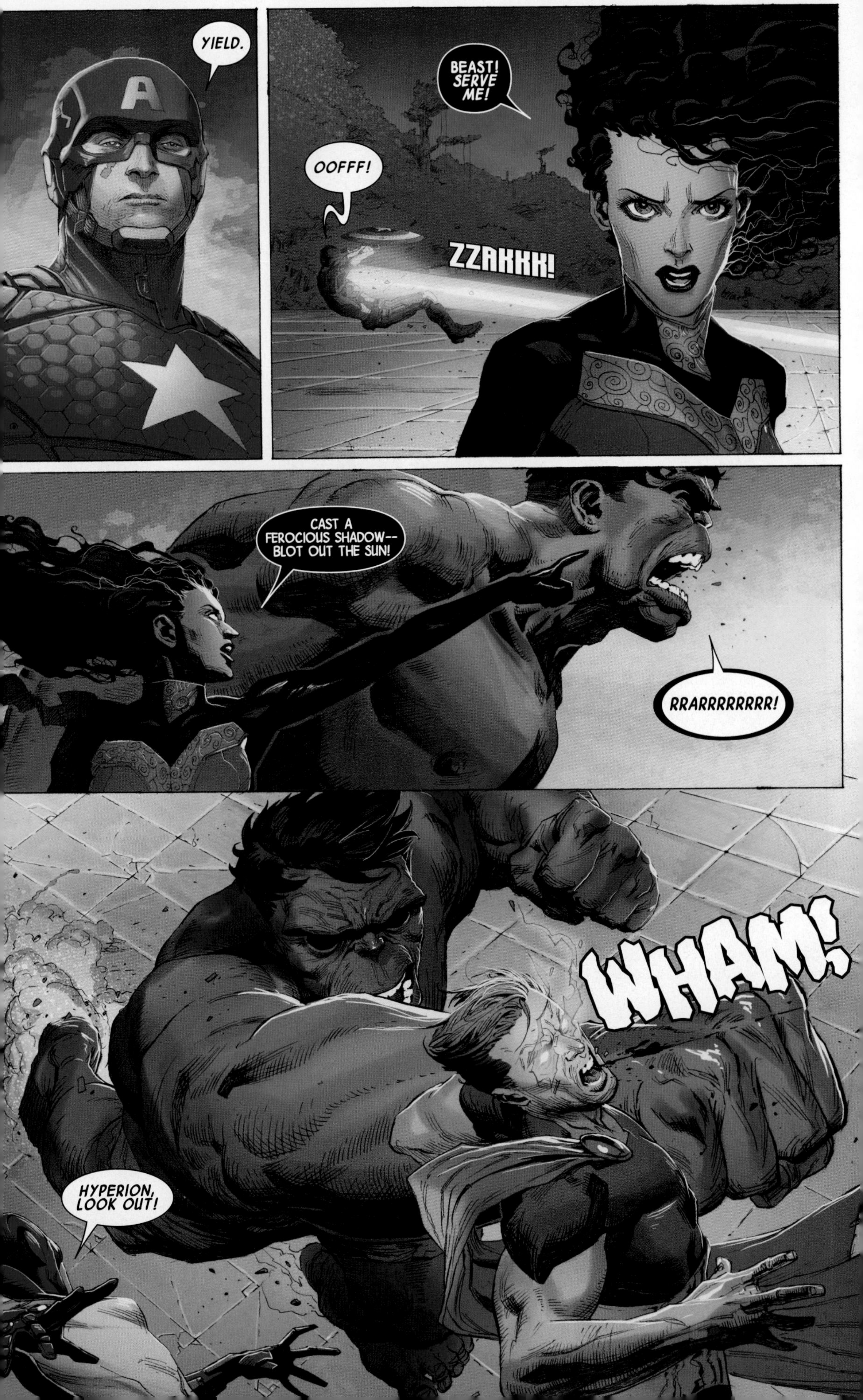
YIELD.
BEAST! SERVE ME!
OOFFF!
ZZAKKK!
CAST A FEROCIOUS SHADOW-- BLOT OUT THE SUN!
RRARRRRRRRR!
WHAM!
HYPERION, LOOK OUT!

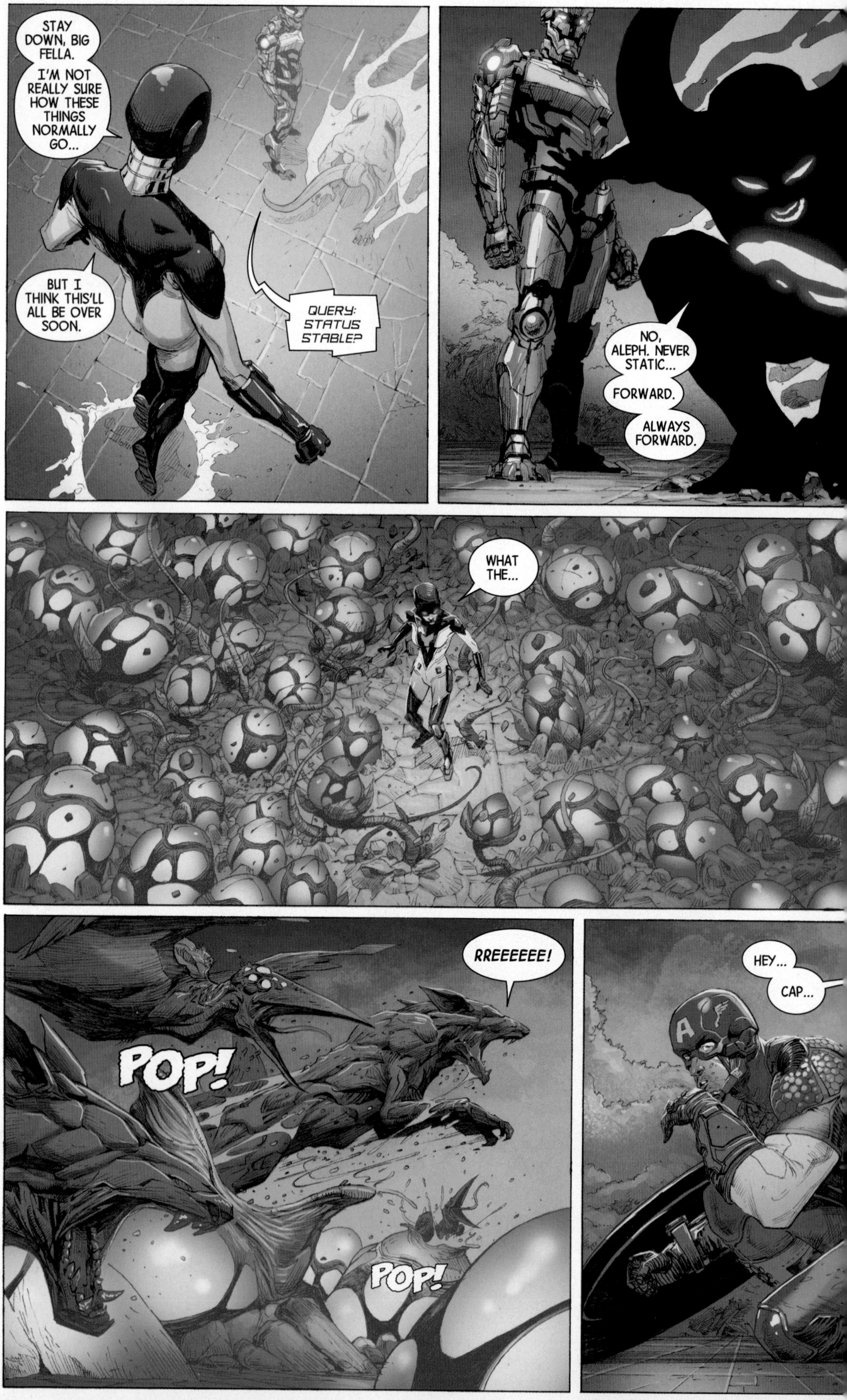
STAY DOWN, BIG FELLA.
I'M NOT REALLY SURE HOW THESE THINGS NORMALLY GO...
BUT I THINK THIS'LL ALL BE OVER SOON.
QUERY: STATUS STABLE?
NO, ALEPH. NEVER STATIC...
FORWARD.
ALWAYS FORWARD.
WHAT THE...
RREEEEEE!
POP!
POP!
HEY...
CAP...

...THE PLAN...

I THOUGHT THE PLAN... WAS TO CALL EVERYONE?

IT WAS. I DID.

CLICK

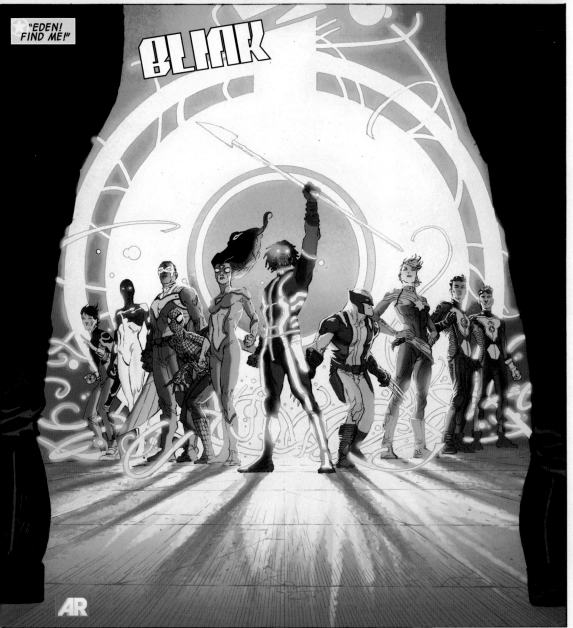

"EDEN! FIND ME!"

BLINK

AR

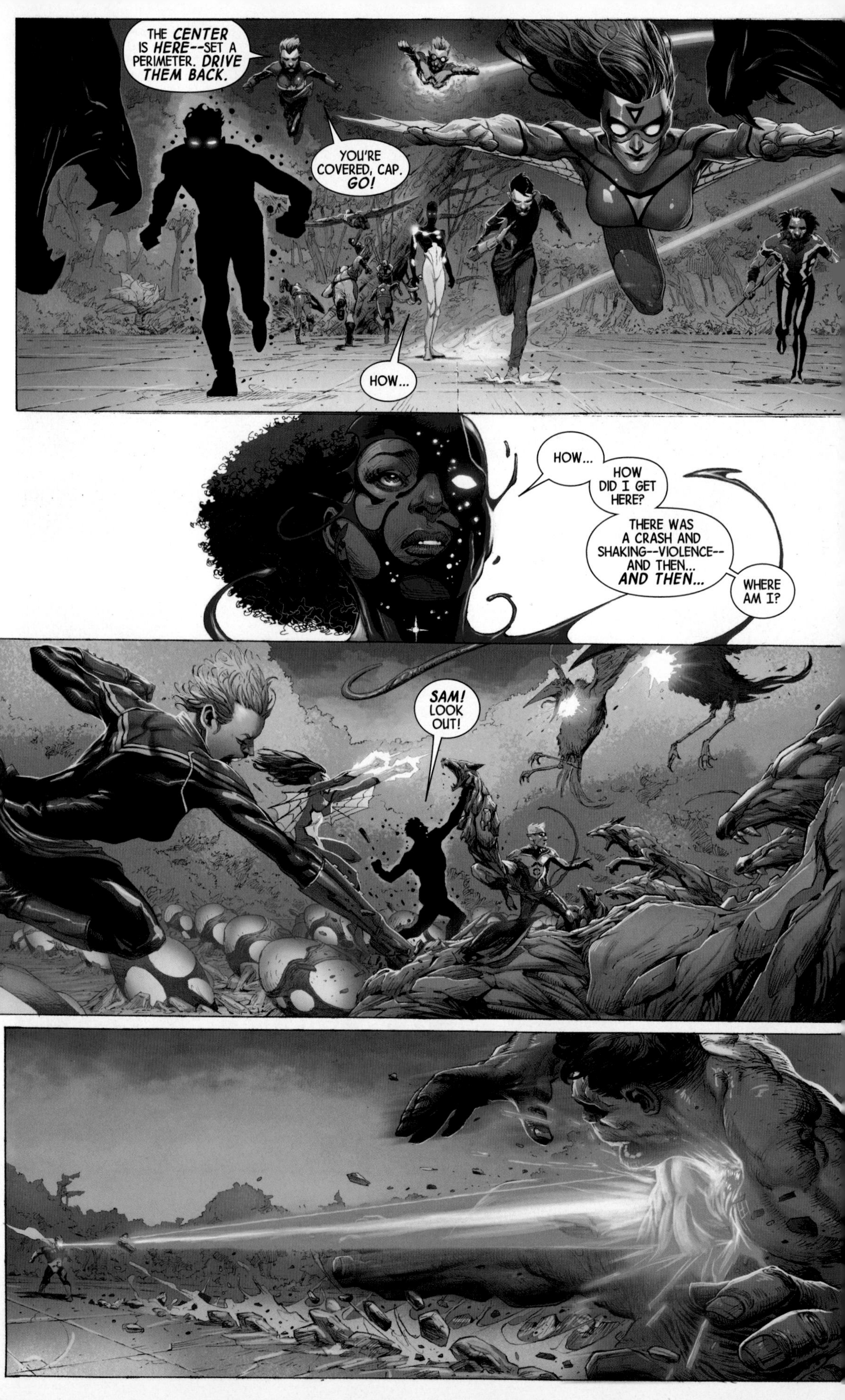
THE CENTER IS HERE--SET A PERIMETER. DRIVE THEM BACK.
YOU'RE COVERED, CAP. GO!
HOW...
HOW...
HOW DID I GET HERE?
THERE WAS A CRASH AND SHAKING--VIOLENCE--AND THEN... AND THEN...
WHERE AM I?
SAM! LOOK OUT!

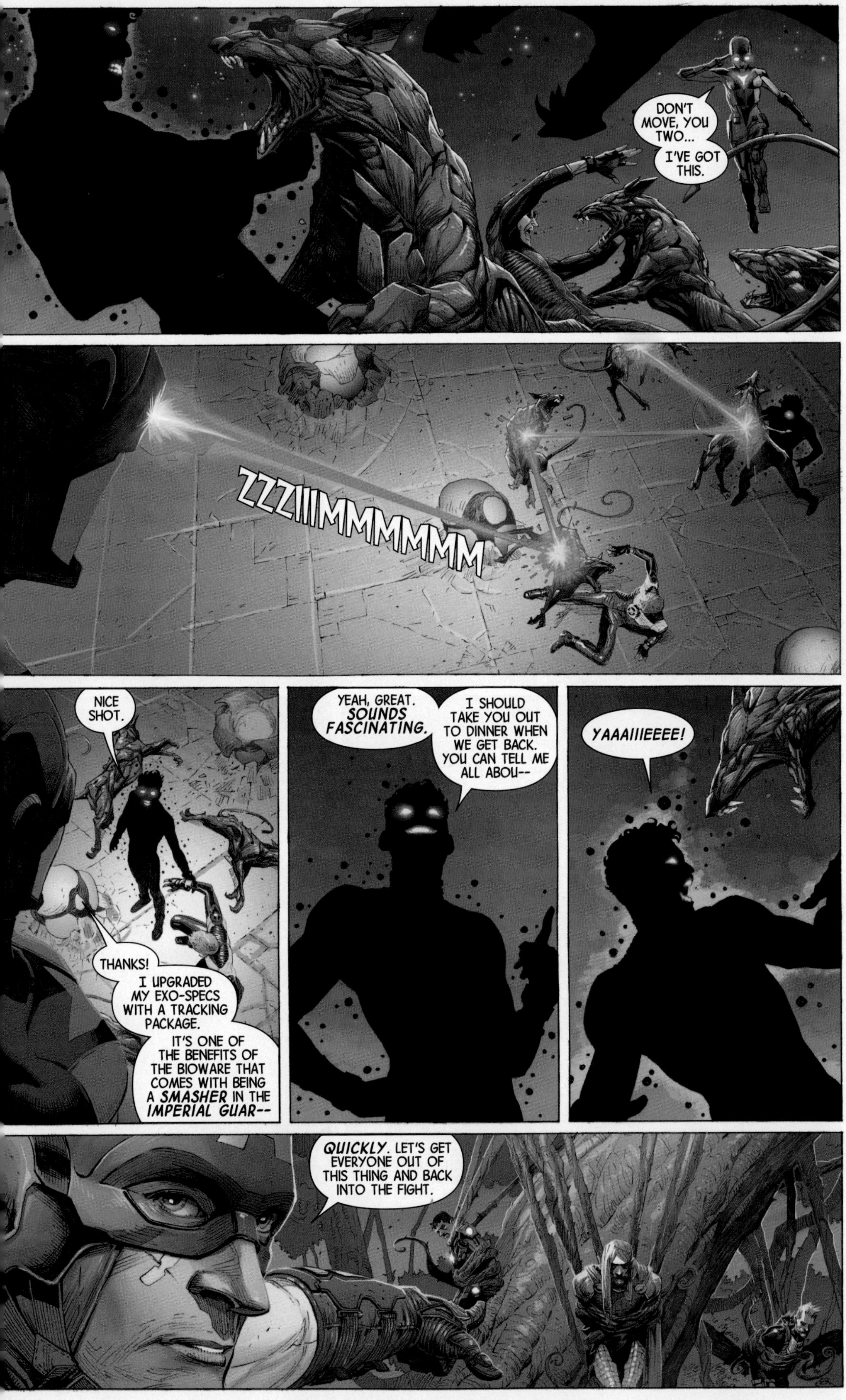
DON'T MOVE, YOU TWO...
I'VE GOT THIS.
ZZZIIIMMMMMMM
NICE SHOT.
THANKS!
I UPGRADED MY EXO-SPECS WITH A TRACKING PACKAGE.
IT'S ONE OF THE BENEFITS OF THE BIOWARE THAT COMES WITH BEING A SMASHER IN THE IMPERIAL GUAR--
YEAH, GREAT. SOUNDS FASCINATING.
I SHOULD TAKE YOU OUT TO DINNER WHEN WE GET BACK. YOU CAN TELL ME ALL ABOU--
YAAAIIIEEEE!
QUICKLY. LET'S GET EVERYONE OUT OF THIS THING AND BACK INTO THE FIGHT.

UUGGGHHH!

OH MAN, THIS STUFF IS LIKE MOLDED TITANIUM. THIS IS GOING TO TAKE TOO LONG TO PULL OFF.

IF ONLY WE HAD SOME WAY TO...

CUT IT.

OR SOMETHING.

RIGHT.

SNIKT

I'VE GOT YOU, TONY.

FALCON, I NEED YOU TO...

SAM!

SNAP OUT OF IT, SAM. WHAT'S WRONG WITH YOU?

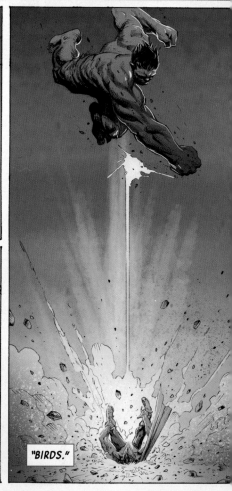

IT TOOK ME A FEW MINUTES TO COMPREHEND WHAT I WAS HEARING--THERE WERE TWO SIDES OF THE CONVERSATION BUT I COULD ONLY MAKE OUT ONE...

I UNDERSTAND IT NOW. THESE TWO ANIMALS WERE MADE TO BE SYMBIOTIC...

AND HE MADE ONE OF THEM BIRDS, STEVE.

"BIRDS."

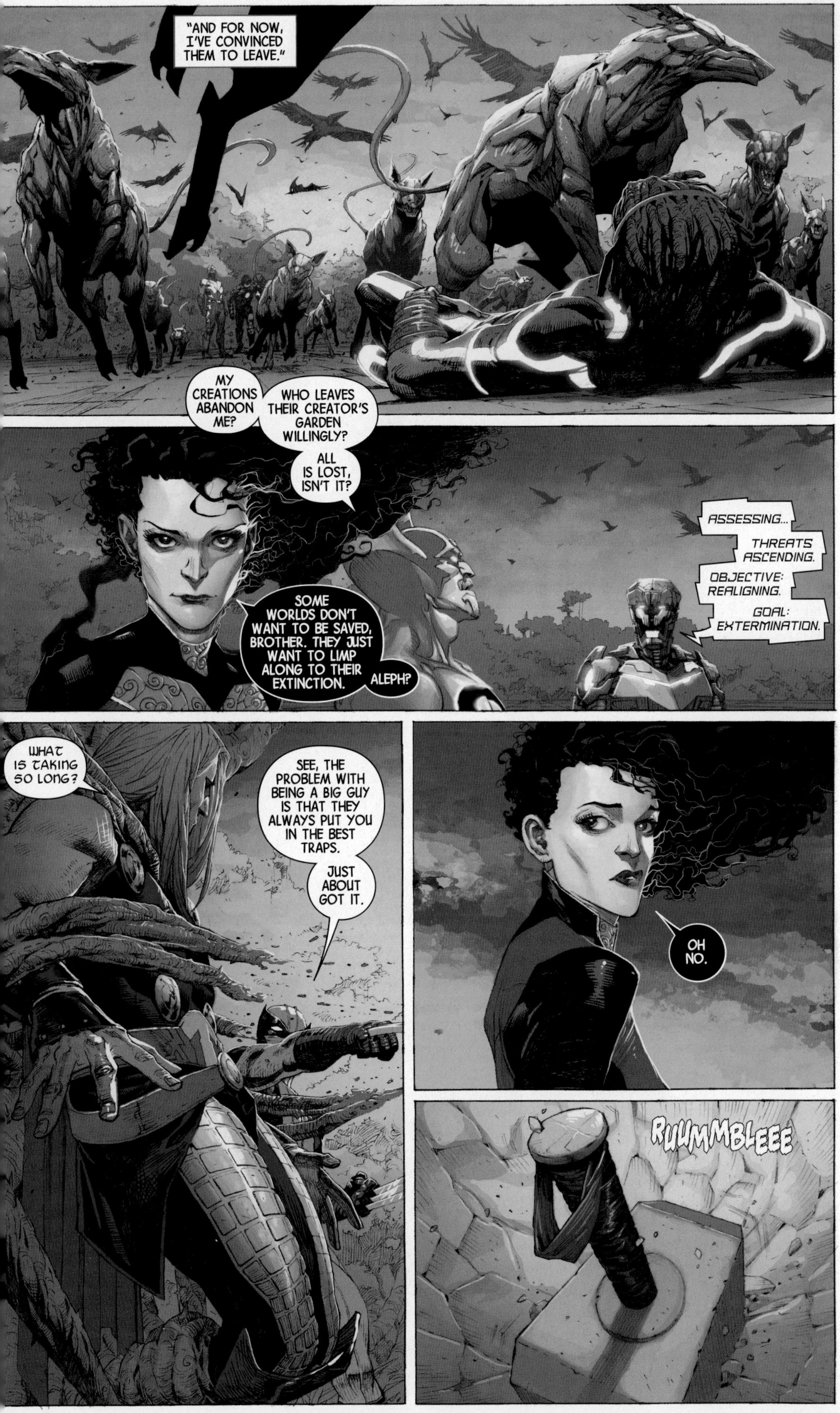
"AND FOR NOW, I'VE CONVINCED THEM TO LEAVE."
MY CREATIONS ABANDON ME?
WHO LEAVES THEIR CREATOR'S GARDEN WILLINGLY?
ALL IS LOST, ISN'T IT?
SOME WORLDS DON'T WANT TO BE SAVED, BROTHER. THEY JUST WANT TO LIMP ALONG TO THEIR EXTINCTION.
ALEPH?
ASSESSING...
THREATS ASCENDING.
OBJECTIVE: REALIGNING.
GOAL: EXTERMINATION.
WHAT IS TAKING SO LONG?
SEE, THE PROBLEM WITH BEING A BIG GUY IS THAT THEY ALWAYS PUT YOU IN THE BEST TRAPS.
JUST ABOUT GOT IT.
OH NO.
RUUMMBLEEE

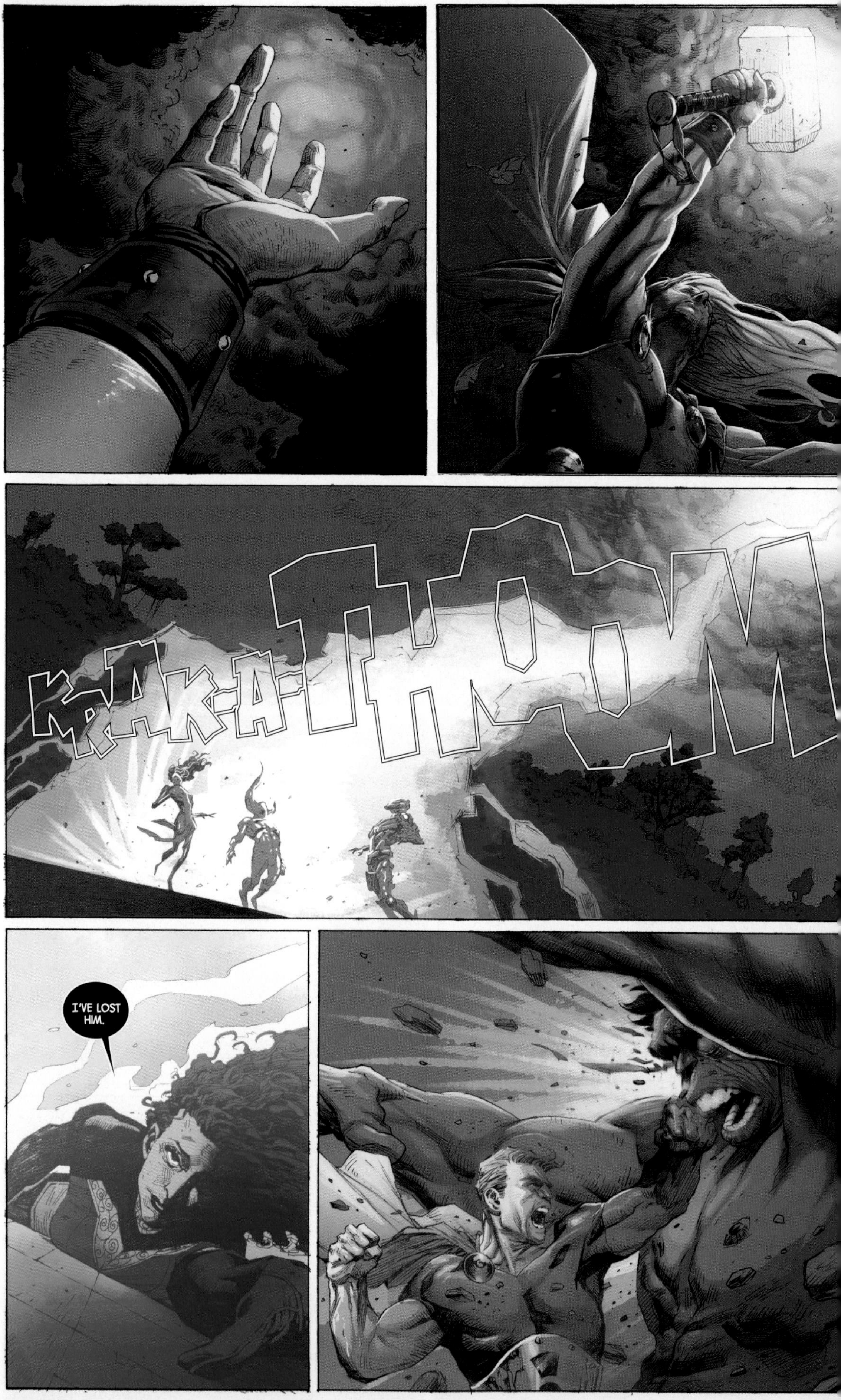
KRAK-A-THOOM
I'VE LOST HIM.

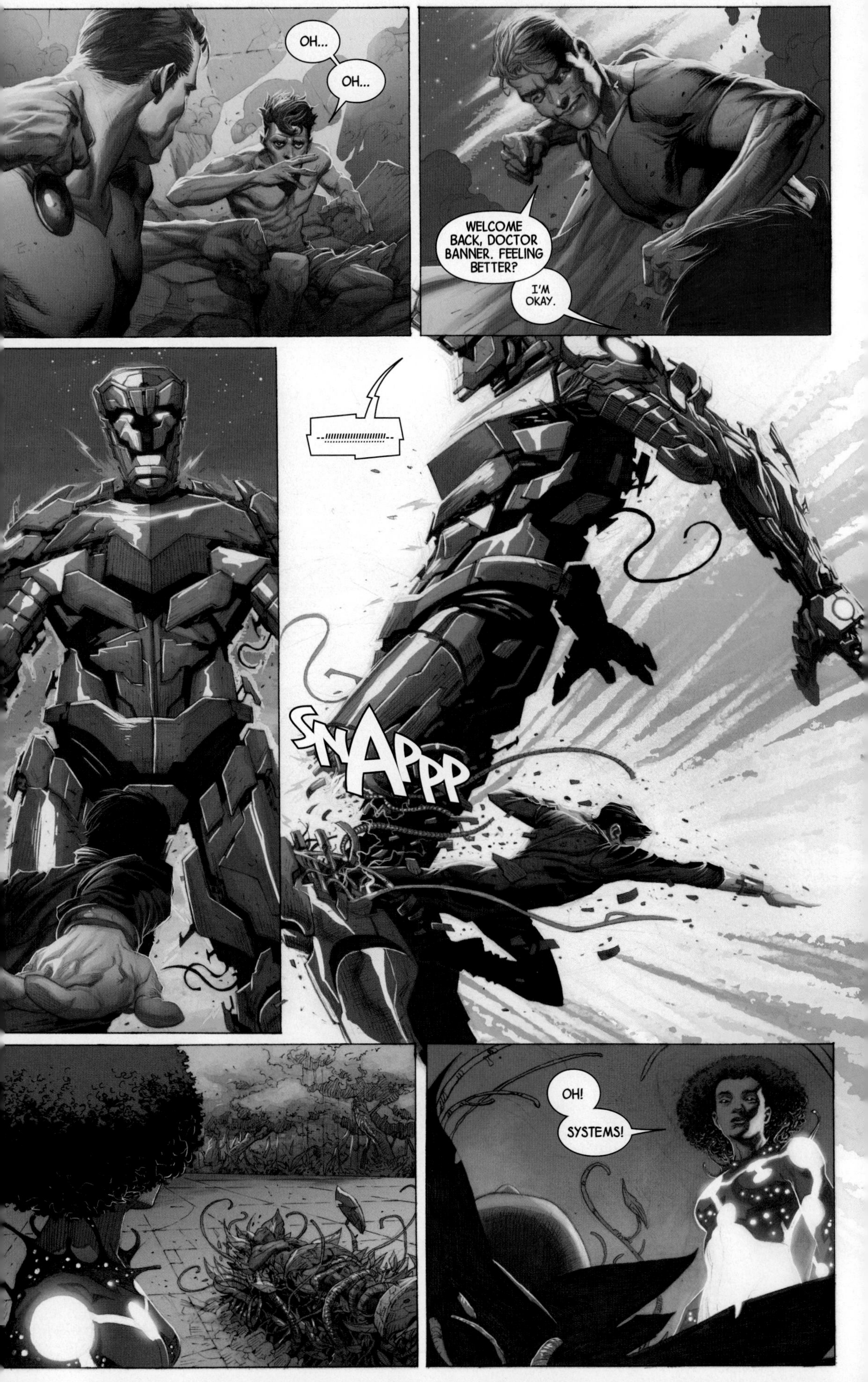
OH...
OH...
WELCOME BACK, DOCTOR BANNER. FEELING BETTER?
I'M OKAY.
SNAPPP
OH!
SYSTEMS!

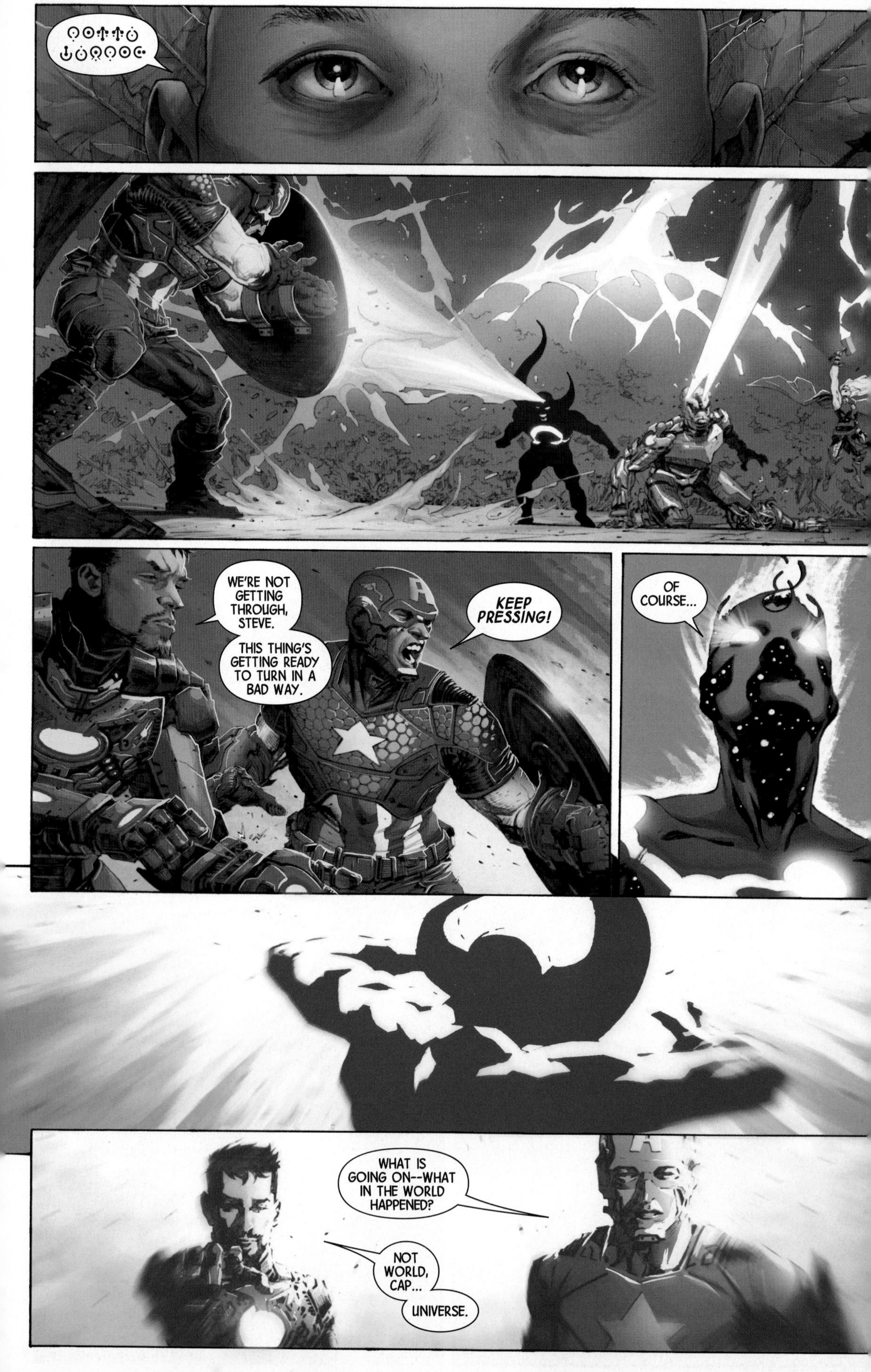
WE'RE NOT GETTING THROUGH, STEVE.
THIS THING'S GETTING READY TO TURN IN A BAD WAY.
KEEP PRESSING!
OF COURSE...
WHAT IS GOING ON--WHAT IN THE WORLD HAPPENED?
NOT WORLD, CAP...
UNIVERSE.

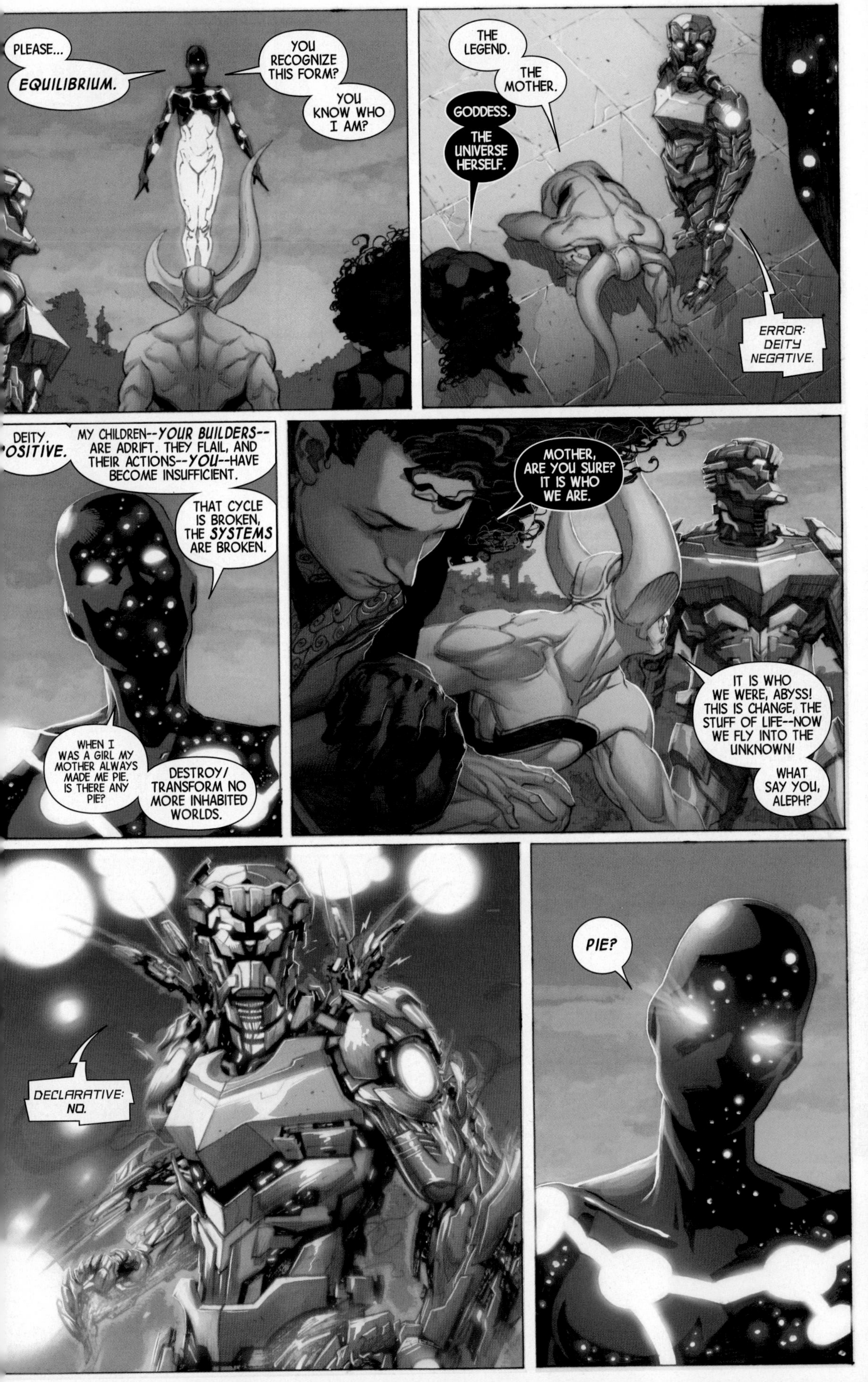
PLEASE...
EQUILIBRIUM.
YOU RECOGNIZE THIS FORM?
YOU KNOW WHO I AM?
THE LEGEND.
THE MOTHER.
GODDESS.
THE UNIVERSE HERSELF.
ERROR: DEITY NEGATIVE.
DEITY. POSITIVE.
MY CHILDREN--YOUR BUILDERS--ARE ADRIFT. THEY FLAIL, AND THEIR ACTIONS--YOU--HAVE BECOME INSUFFICIENT.
THAT CYCLE IS BROKEN, THE SYSTEMS ARE BROKEN.
WHEN I WAS A GIRL MY MOTHER ALWAYS MADE ME PIE. IS THERE ANY PIE?
DESTROY/ TRANSFORM NO MORE INHABITED WORLDS.
MOTHER, ARE YOU SURE? IT IS WHO WE ARE.
IT IS WHO WE WERE, ABYSS! THIS IS CHANGE, THE STUFF OF LIFE--NOW WE FLY INTO THE UNKNOWN!
WHAT SAY YOU, ALEPH?
DECLARATIVE: NO.
PIE?

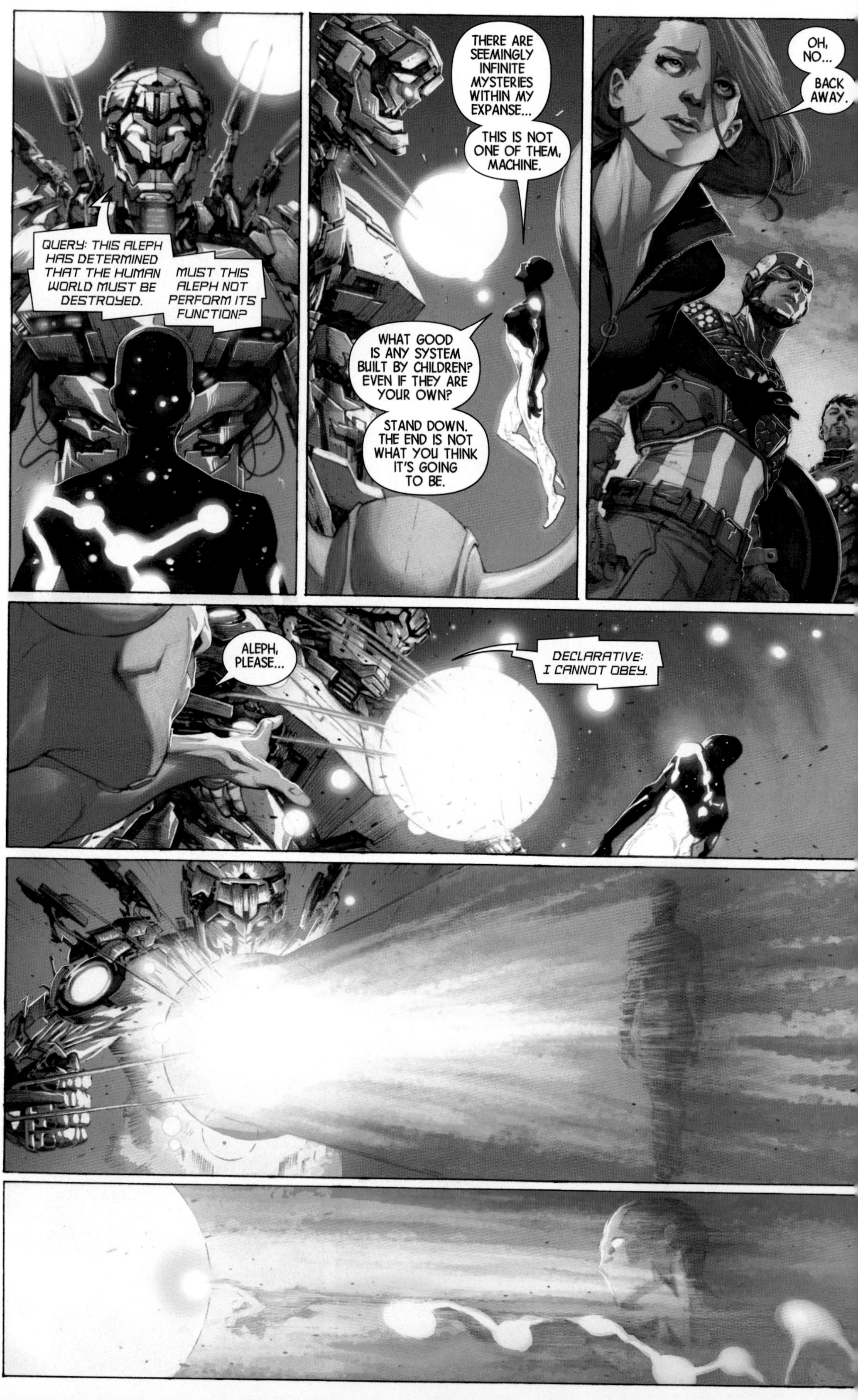
QUERY: THIS ALEPH HAS DETERMINED THAT THE HUMAN WORLD MUST BE DESTROYED.
MUST THIS ALEPH NOT PERFORM ITS FUNCTION?
THERE ARE SEEMINGLY INFINITE MYSTERIES WITHIN MY EXPANSE...
THIS IS NOT ONE OF THEM, MACHINE.
WHAT GOOD IS ANY SYSTEM BUILT BY CHILDREN? EVEN IF THEY ARE YOUR OWN?
STAND DOWN. THE END IS NOT WHAT YOU THINK IT'S GOING TO BE.
OH, NO...
BACK AWAY.
ALEPH, PLEASE...
DECLARATIVE: I CANNOT OBEY.

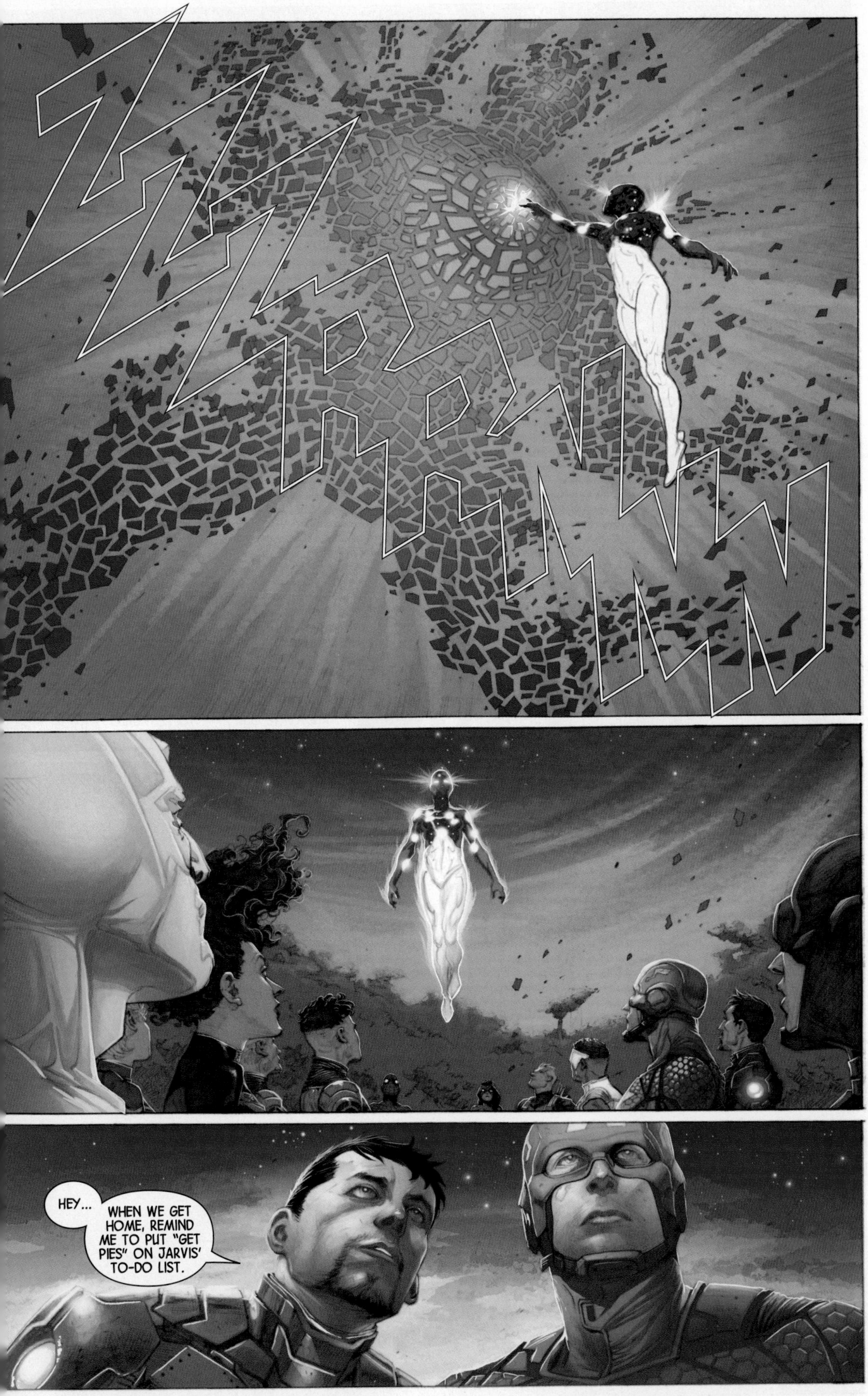
ZZZRAWWW
HEY...
WHEN WE GET HOME, REMIND ME TO PUT "GET PIES" ON JARVIS' TO-DO LIST.

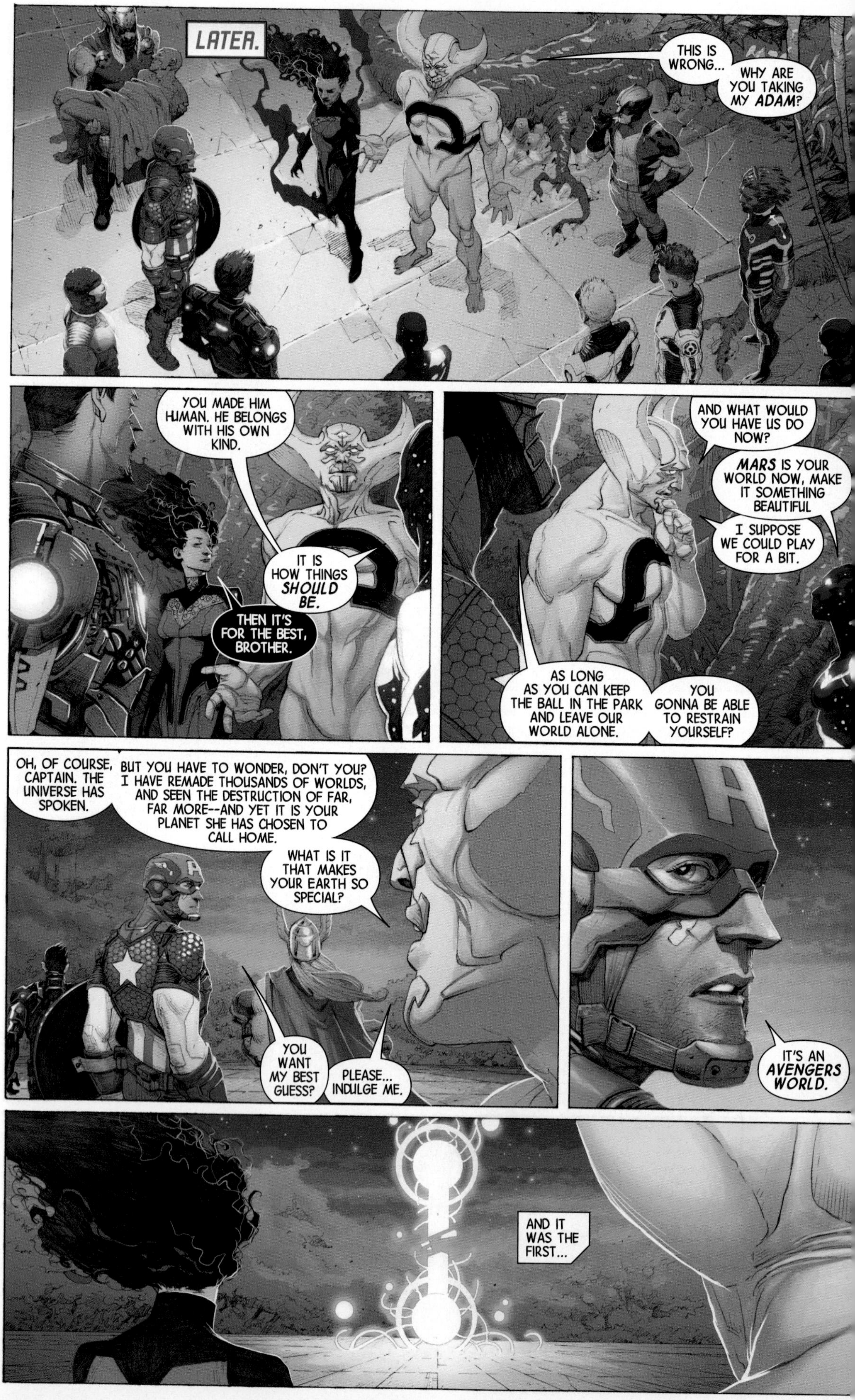
LATER.
THIS IS WRONG...
WHY ARE YOU TAKING MY ADAM?
YOU MADE HIM HUMAN. HE BELONGS WITH HIS OWN KIND.
IT IS HOW THINGS SHOULD BE.
THEN IT'S FOR THE BEST, BROTHER.
AND WHAT WOULD YOU HAVE US DO NOW?
MARS IS YOUR WORLD NOW, MAKE IT SOMETHING BEAUTIFUL
I SUPPOSE WE COULD PLAY FOR A BIT.
AS LONG AS YOU CAN KEEP THE BALL IN THE PARK AND LEAVE OUR WORLD ALONE.
YOU GONNA BE ABLE TO RESTRAIN YOURSELF?
OH, OF COURSE, CAPTAIN. THE UNIVERSE HAS SPOKEN.
BUT YOU HAVE TO WONDER, DON'T YOU? I HAVE REMADE THOUSANDS OF WORLDS, AND SEEN THE DESTRUCTION OF FAR, FAR MORE--AND YET IT IS YOUR PLANET SHE HAS CHOSEN TO CALL HOME.
WHAT IS IT THAT MAKES YOUR EARTH SO SPECIAL?
YOU WANT MY BEST GUESS?
PLEASE... INDULGE ME.
IT'S AN AVENGERS WORLD.
AND IT WAS THE FIRST...

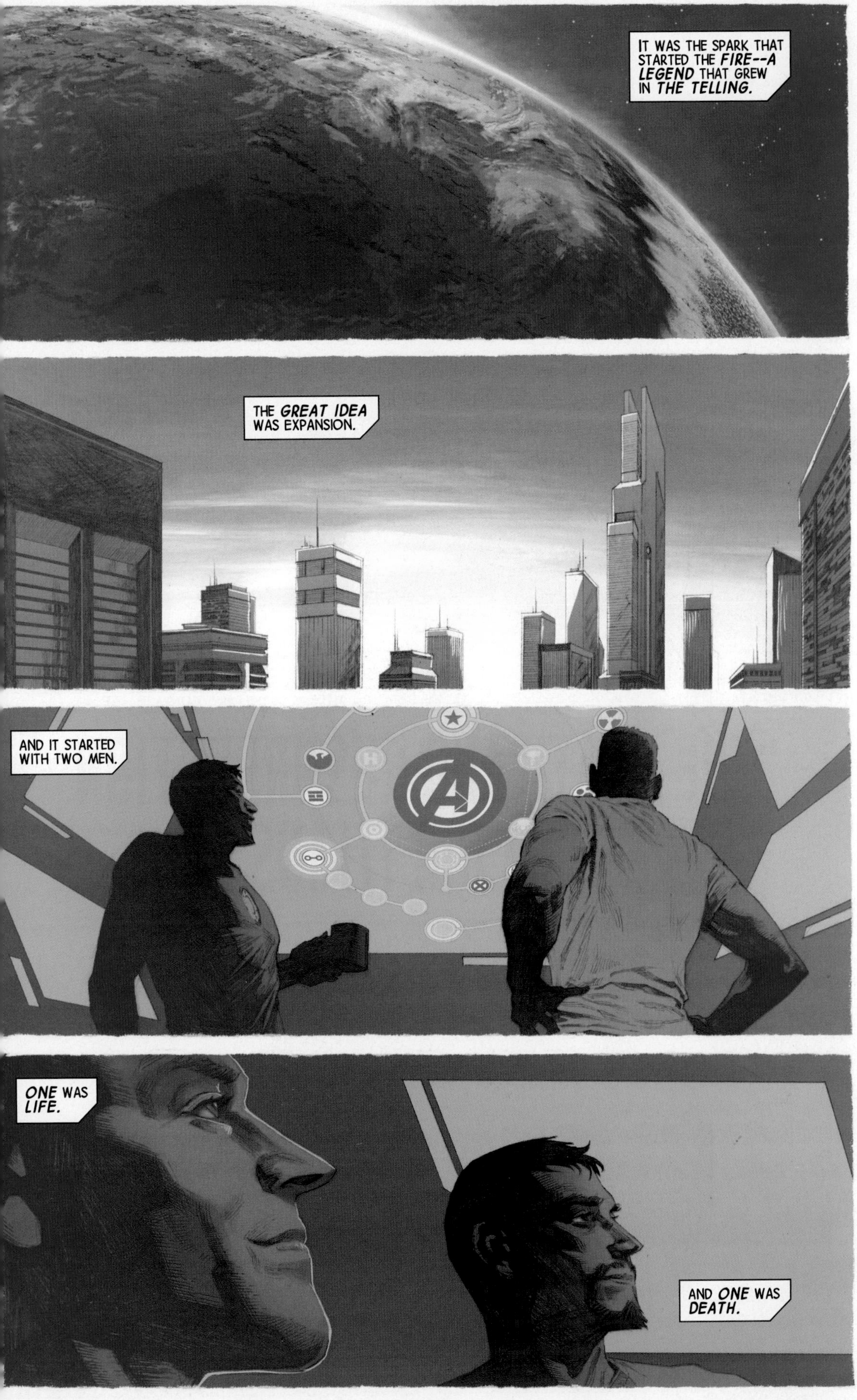
IT WAS THE SPARK THAT STARTED THE FIRE--A LEGEND THAT GREW IN THE TELLING.
THE GREAT IDEA WAS EXPANSION.
AND IT STARTED WITH TWO MEN.
ONE WAS LIFE.
AND ONE WAS DEATH.

"THE DEATH AND RESURRECTION OF MAJOR TITANS"

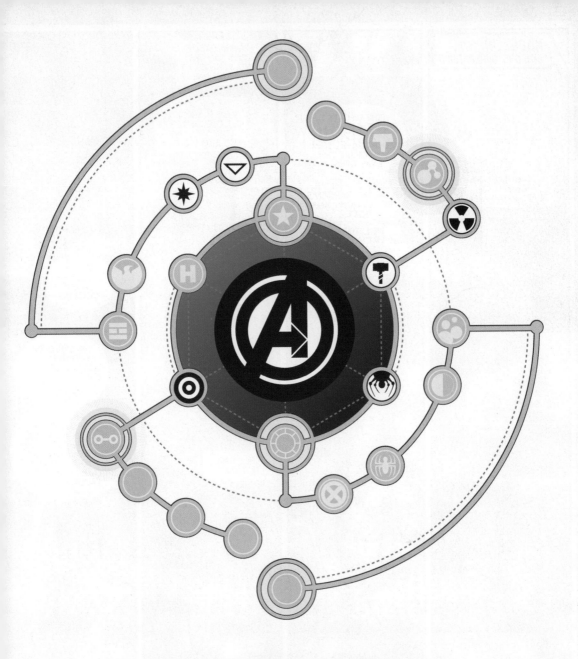

EARTH'S MIGHTIEST HEROES

CAPTAIN AMERICA · IRON MAN · THOR · HAWKEYE · BLACK WIDOW · HULK
WOLVERINE · SPIDER-MAN · CAPTAIN MARVEL · SPIDER-WOMAN
FALCON · SHANG-CHI · SUNSPOT · CANNONBALL · MANIFOLD
SMASHER · CAPTAIN UNIVERSE · HYPERION

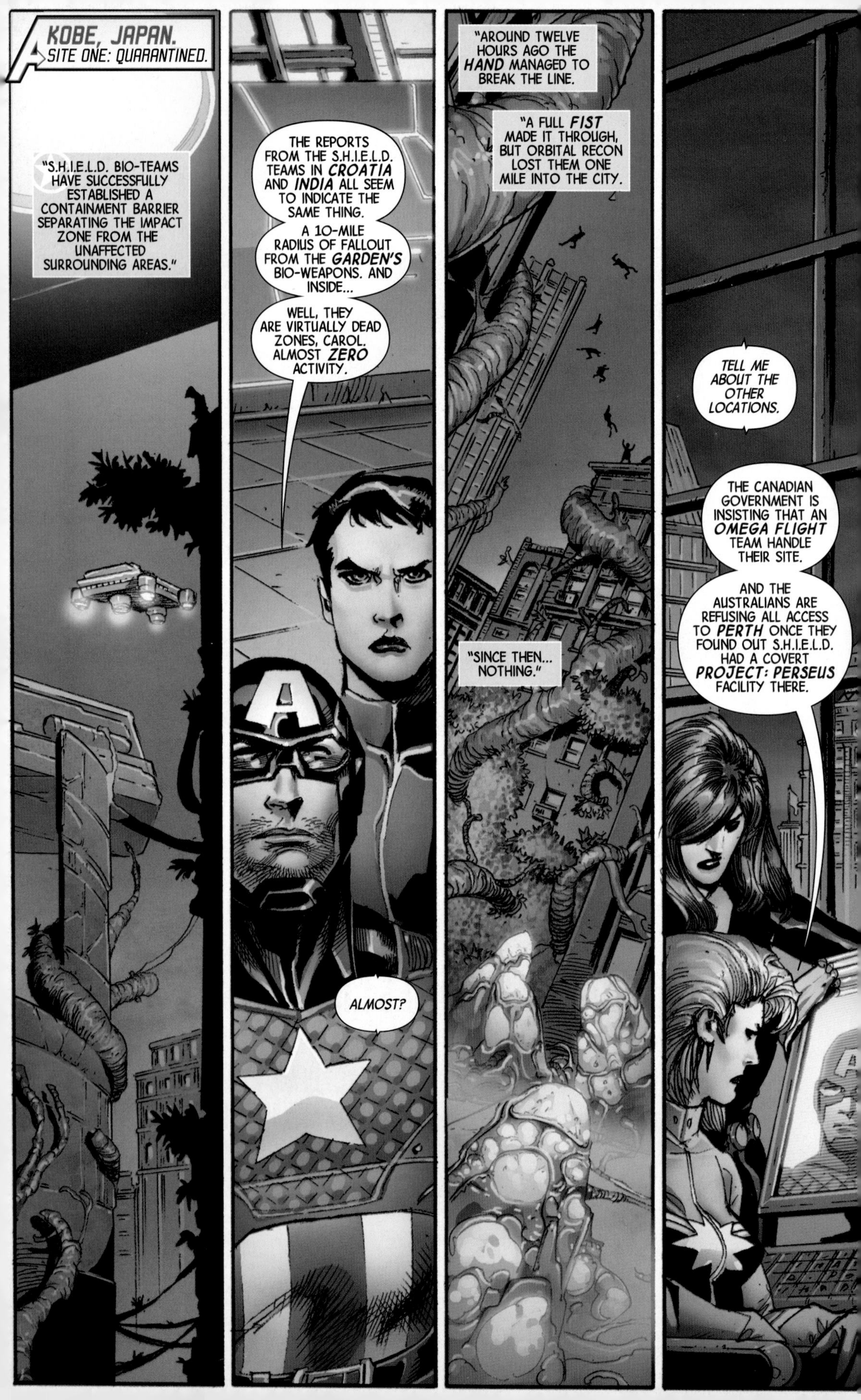
KOBE, JAPAN.
SITE ONE: QUARANTINED.
"S.H.I.E.L.D. BIO-TEAMS HAVE SUCCESSFULLY ESTABLISHED A CONTAINMENT BARRIER SEPARATING THE IMPACT ZONE FROM THE UNAFFECTED SURROUNDING AREAS."
THE REPORTS FROM THE S.H.I.E.L.D. TEAMS IN CROATIA AND INDIA ALL SEEM TO INDICATE THE SAME THING.
A 10-MILE RADIUS OF FALLOUT FROM THE GARDEN'S BIO-WEAPONS. AND INSIDE...
WELL, THEY ARE VIRTUALLY DEAD ZONES, CAROL. ALMOST ZERO ACTIVITY.
ALMOST?
"AROUND TWELVE HOURS AGO THE HAND MANAGED TO BREAK THE LINE.
"A FULL FIST MADE IT THROUGH, BUT ORBITAL RECON LOST THEM ONE MILE INTO THE CITY.
"SINCE THEN... NOTHING."
TELL ME ABOUT THE OTHER LOCATIONS.
THE CANADIAN GOVERNMENT IS INSISTING THAT AN OMEGA FLIGHT TEAM HANDLE THEIR SITE.
AND THE AUSTRALIANS ARE REFUSING ALL ACCESS TO PERTH ONCE THEY FOUND OUT S.H.I.E.L.D. HAD A COVERT PROJECT: PERSEUS FACILITY THERE.

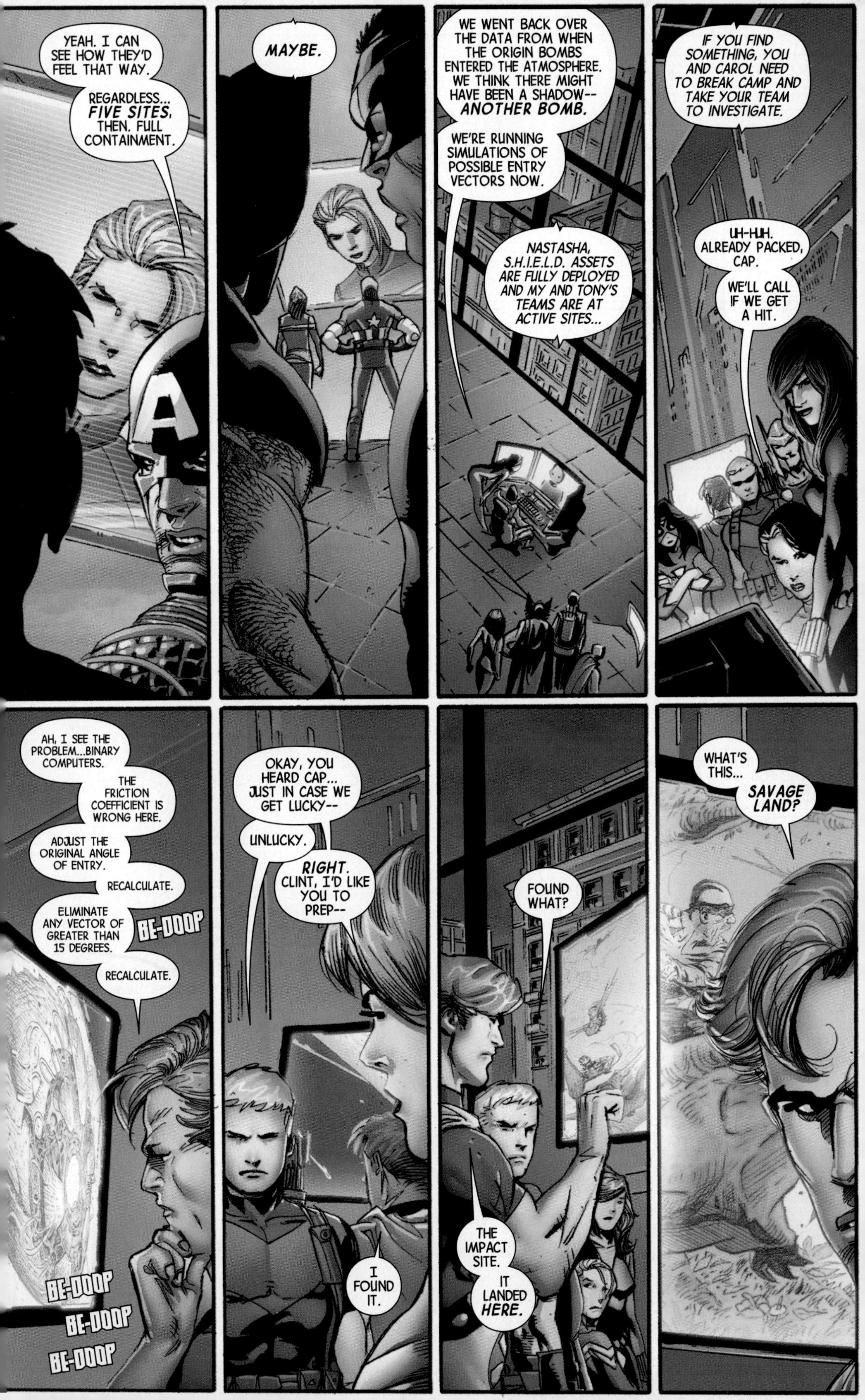
YEAH. I CAN SEE HOW THEY'D FEEL THAT WAY.
REGARDLESS... FIVE SITES, THEN. FULL CONTAINMENT.
MAYBE.
WE WENT BACK OVER THE DATA FROM WHEN THE ORIGIN BOMBS ENTERED THE ATMOSPHERE. WE THINK THERE MIGHT HAVE BEEN A SHADOW-- ANOTHER BOMB.
WE'RE RUNNING SIMULATIONS OF POSSIBLE ENTRY VECTORS NOW.
NASTASHA, S.H.I.E.L.D. ASSETS ARE FULLY DEPLOYED AND MY AND TONY'S TEAMS ARE AT ACTIVE SITES...
IF YOU FIND SOMETHING, YOU AND CAROL NEED TO BREAK CAMP AND TAKE YOUR TEAM TO INVESTIGATE.
UH-HUH. ALREADY PACKED, CAP.
WE'LL CALL IF WE GET A HIT.
AH, I SEE THE PROBLEM...BINARY COMPUTERS.
THE FRICTION COEFFICIENT IS WRONG HERE.
ADJUST THE ORIGINAL ANGLE OF ENTRY.
RECALCULATE.
ELIMINATE ANY VECTOR OF GREATER THAN 15 DEGREES.
BE-DOOP
RECALCULATE.
BE-DOOP
BE-DOOP
BE-DOOP
OKAY, YOU HEARD CAP... JUST IN CASE WE GET LUCKY--
UNLUCKY.
RIGHT. CLINT, I'D LIKE YOU TO PREP--
I FOUND IT.
FOUND WHAT?
THE IMPACT SITE.
IT LANDED HERE.
WHAT'S THIS... SAVAGE LAND?

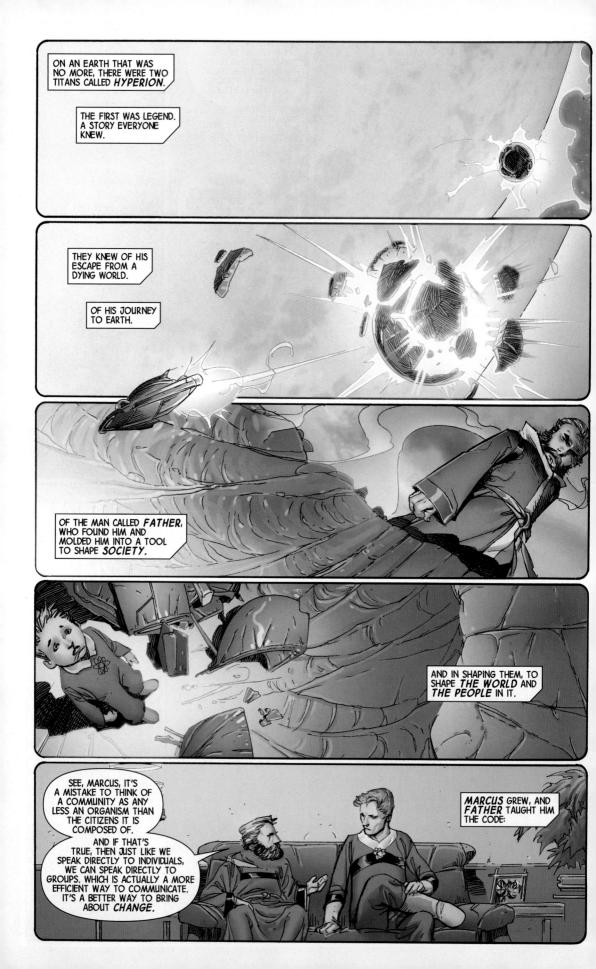

ON AN EARTH THAT WAS NO MORE, THERE WERE TWO TITANS CALLED *HYPERION*.

THE FIRST WAS LEGEND. A STORY EVERYONE KNEW.

THEY KNEW OF HIS ESCAPE FROM A DYING WORLD.

OF HIS JOURNEY TO EARTH.

OF THE MAN CALLED *FATHER*, WHO FOUND HIM AND MOLDED HIM INTO A TOOL TO SHAPE *SOCIETY*.

AND IN SHAPING THEM, TO SHAPE *THE WORLD* AND *THE PEOPLE* IN IT.

SEE, MARCUS, IT'S A MISTAKE TO THINK OF A COMMUNITY AS ANY LESS AN ORGANISM THAN THE CITIZENS IT IS COMPOSED OF.

AND IF THAT'S TRUE, THEN JUST LIKE WE SPEAK DIRECTLY TO INDIVIDUALS, WE CAN SPEAK DIRECTLY TO GROUPS. WHICH IS ACTUALLY A MORE EFFICIENT WAY TO COMMUNICATE. IT'S A BETTER WAY TO BRING ABOUT *CHANGE*.

MARCUS GREW, AND *FATHER* TAUGHT HIM THE CODE:

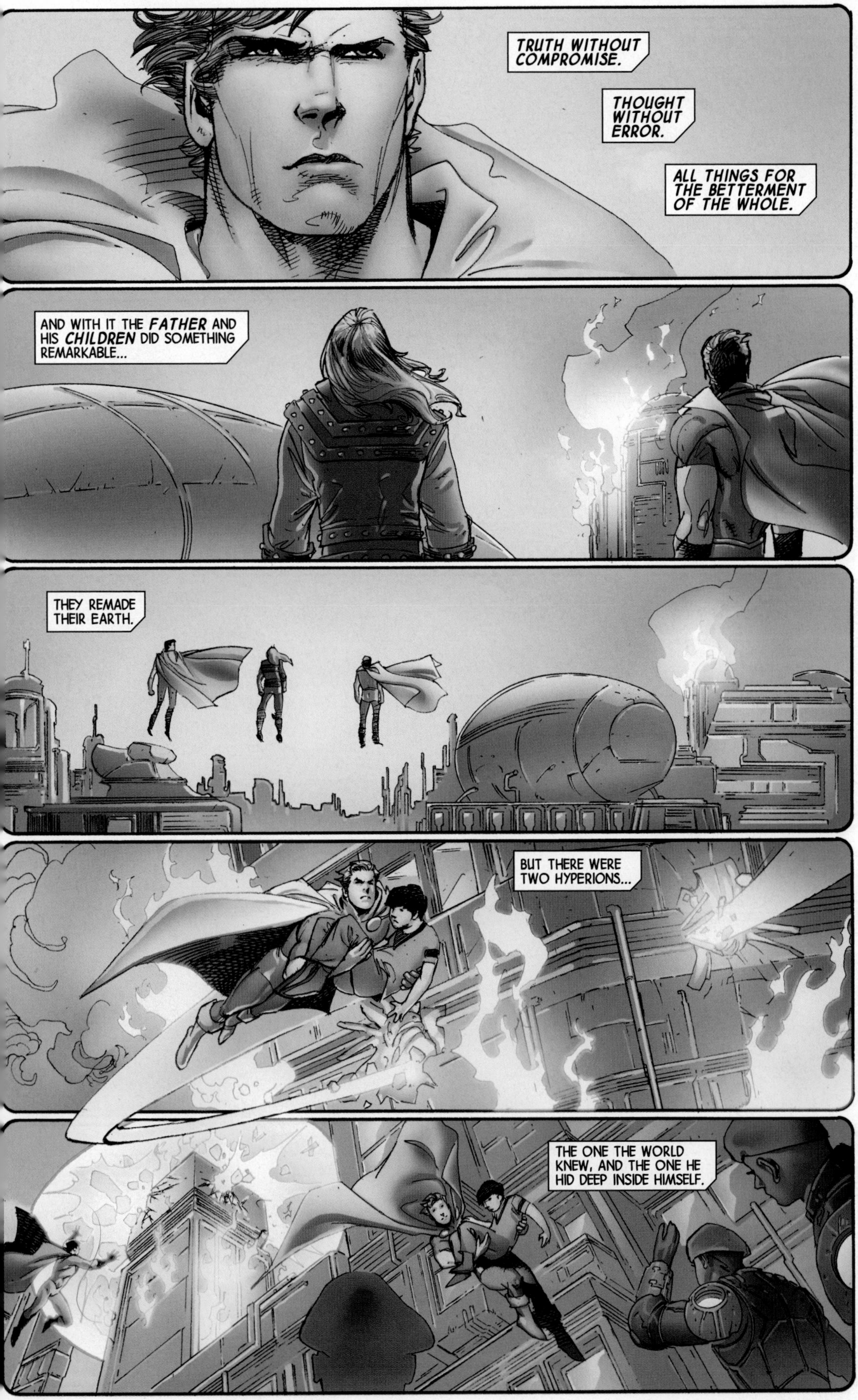
TRUTH WITHOUT COMPROMISE.
THOUGHT WITHOUT ERROR.
ALL THINGS FOR THE BETTERMENT OF THE WHOLE.
AND WITH IT THE FATHER AND HIS CHILDREN DID SOMETHING REMARKABLE...
THEY REMADE THEIR EARTH.
BUT THERE WERE TWO HYPERIONS...
THE ONE THE WORLD KNEW, AND THE ONE HE HID DEEP INSIDE HIMSELF.

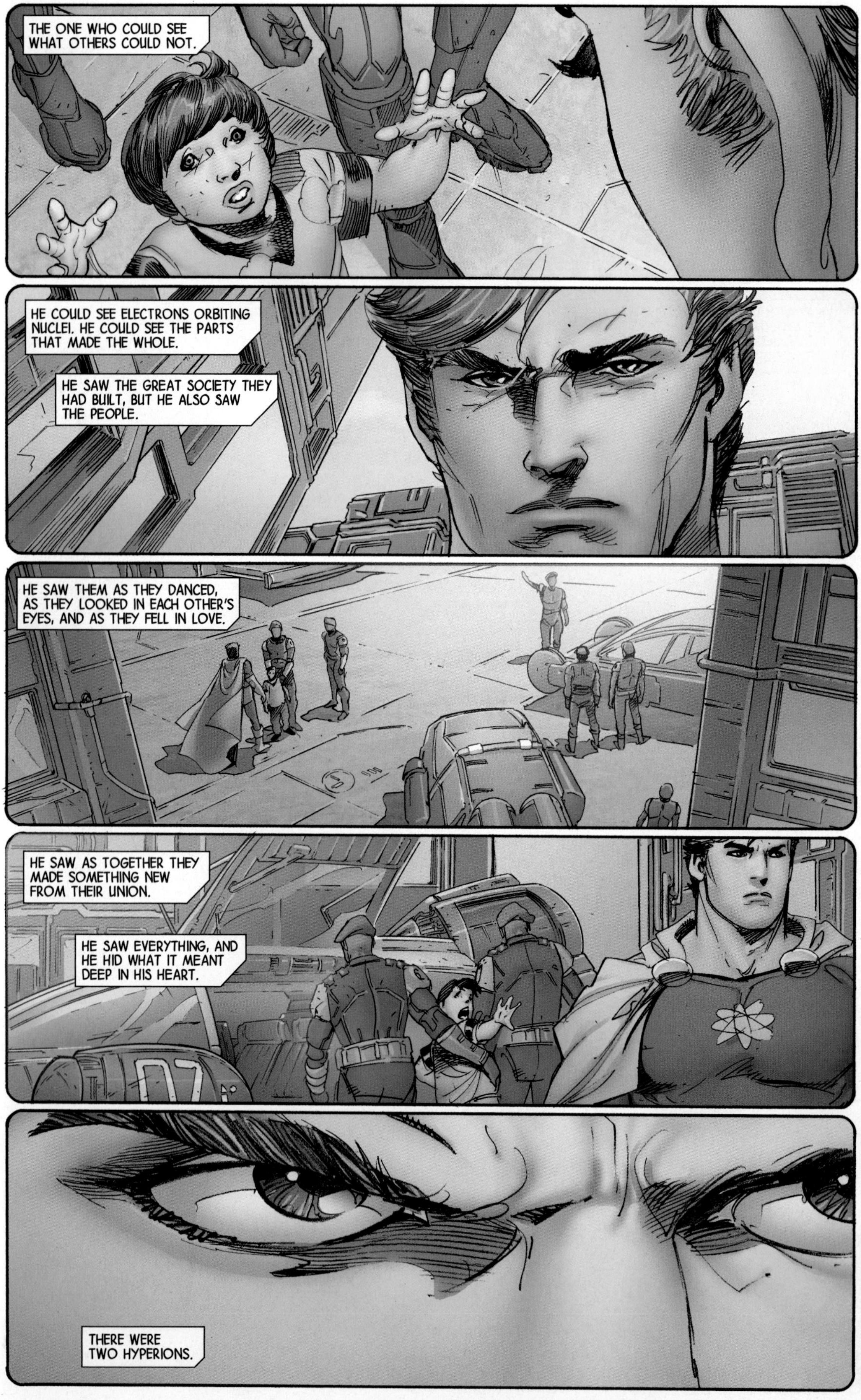
THE ONE WHO COULD SEE WHAT OTHERS COULD NOT.
HE COULD SEE ELECTRONS ORBITING NUCLEI. HE COULD SEE THE PARTS THAT MADE THE WHOLE.
HE SAW THE GREAT SOCIETY THEY HAD BUILT, BUT HE ALSO SAW THE PEOPLE.
HE SAW THEM AS THEY DANCED, AS THEY LOOKED IN EACH OTHER'S EYES, AND AS THEY FELL IN LOVE.
HE SAW AS TOGETHER THEY MADE SOMETHING NEW FROM THEIR UNION.
HE SAW EVERYTHING, AND HE HID WHAT IT MEANT DEEP IN HIS HEART.
THERE WERE TWO HYPERIONS.

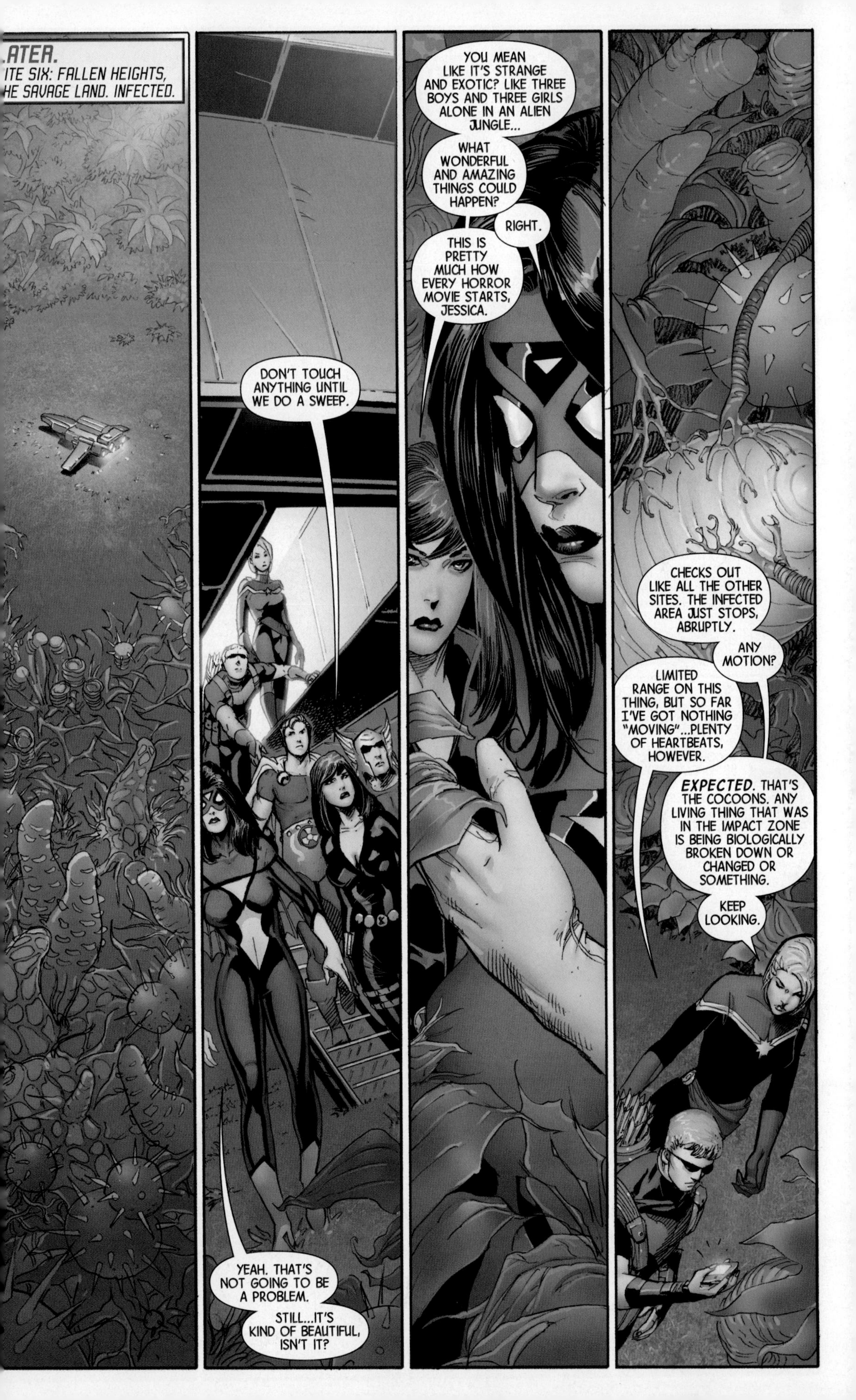

LATER.
ITE SIX: FALLEN HEIGHTS, HE SAVAGE LAND. INFECTED.
DON'T TOUCH ANYTHING UNTIL WE DO A SWEEP.
YEAH. THAT'S NOT GOING TO BE A PROBLEM.
STILL...IT'S KIND OF BEAUTIFUL, ISN'T IT?
YOU MEAN LIKE IT'S STRANGE AND EXOTIC? LIKE THREE BOYS AND THREE GIRLS ALONE IN AN ALIEN JUNGLE...
WHAT WONDERFUL AND AMAZING THINGS COULD HAPPEN?
RIGHT.
THIS IS PRETTY MUCH HOW EVERY HORROR MOVIE STARTS, JESSICA.
CHECKS OUT LIKE ALL THE OTHER SITES. THE INFECTED AREA JUST STOPS, ABRUPTLY.
ANY MOTION?
LIMITED RANGE ON THIS THING, BUT SO FAR I'VE GOT NOTHING "MOVING"...PLENTY OF HEARTBEATS, HOWEVER.
EXPECTED. THAT'S THE COCOONS. ANY LIVING THING THAT WAS IN THE IMPACT ZONE IS BEING BIOLOGICALLY BROKEN DOWN OR CHANGED OR SOMETHING.
KEEP LOOKING.

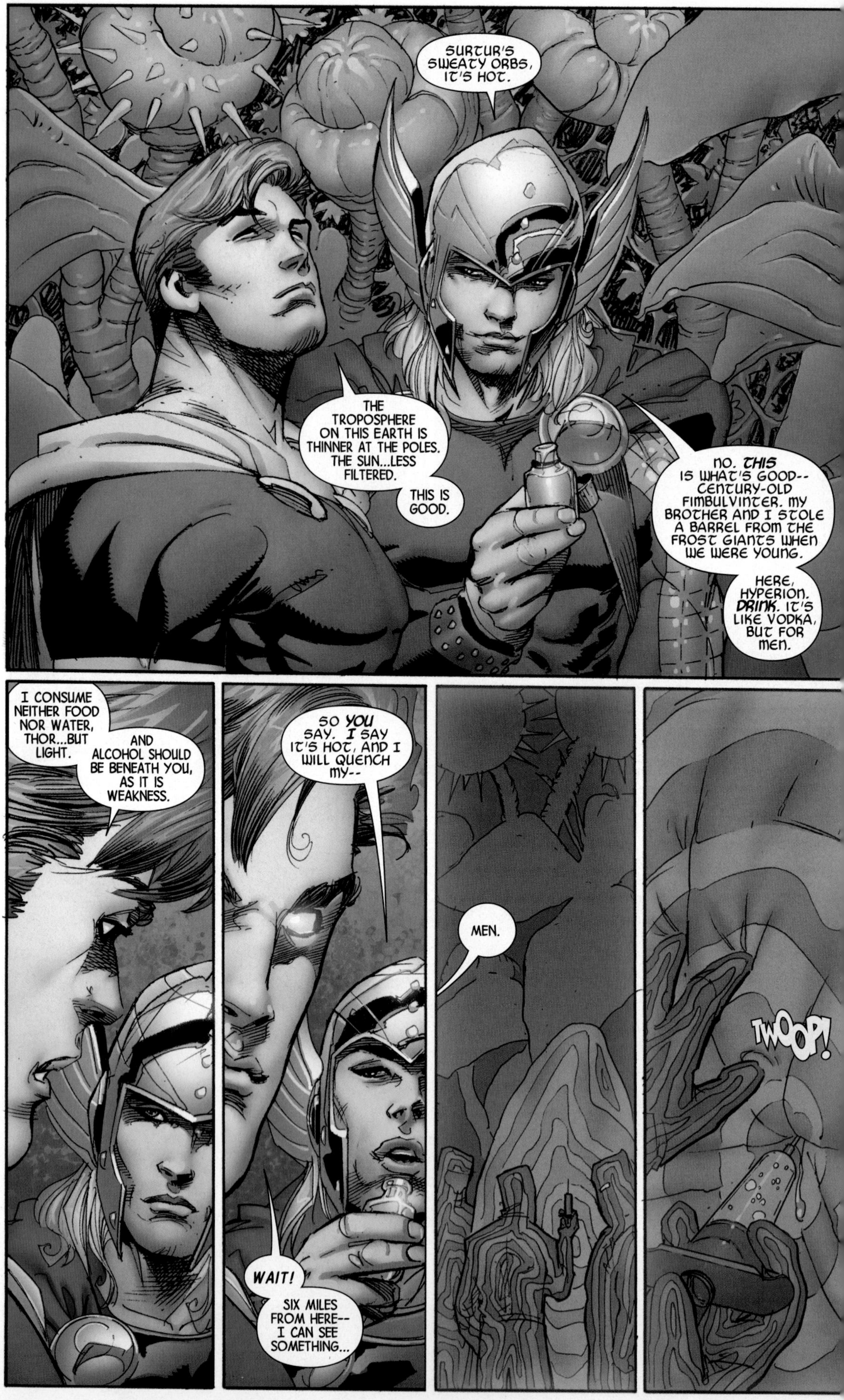
SURTUR'S SWEATY ORBS, IT'S HOT.
THE TROPOSPHERE ON THIS EARTH IS THINNER AT THE POLES. THE SUN...LESS FILTERED.
THIS IS GOOD.
NO. THIS IS WHAT'S GOOD-- CENTURY-OLD FIMBULVINTER. MY BROTHER AND I STOLE A BARREL FROM THE FROST GIANTS WHEN WE WERE YOUNG.
HERE, HYPERION. DRINK. IT'S LIKE VODKA, BUT FOR MEN.
I CONSUME NEITHER FOOD NOR WATER, THOR...BUT LIGHT.
AND ALCOHOL SHOULD BE BENEATH YOU, AS IT IS WEAKNESS.
SO YOU SAY. I SAY IT'S HOT, AND I WILL QUENCH MY--
WAIT!
SIX MILES FROM HERE-- I CAN SEE SOMETHING...
MEN.
TWOOP!

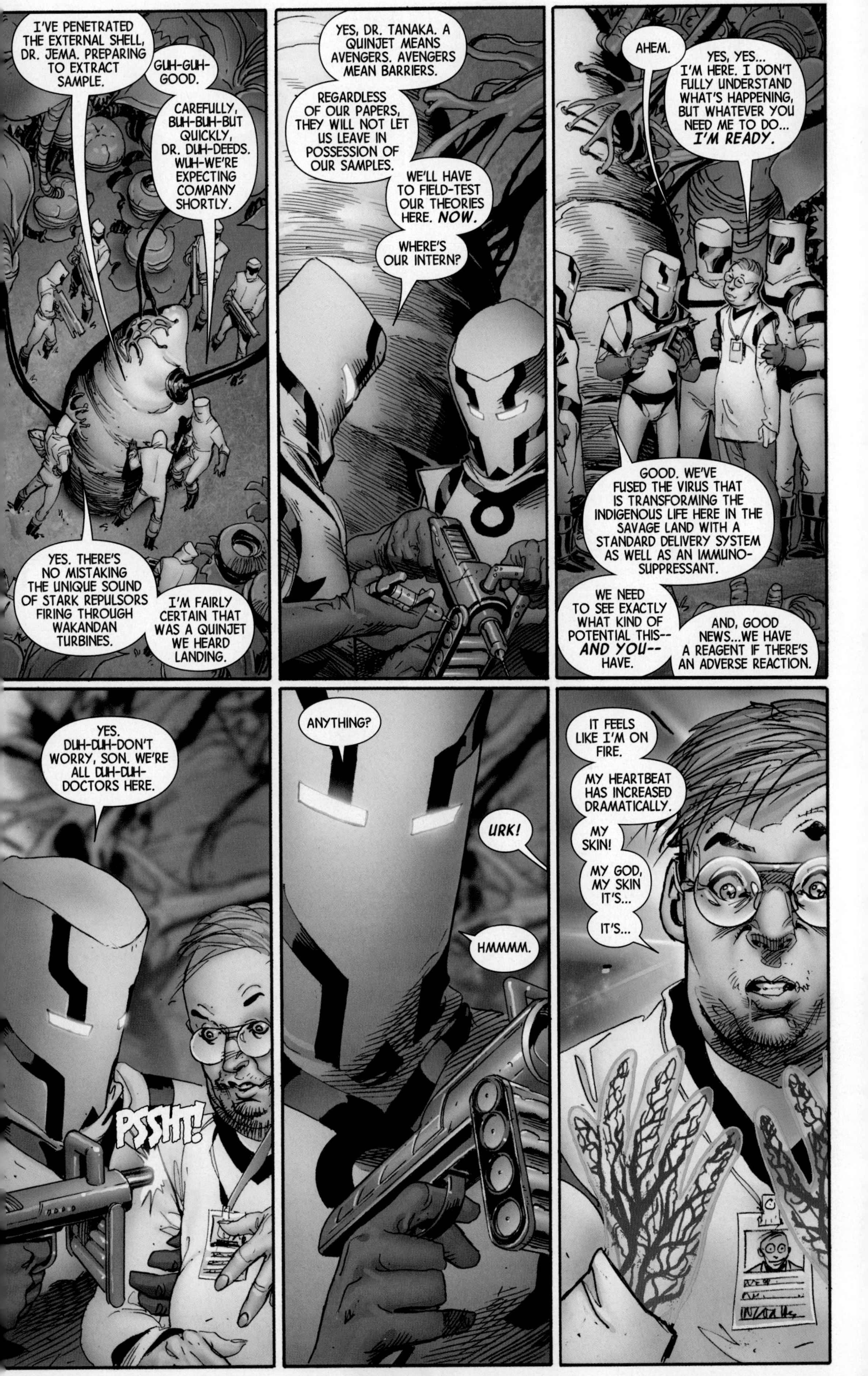
I'VE PENETRATED THE EXTERNAL SHELL, DR. JEMA. PREPARING TO EXTRACT SAMPLE.
GUH-GUH-GOOD.
CAREFULLY, BUH-BUH-BUT QUICKLY, DR. DUH-DEEDS. WUH-WE'RE EXPECTING COMPANY SHORTLY.
YES. THERE'S NO MISTAKING THE UNIQUE SOUND OF STARK REPULSORS FIRING THROUGH WAKANDAN TURBINES.
I'M FAIRLY CERTAIN THAT WAS A QUINJET WE HEARD LANDING.
YES, DR. TANAKA. A QUINJET MEANS AVENGERS. AVENGERS MEAN BARRIERS.
REGARDLESS OF OUR PAPERS, THEY WILL NOT LET US LEAVE IN POSSESSION OF OUR SAMPLES.
WE'LL HAVE TO FIELD-TEST OUR THEORIES HERE. NOW.
WHERE'S OUR INTERN?
AHEM.
YES, YES... I'M HERE. I DON'T FULLY UNDERSTAND WHAT'S HAPPENING, BUT WHATEVER YOU NEED ME TO DO... I'M READY.
GOOD. WE'VE FUSED THE VIRUS THAT IS TRANSFORMING THE INDIGENOUS LIFE HERE IN THE SAVAGE LAND WITH A STANDARD DELIVERY SYSTEM AS WELL AS AN IMMUNO-SUPPRESSANT.
WE NEED TO SEE EXACTLY WHAT KIND OF POTENTIAL THIS-- AND YOU-- HAVE.
AND, GOOD NEWS...WE HAVE A REAGENT IF THERE'S AN ADVERSE REACTION.
YES. DUH-DUH-DON'T WORRY, SON. WE'RE ALL DUH-DUH-DOCTORS HERE.
PSSHT!
ANYTHING?
URK!
HMMMM.
IT FEELS LIKE I'M ON FIRE.
MY HEARTBEAT HAS INCREASED DRAMATICALLY.
MY SKIN!
MY GOD, MY SKIN IT'S...
IT'S...

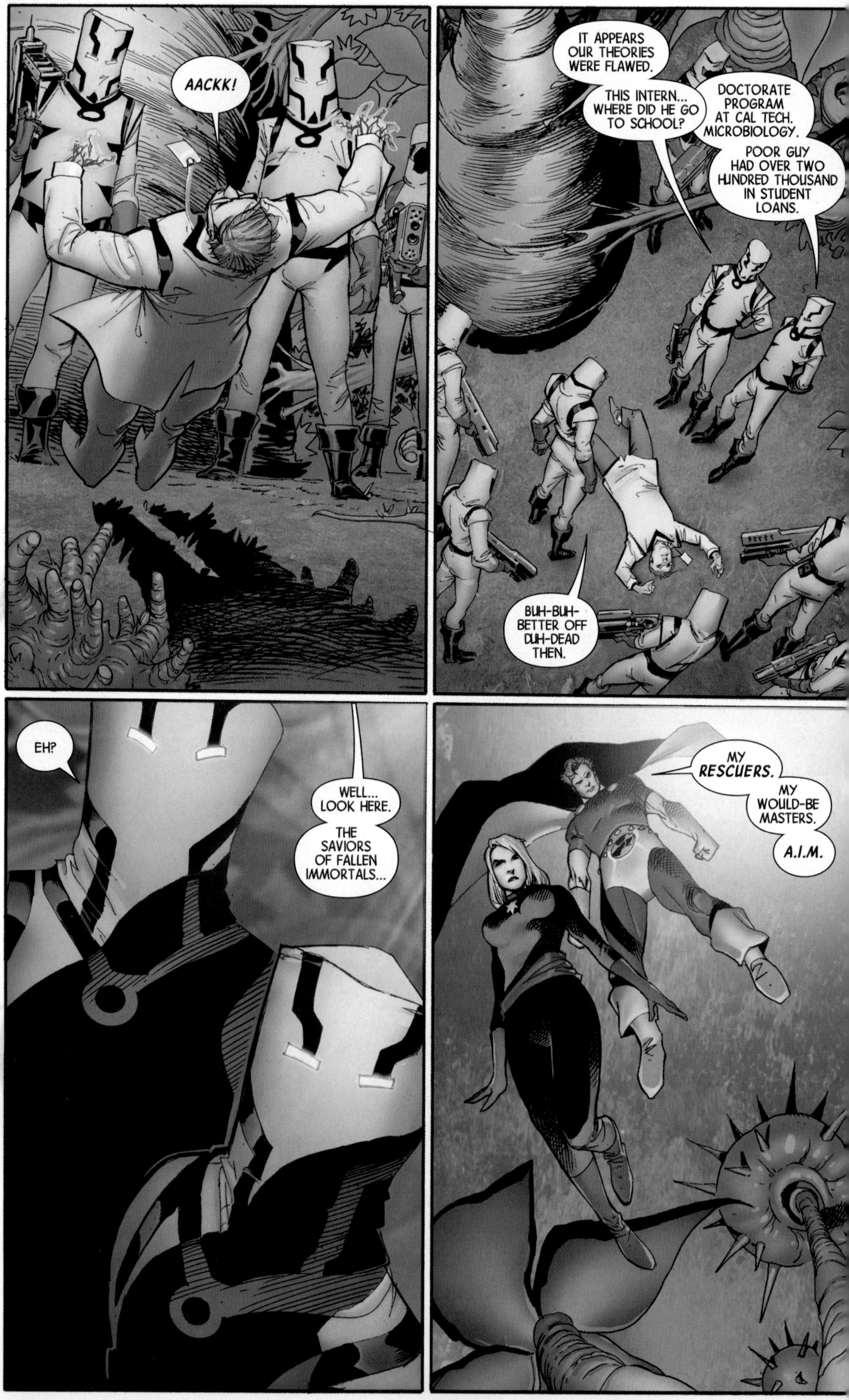
AACKK!
IT APPEARS OUR THEORIES WERE FLAWED.
THIS INTERN... WHERE DID HE GO TO SCHOOL?
DOCTORATE PROGRAM AT CAL TECH. MICROBIOLOGY.
POOR GUY HAD OVER TWO HUNDRED THOUSAND IN STUDENT LOANS.
BUH-BUH-BETTER OFF DUH-DEAD THEN.
EH?
WELL... LOOK HERE.
THE SAVIORS OF FALLEN IMMORTALS...
MY RESCUERS.
MY WOULD-BE MASTERS.
A.I.M.

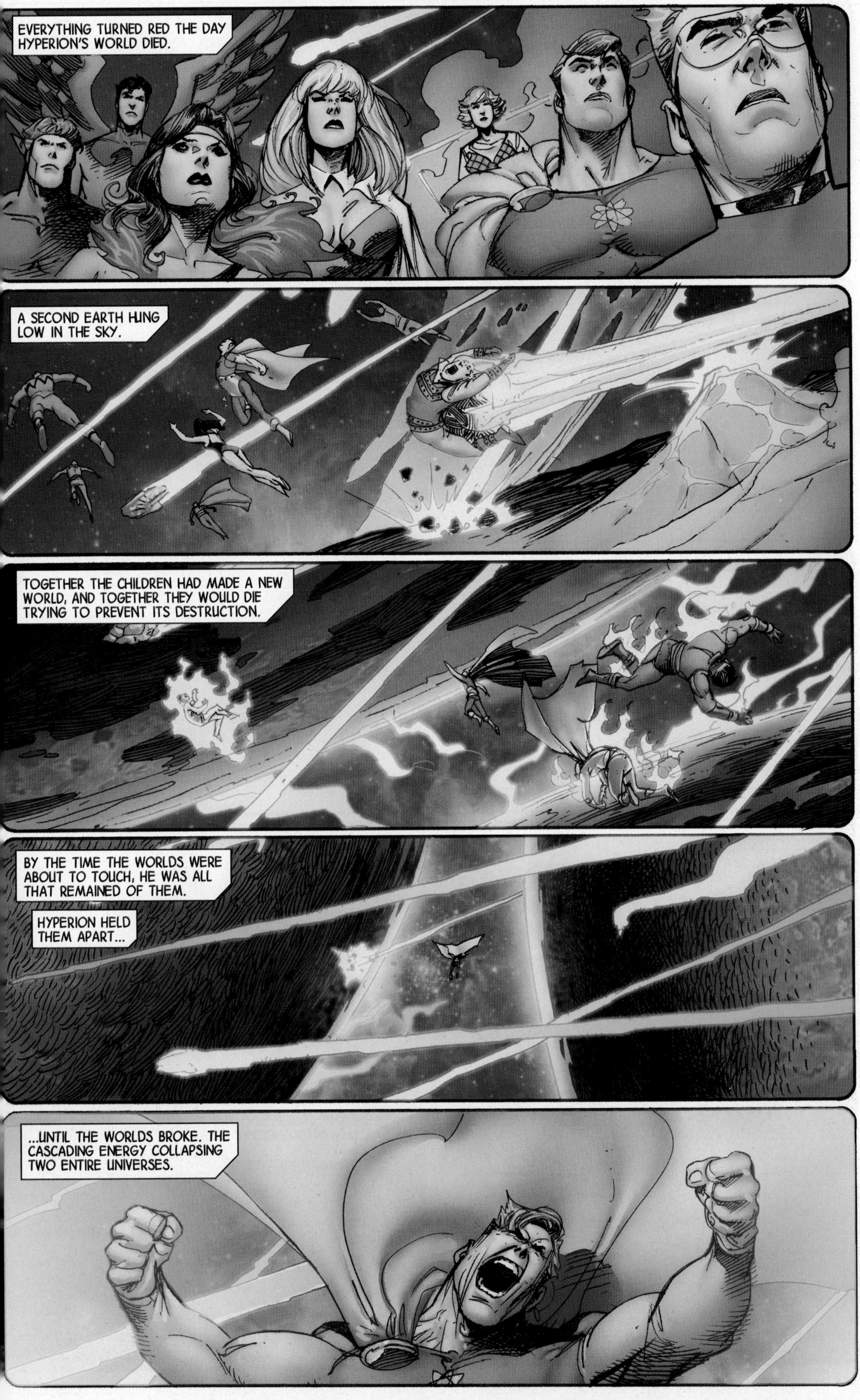
EVERYTHING TURNED RED THE DAY HYPERION'S WORLD DIED.
A SECOND EARTH HUNG LOW IN THE SKY.
TOGETHER THE CHILDREN HAD MADE A NEW WORLD, AND TOGETHER THEY WOULD DIE TRYING TO PREVENT ITS DESTRUCTION.
BY THE TIME THE WORLDS WERE ABOUT TO TOUCH, HE WAS ALL THAT REMAINED OF THEM.
HYPERION HELD THEM APART...
...UNTIL THE WORLDS BROKE. THE CASCADING ENERGY COLLAPSING TWO ENTIRE UNIVERSES.

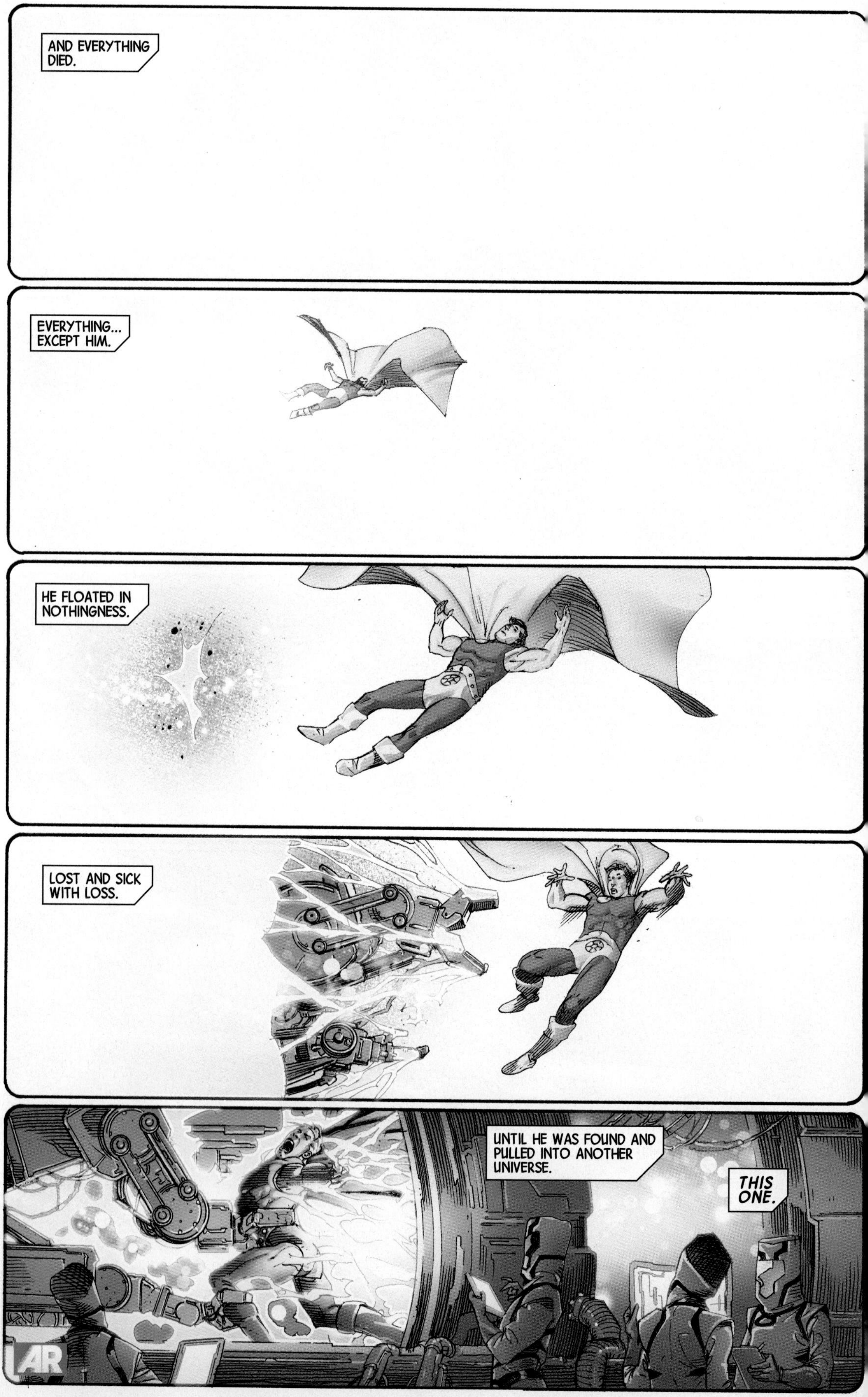
AND EVERYTHING DIED.
EVERYTHING... EXCEPT HIM.
HE FLOATED IN NOTHINGNESS.
LOST AND SICK WITH LOSS.
UNTIL HE WAS FOUND AND PULLED INTO ANOTHER UNIVERSE.
THIS ONE.

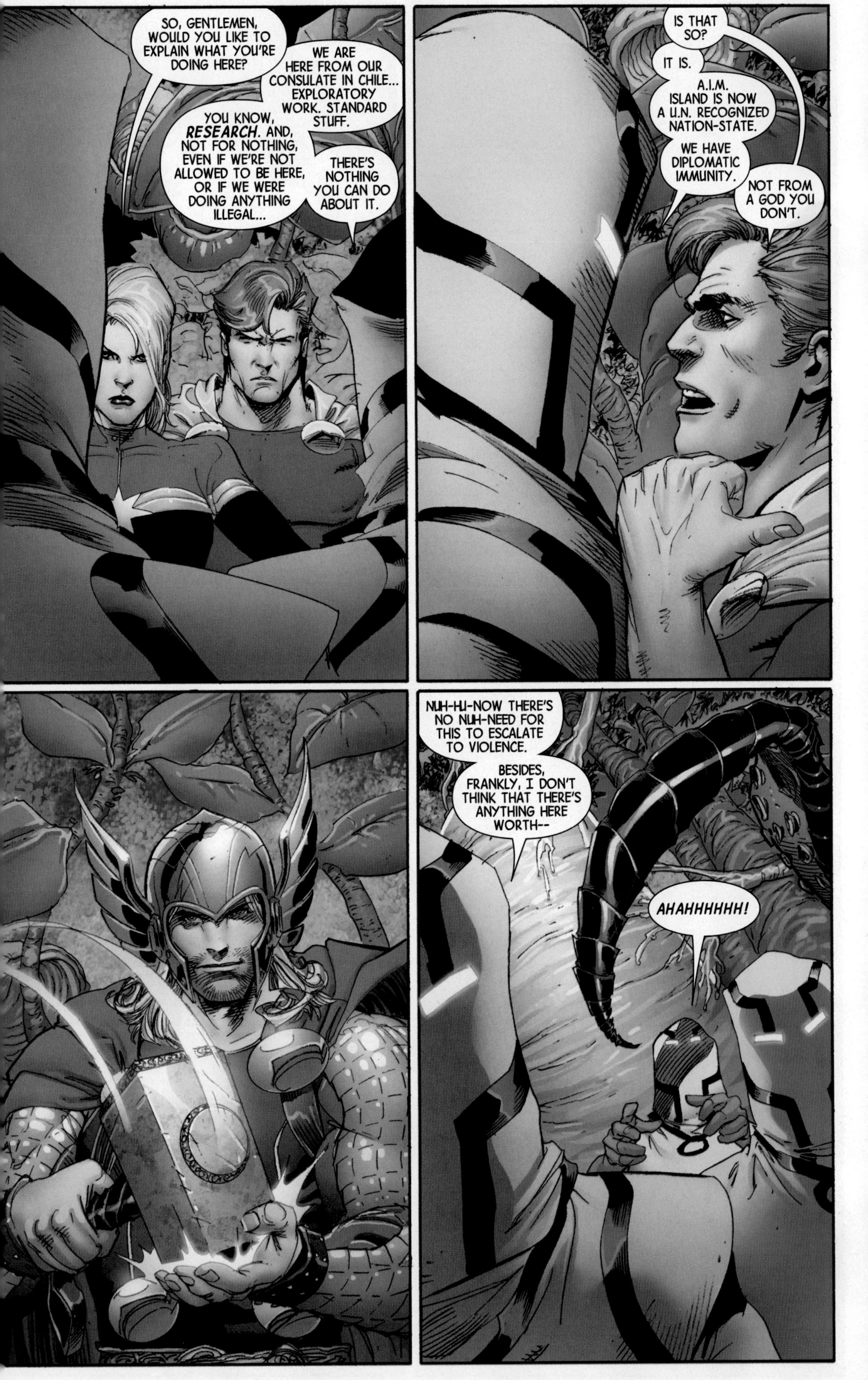
SO, GENTLEMEN, WOULD YOU LIKE TO EXPLAIN WHAT YOU'RE DOING HERE?
WE ARE HERE FROM OUR CONSULATE IN CHILE... EXPLORATORY WORK. STANDARD STUFF.
YOU KNOW, RESEARCH. AND, NOT FOR NOTHING, EVEN IF WE'RE NOT ALLOWED TO BE HERE, OR IF WE WERE DOING ANYTHING ILLEGAL...
THERE'S NOTHING YOU CAN DO ABOUT IT.
IS THAT SO?
IT IS.
A.I.M. ISLAND IS NOW A U.N. RECOGNIZED NATION-STATE.
WE HAVE DIPLOMATIC IMMUNITY.
NOT FROM A GOD YOU DON'T.
NUH-HU-NOW THERE'S NO NUH-NEED FOR THIS TO ESCALATE TO VIOLENCE.
BESIDES, FRANKLY, I DON'T THINK THAT THERE'S ANYTHING HERE WORTH--
AHAHHHHHH!

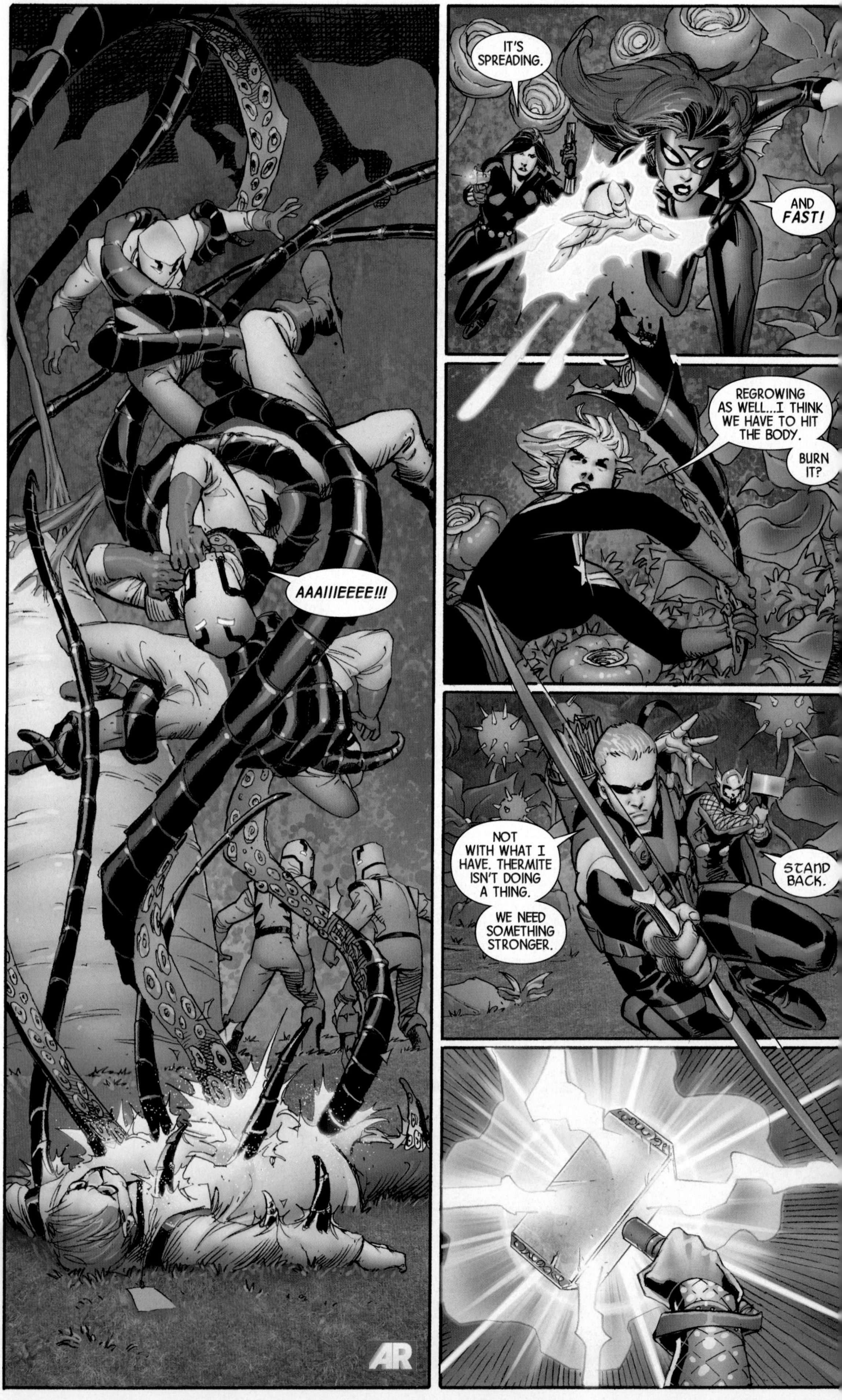
AAAIIIEEEE!!!
IT'S SPREADING.
AND FAST!
REGROWING AS WELL...I THINK WE HAVE TO HIT THE BODY.
BURN IT?
NOT WITH WHAT I HAVE. THERMITE ISN'T DOING A THING.
WE NEED SOMETHING STRONGER.
STAND BACK.
AR

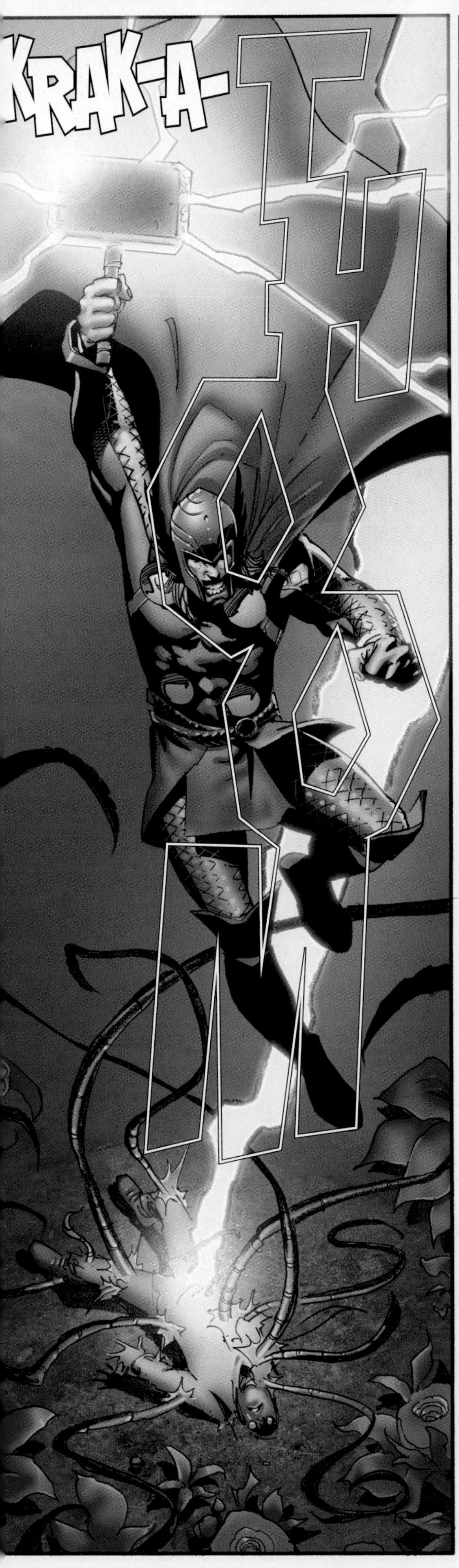
KRAK-A-THOOM

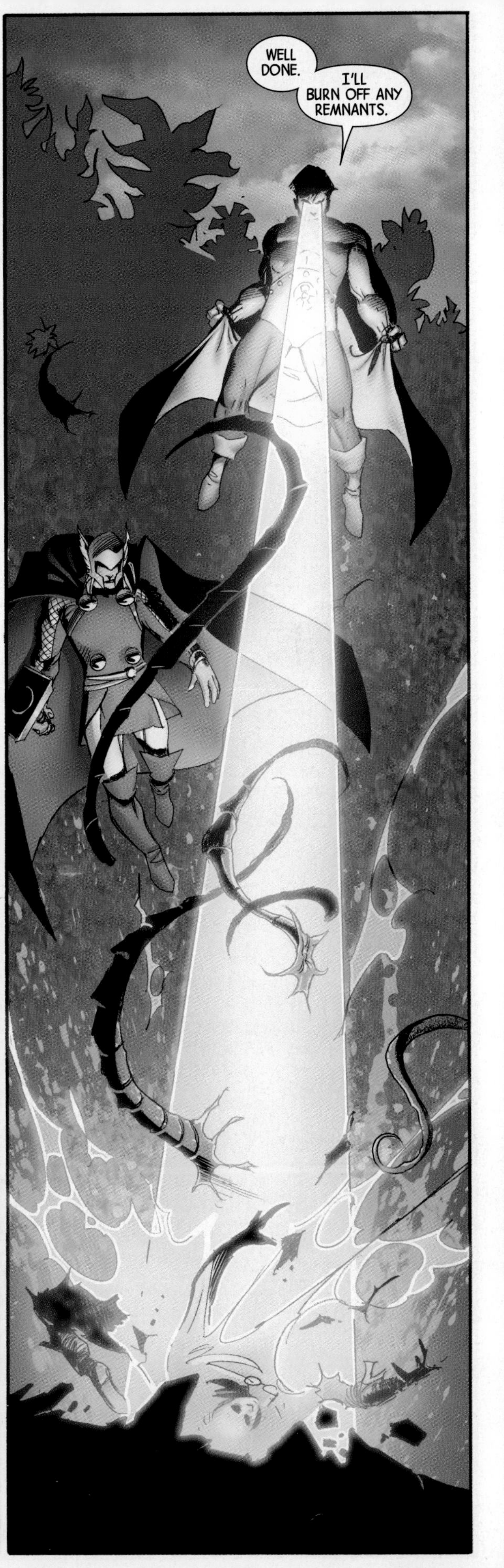
WELL DONE.
I'LL BURN OFF ANY REMNANTS.

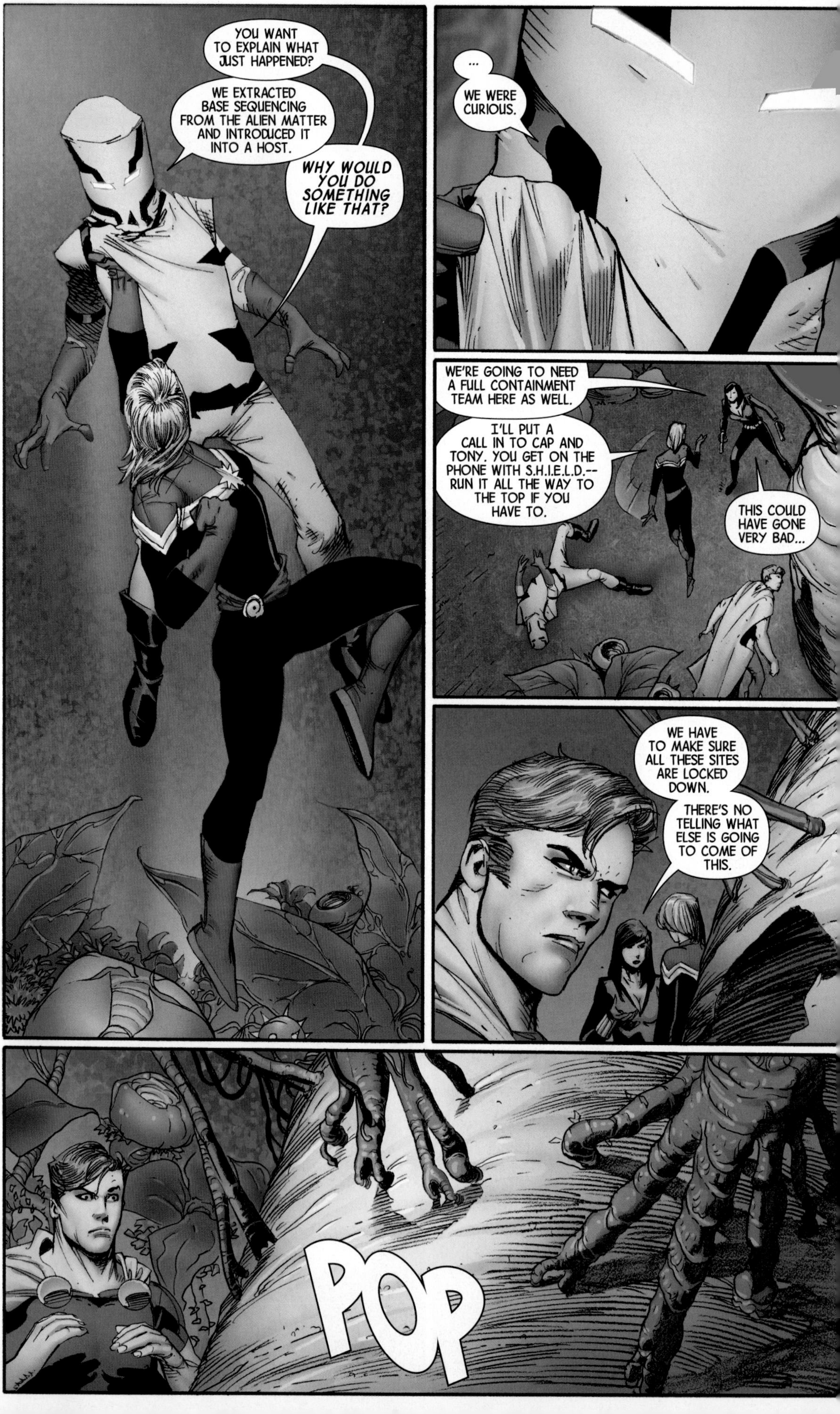
YOU WANT TO EXPLAIN WHAT JUST HAPPENED?
WE EXTRACTED BASE SEQUENCING FROM THE ALIEN MATTER AND INTRODUCED IT INTO A HOST.
WHY WOULD YOU DO SOMETHING LIKE THAT?
...
WE WERE CURIOUS.
WE'RE GOING TO NEED A FULL CONTAINMENT TEAM HERE AS WELL.
I'LL PUT A CALL IN TO CAP AND TONY. YOU GET ON THE PHONE WITH S.H.I.E.L.D.-- RUN IT ALL THE WAY TO THE TOP IF YOU HAVE TO.
THIS COULD HAVE GONE VERY BAD...
WE HAVE TO MAKE SURE ALL THESE SITES ARE LOCKED DOWN.
THERE'S NO TELLING WHAT ELSE IS GOING TO COME OF THIS.
POP

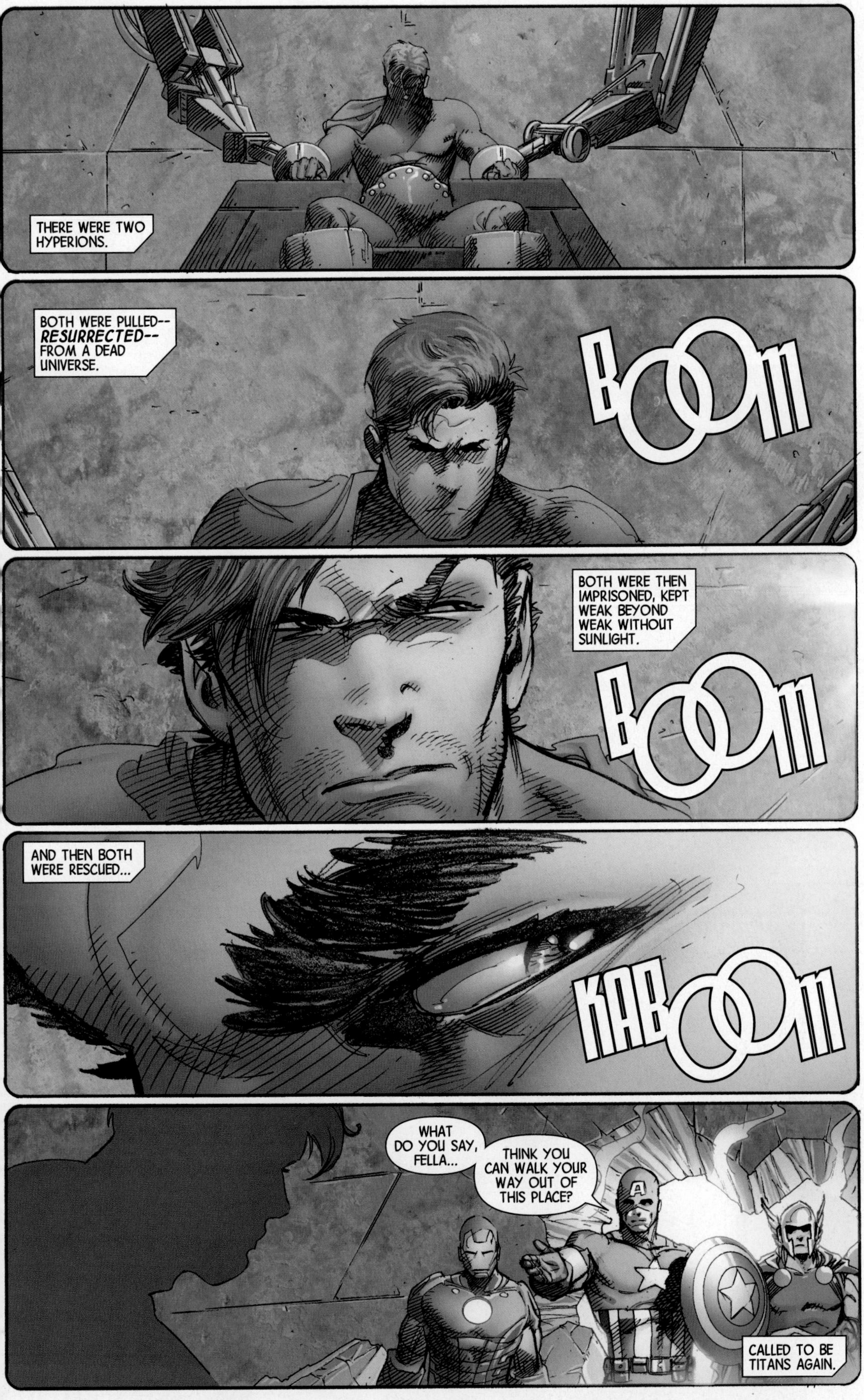

THERE WERE TWO HYPERIONS.
BOTH WERE PULLED-- *RESURRECTED--* FROM A DEAD UNIVERSE.
BOOM
BOTH WERE THEN IMPRISONED, KEPT WEAK BEYOND WEAK WITHOUT SUNLIGHT.
BOOM
AND THEN BOTH WERE RESCUED...
KABOOM
WHAT DO YOU SAY, FELLA...
THINK YOU CAN WALK YOUR WAY OUT OF THIS PLACE?
CALLED TO BE TITANS AGAIN.

TITANS, TOWERING OVER MORTAL MEN AND WOMEN.

TITANS, SHAPING THE WORLD INTO SOMETHING BETTER.

POP

HE REMEMBERED HIS *FATHER'S* WORDS:

TRUTH WITHOUT COMPROMISE.

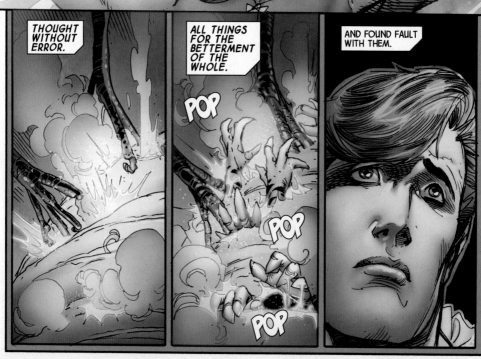

THOUGHT WITHOUT ERROR.

ALL THINGS FOR THE BETTERMENT OF THE WHOLE.

AND FOUND FAULT WITH THEM.

POP

POP

POP

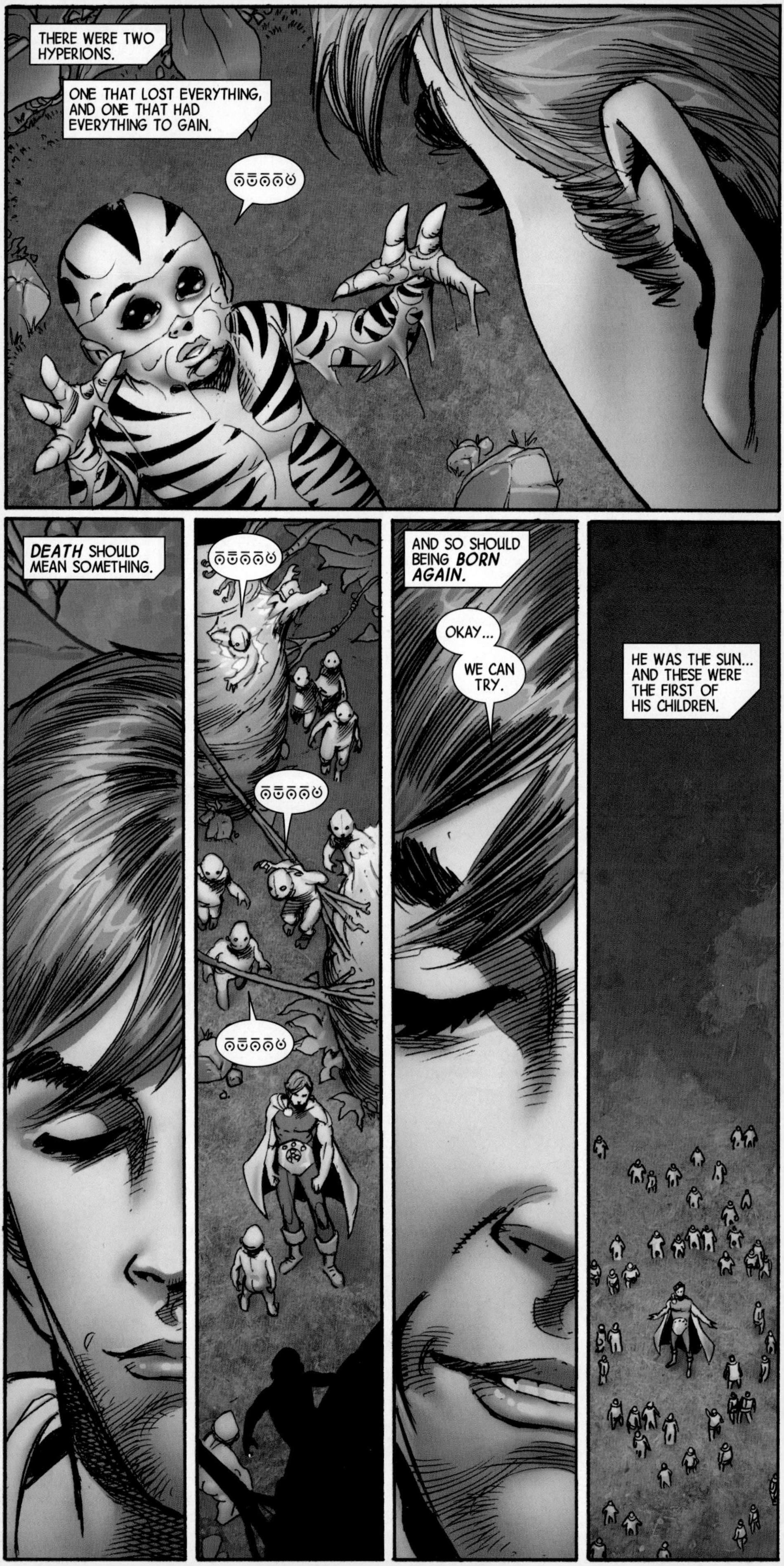
THERE WERE TWO HYPERIONS.
ONE THAT LOST EVERYTHING, AND ONE THAT HAD EVERYTHING TO GAIN.
DEATH SHOULD MEAN SOMETHING.
AND SO SHOULD BEING BORN AGAIN.
OKAY...
WE CAN TRY.
HE WAS THE SUN... AND THESE WERE THE FIRST OF HIS CHILDREN.

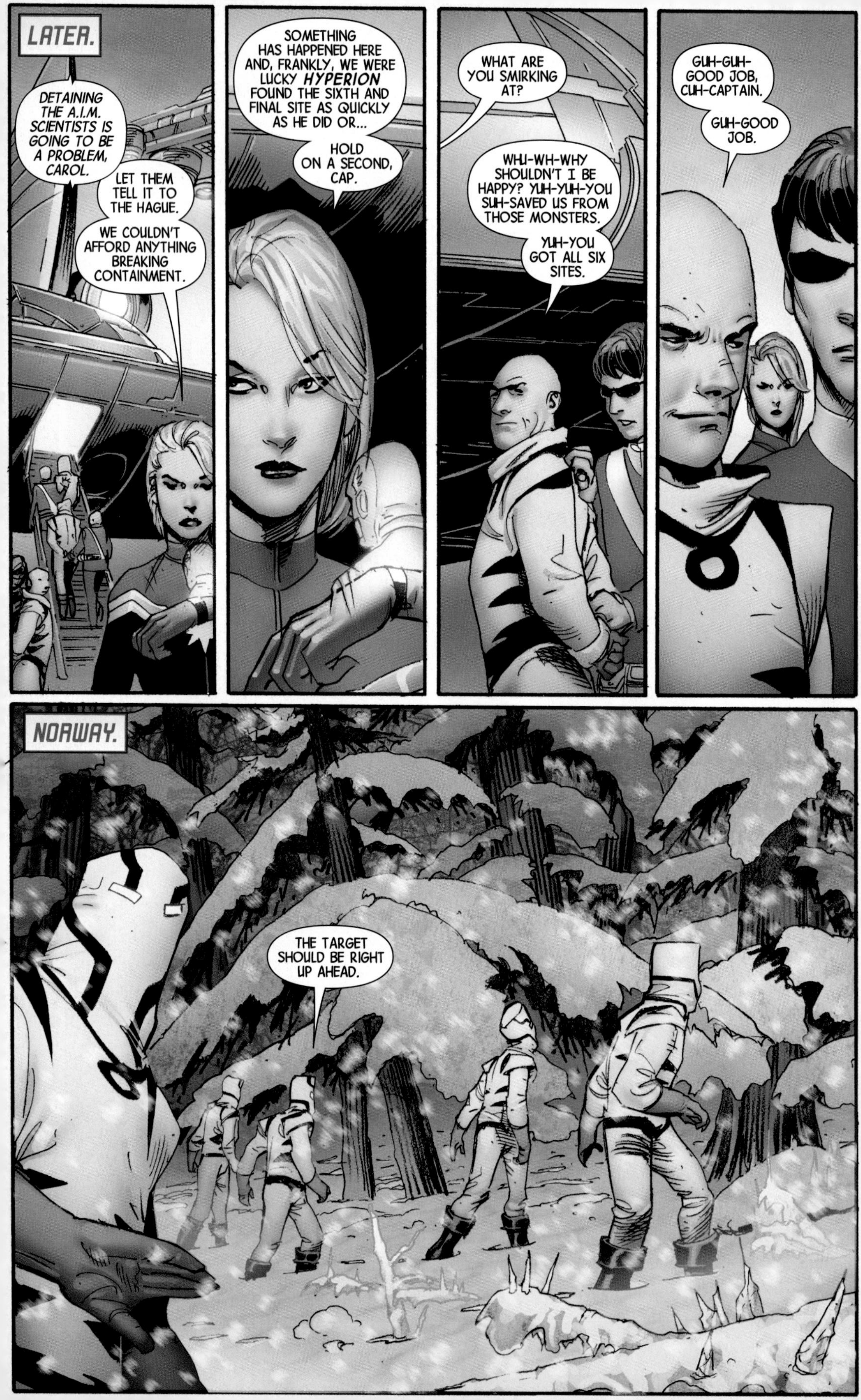
LATER.
DETAINING THE A.I.M. SCIENTISTS IS GOING TO BE A PROBLEM, CAROL.
LET THEM TELL IT TO THE HAGUE.
WE COULDN'T AFFORD ANYTHING BREAKING CONTAINMENT.
SOMETHING HAS HAPPENED HERE AND, FRANKLY, WE WERE LUCKY HYPERION FOUND THE SIXTH AND FINAL SITE AS QUICKLY AS HE DID OR...
HOLD ON A SECOND, CAP.
WHAT ARE YOU SMIRKING AT?
WHU-WH-WHY SHOULDN'T I BE HAPPY? YUH-YUH-YOU SUH-SAVED US FROM THOSE MONSTERS.
YUH-YOU GOT ALL SIX SITES.
GUH-GUH-GOOD JOB, CUH-CAPTAIN.
GUH-GOOD JOB.
NORWAY.
THE TARGET SHOULD BE RIGHT UP AHEAD.

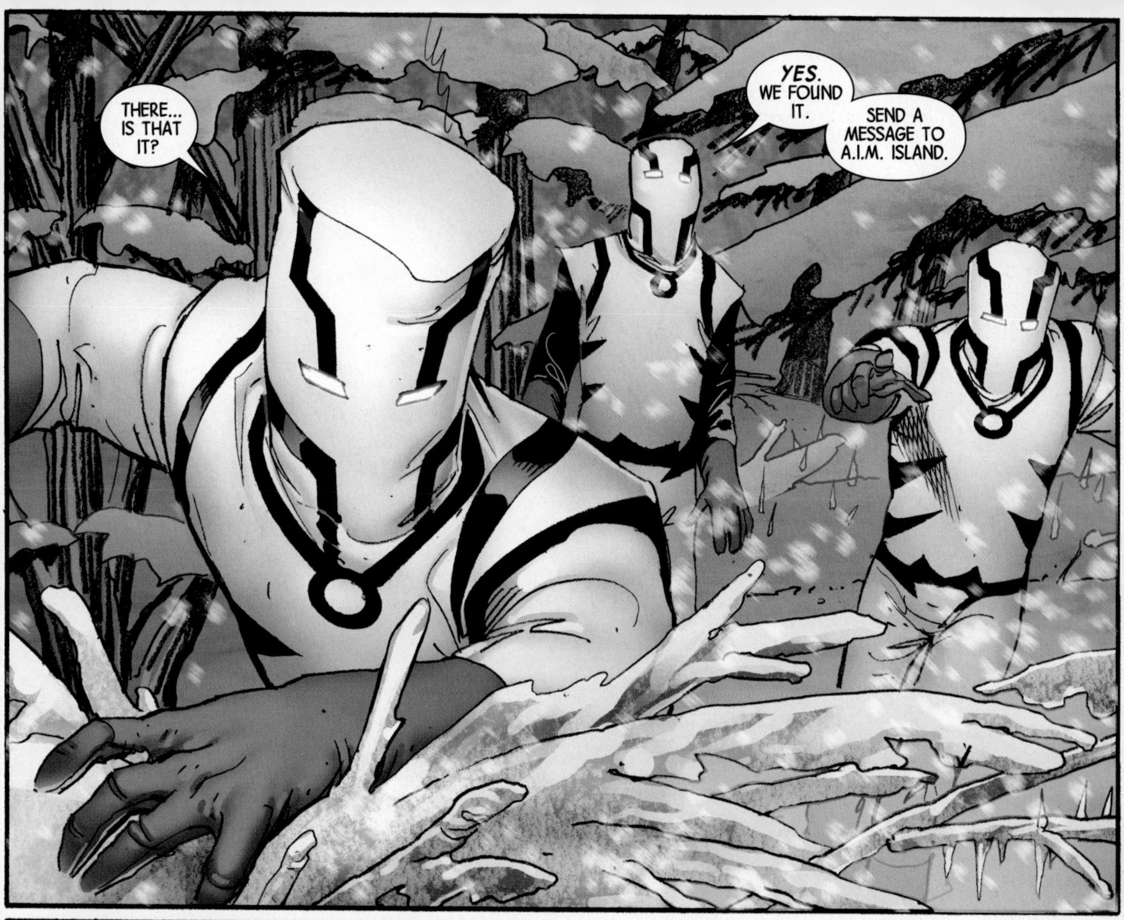
THERE... IS THAT IT?
YES. WE FOUND IT.
SEND A MESSAGE TO A.I.M. ISLAND.

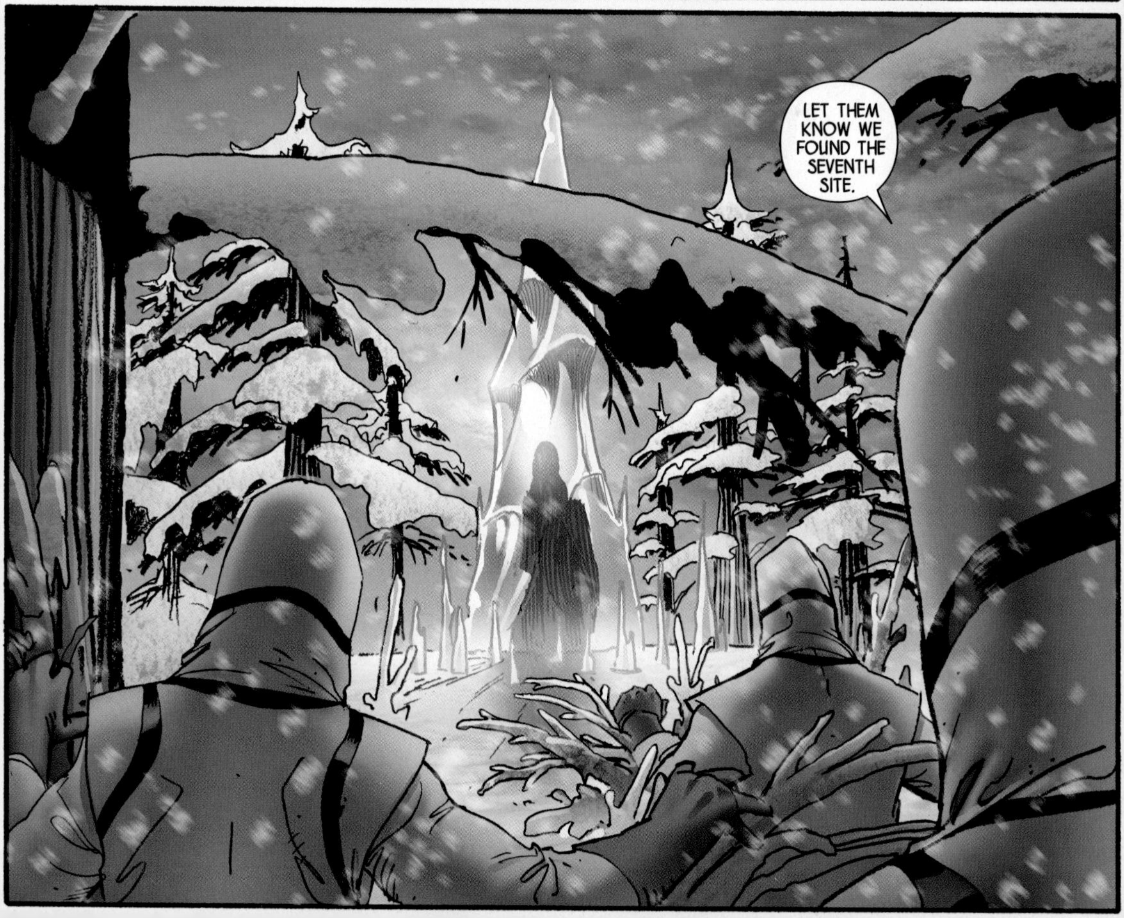
LET THEM KNOW WE FOUND THE SEVENTH SITE.

"SUPERGUARDIAN"

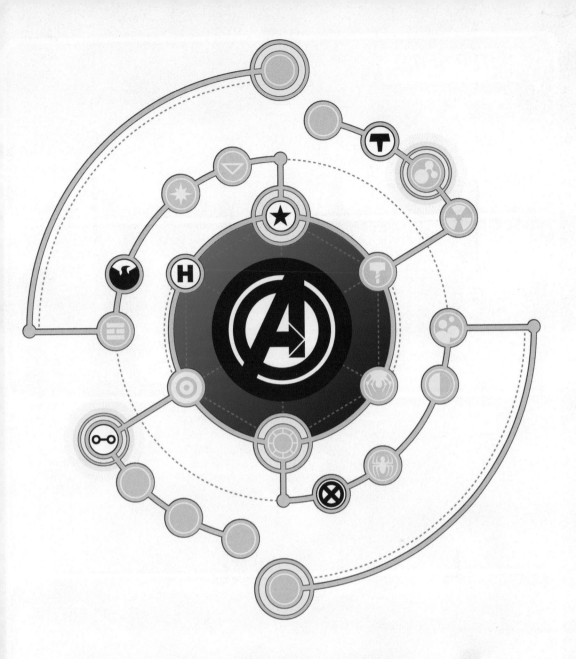

EARTH'S MIGHTIEST HEROES

CAPTAIN AMERICA · IRON MAN · THOR · HAWKEYE · BLACK WIDOW · HULK
WOLVERINE · SPIDER-MAN · CAPTAIN MARVEL · SPIDER-WOMAN
FALCON · SHANG-CHI · SUNSPOT · CANNONBALL · MANIFOLD
SMASHER · CAPTAIN UNIVERSE · HYPERION

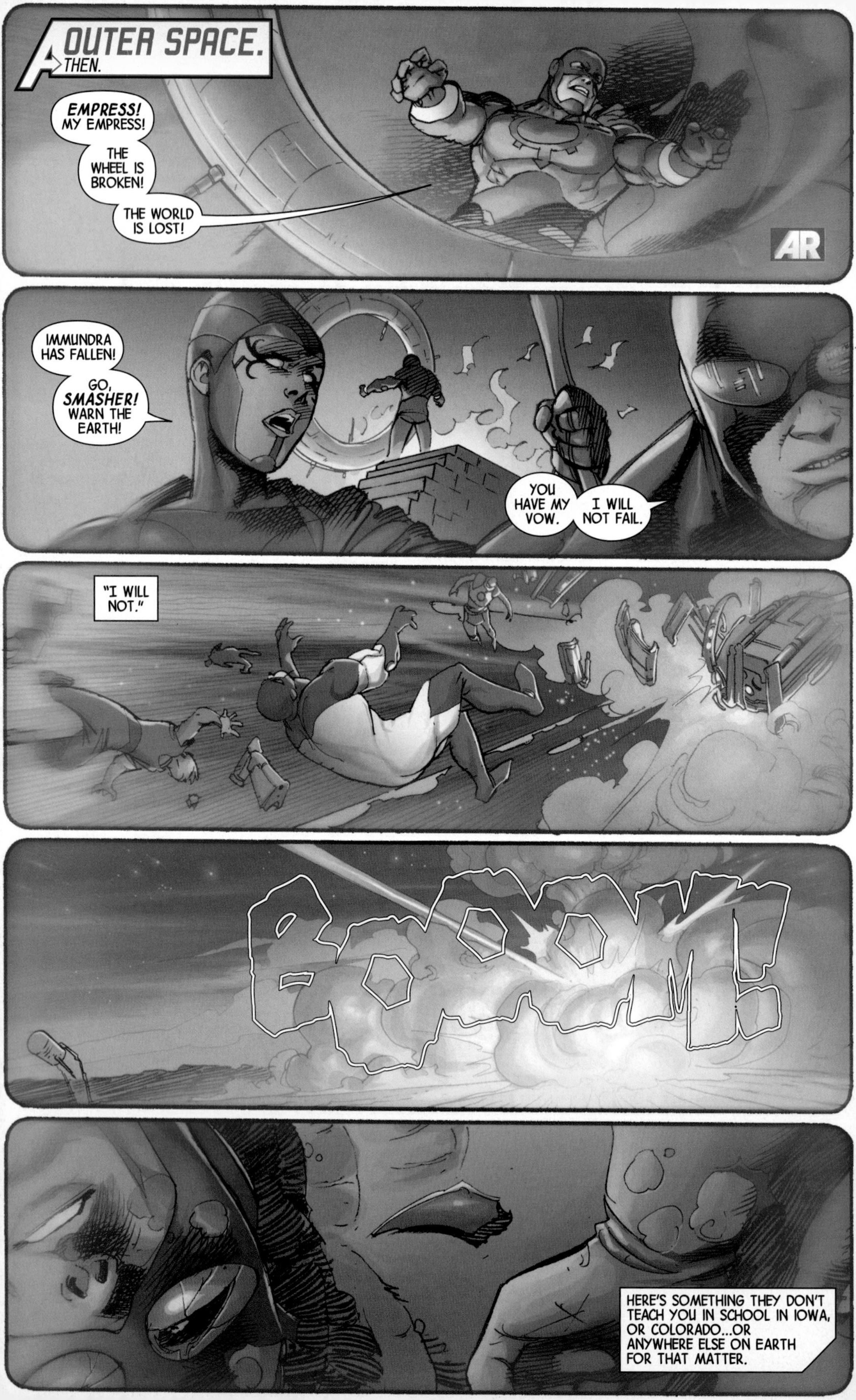

OUTER SPACE.
THEN.
EMPRESS! MY EMPRESS!
THE WHEEL IS BROKEN!
THE WORLD IS LOST!
IMMUNDRA HAS FALLEN!
GO, SMASHER! WARN THE EARTH!
YOU HAVE MY VOW.
I WILL NOT FAIL.
"I WILL NOT."
BOOOM!
HERE'S SOMETHING THEY DON'T TEACH YOU IN SCHOOL IN IOWA, OR COLORADO...OR ANYWHERE ELSE ON EARTH FOR THAT MATTER.

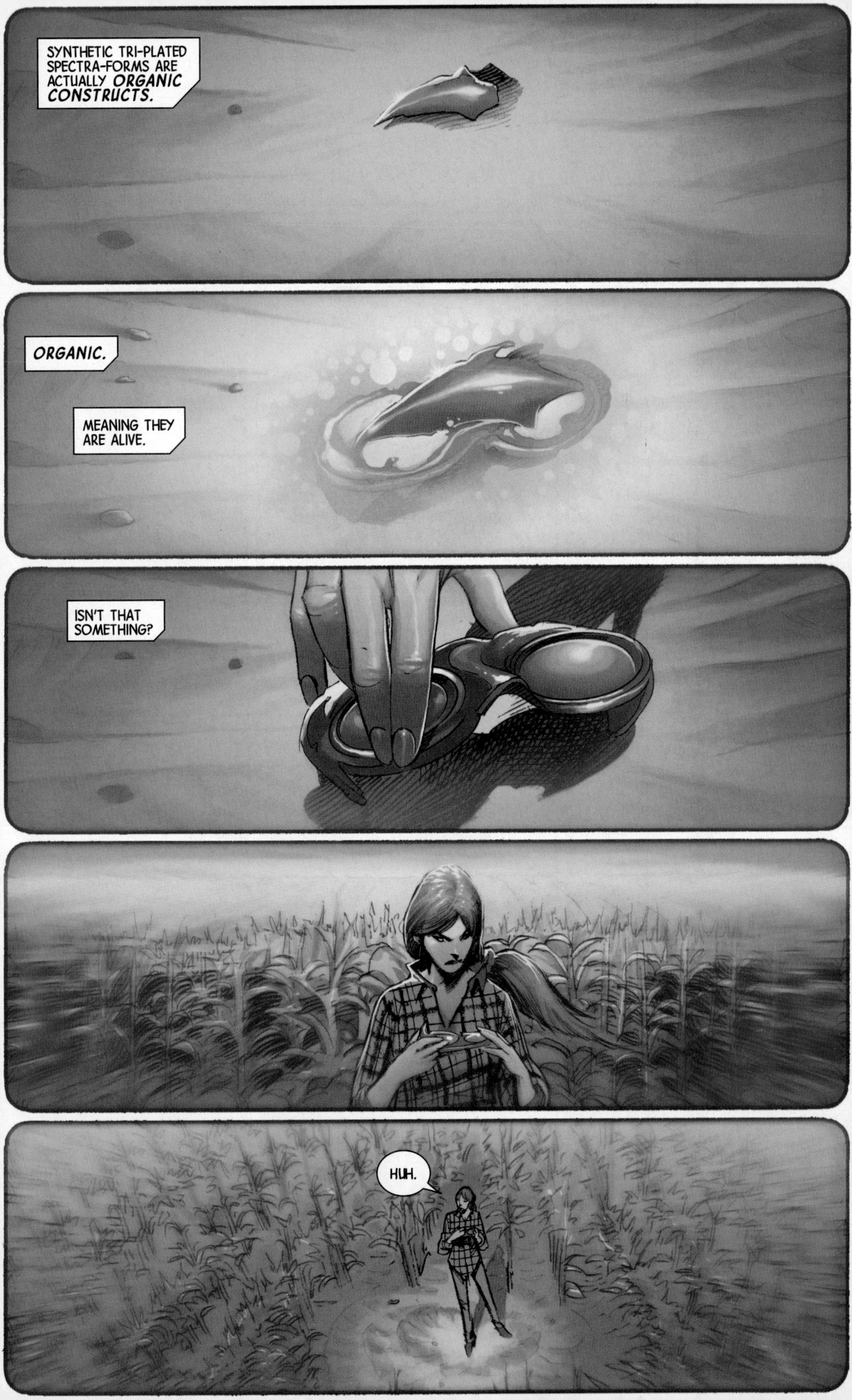
SYNTHETIC TRI-PLATED SPECTRA-FORMS ARE ACTUALLY *ORGANIC CONSTRUCTS.*
ORGANIC.
MEANING THEY ARE ALIVE.
ISN'T THAT SOMETHING?
HUH.

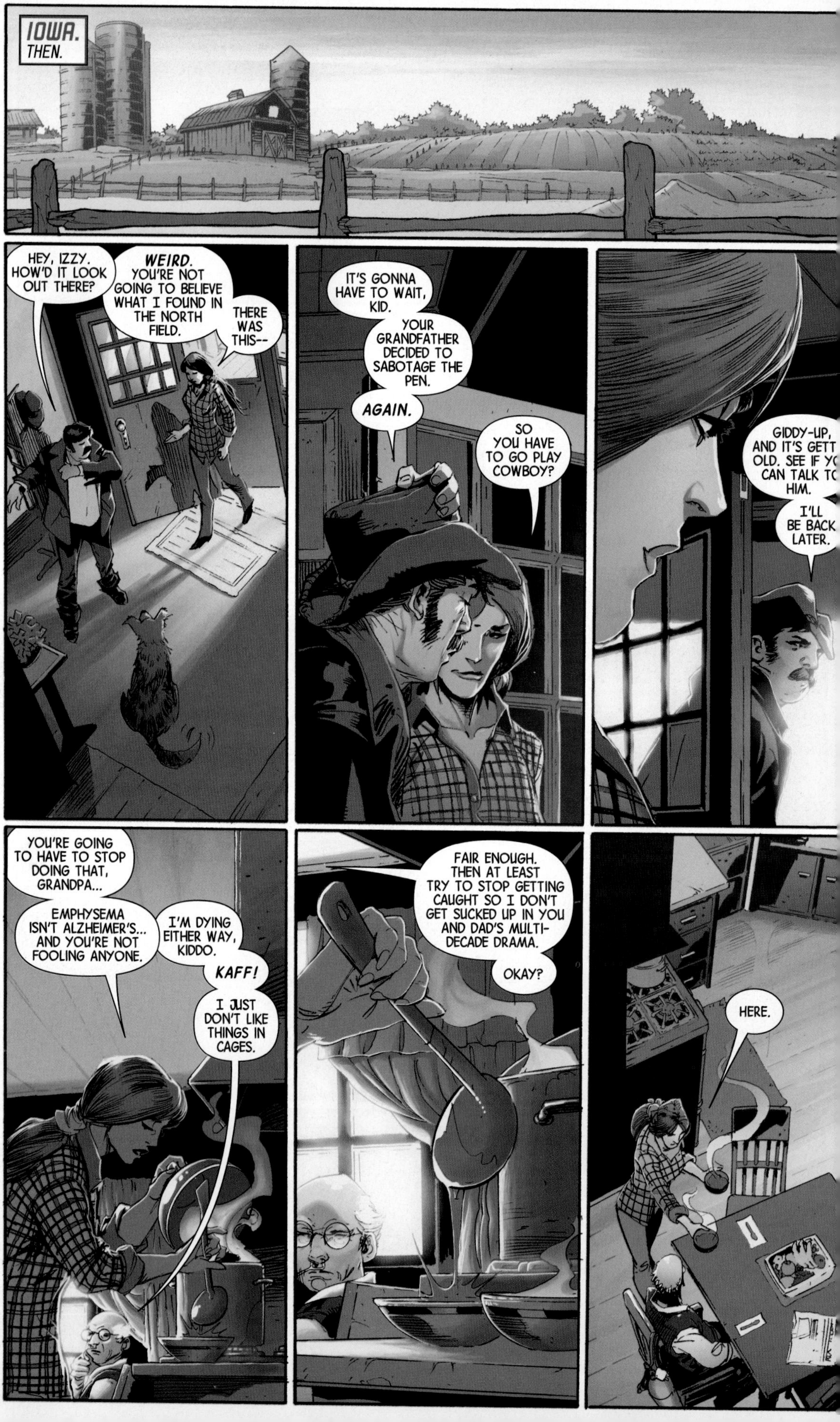
IOWA. THEN.
HEY, IZZY. HOW'D IT LOOK OUT THERE?
WEIRD. YOU'RE NOT GOING TO BELIEVE WHAT I FOUND IN THE NORTH FIELD.
THERE WAS THIS--
IT'S GONNA HAVE TO WAIT, KID.
YOUR GRANDFATHER DECIDED TO SABOTAGE THE PEN.
AGAIN.
SO YOU HAVE TO GO PLAY COWBOY?
GIDDY-UP, AND IT'S GETT OLD. SEE IF YO CAN TALK TO HIM.
I'LL BE BACK LATER.
YOU'RE GOING TO HAVE TO STOP DOING THAT, GRANDPA...
EMPHYSEMA ISN'T ALZHEIMER'S... AND YOU'RE NOT FOOLING ANYONE.
I'M DYING EITHER WAY, KIDDO.
KAFF!
I JUST DON'T LIKE THINGS IN CAGES.
FAIR ENOUGH. THEN AT LEAST TRY TO STOP GETTING CAUGHT SO I DON'T GET SUCKED UP IN YOU AND DAD'S MULTI-DECADE DRAMA.
OKAY?
HERE.

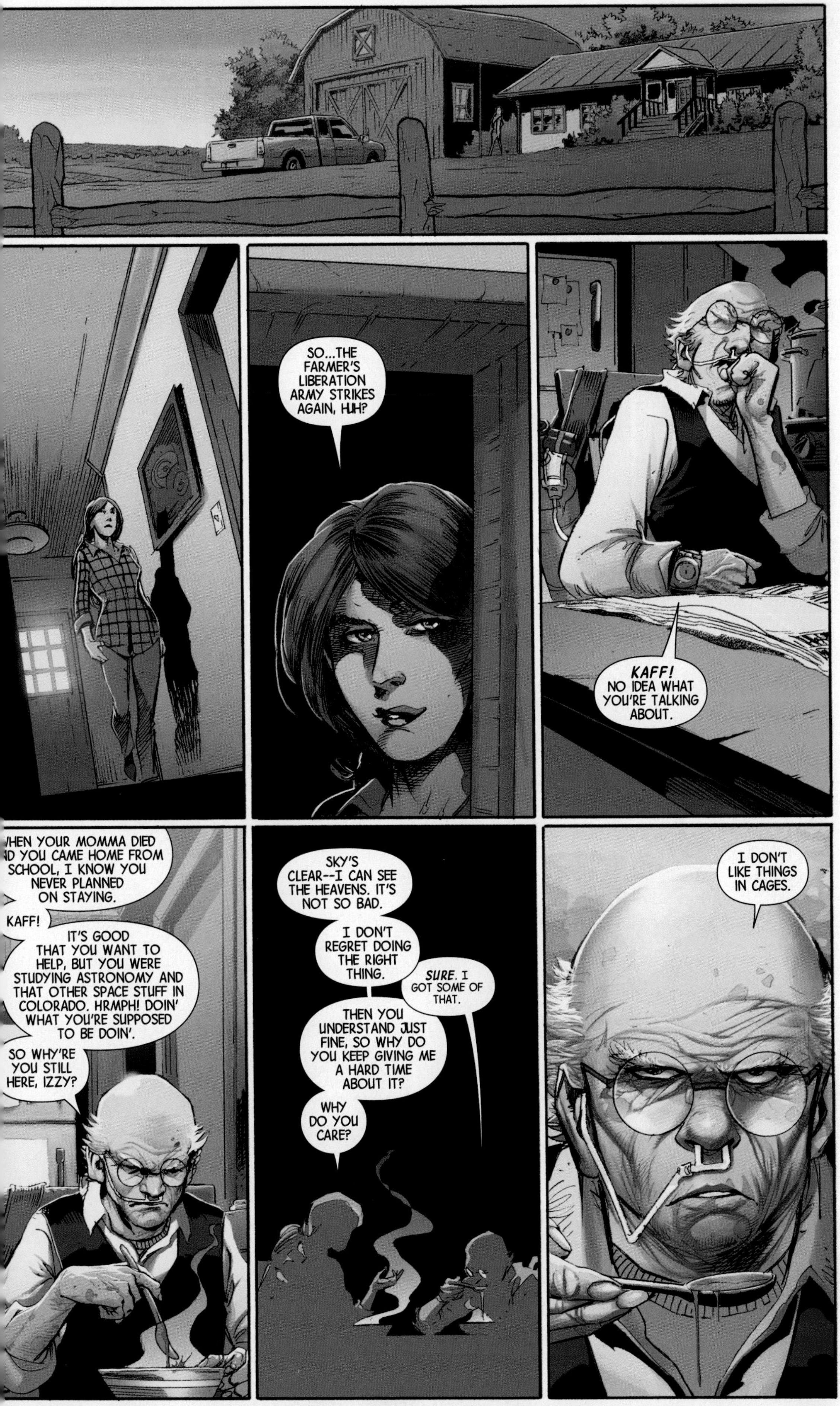

SO...THE FARMER'S LIBERATION ARMY STRIKES AGAIN, HUH?
KAFF! NO IDEA WHAT YOU'RE TALKING ABOUT.
HEN YOUR MOMMA DIED D YOU CAME HOME FROM SCHOOL, I KNOW YOU NEVER PLANNED ON STAYING.
KAFF!
IT'S GOOD THAT YOU WANT TO HELP, BUT YOU WERE STUDYING ASTRONOMY AND THAT OTHER SPACE STUFF IN COLORADO. HRMPH! DOIN' WHAT YOU'RE SUPPOSED TO BE DOIN'.
SO WHY'RE YOU STILL HERE, IZZY?
SKY'S CLEAR--I CAN SEE THE HEAVENS. IT'S NOT SO BAD.
I DON'T REGRET DOING THE RIGHT THING.
SURE. I GOT SOME OF THAT.
THEN YOU UNDERSTAND JUST FINE, SO WHY DO YOU KEEP GIVING ME A HARD TIME ABOUT IT?
WHY DO YOU CARE?
I DON'T LIKE THINGS IN CAGES.

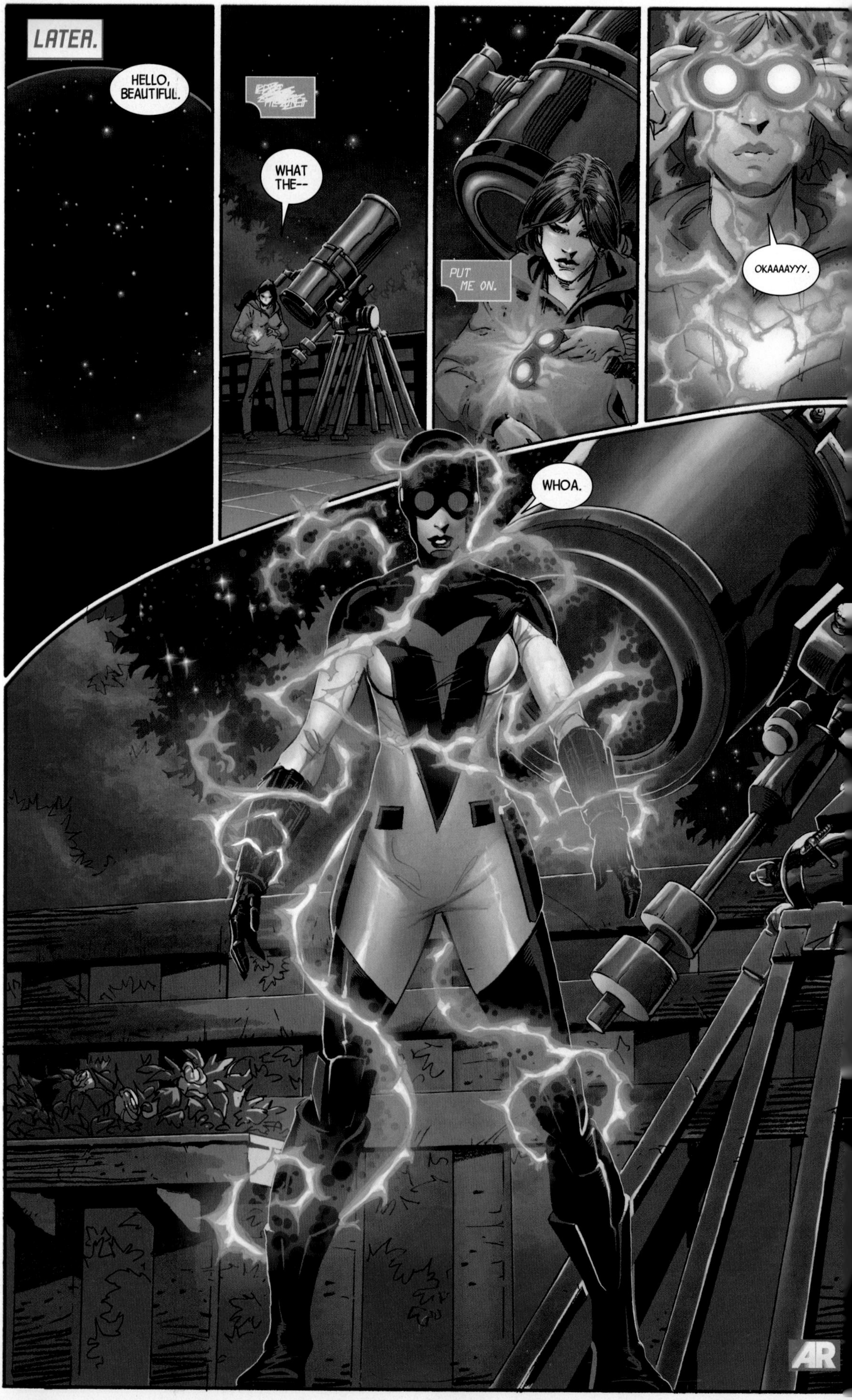
LATER.
HELLO, BEAUTIFUL.
WHAT THE--
PUT ME ON.
OKAAAAYYY.
WHOA.

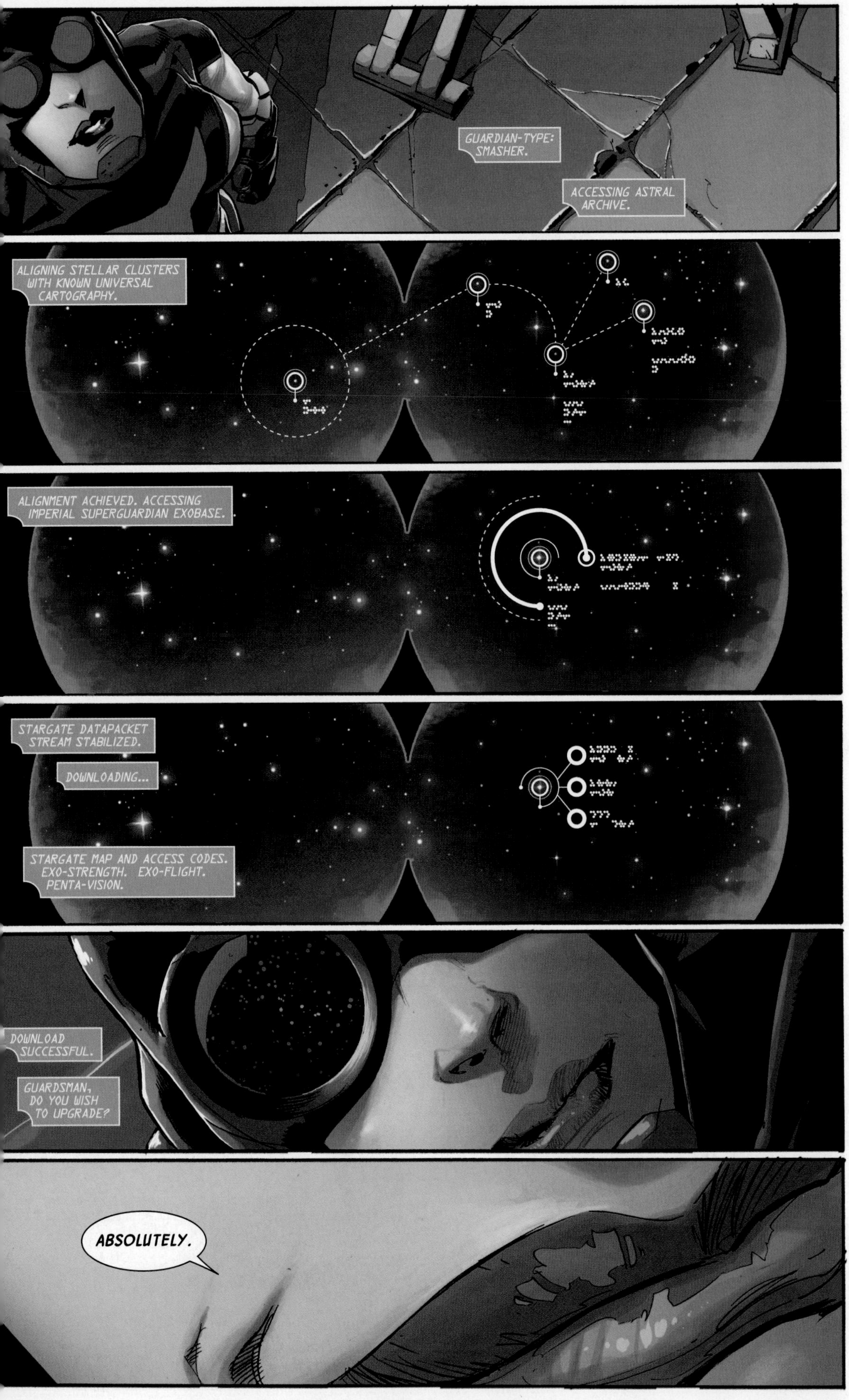
GUARDIAN-TYPE: SMASHER.
ACCESSING ASTRAL ARCHIVE.
ALIGNING STELLAR CLUSTERS WITH KNOWN UNIVERSAL CARTOGRAPHY.
ALIGNMENT ACHIEVED. ACCESSING IMPERIAL SUPERGUARDIAN EXOBASE.
STARGATE DATAPACKET STREAM STABILIZED.
DOWNLOADING...
STARGATE MAP AND ACCESS CODES. EXO-STRENGTH. EXO-FLIGHT. PENTA-VISION.
DOWNLOAD SUCCESSFUL.
GUARDSMAN, DO YOU WISH TO UPGRADE?
ABSOLUTELY.

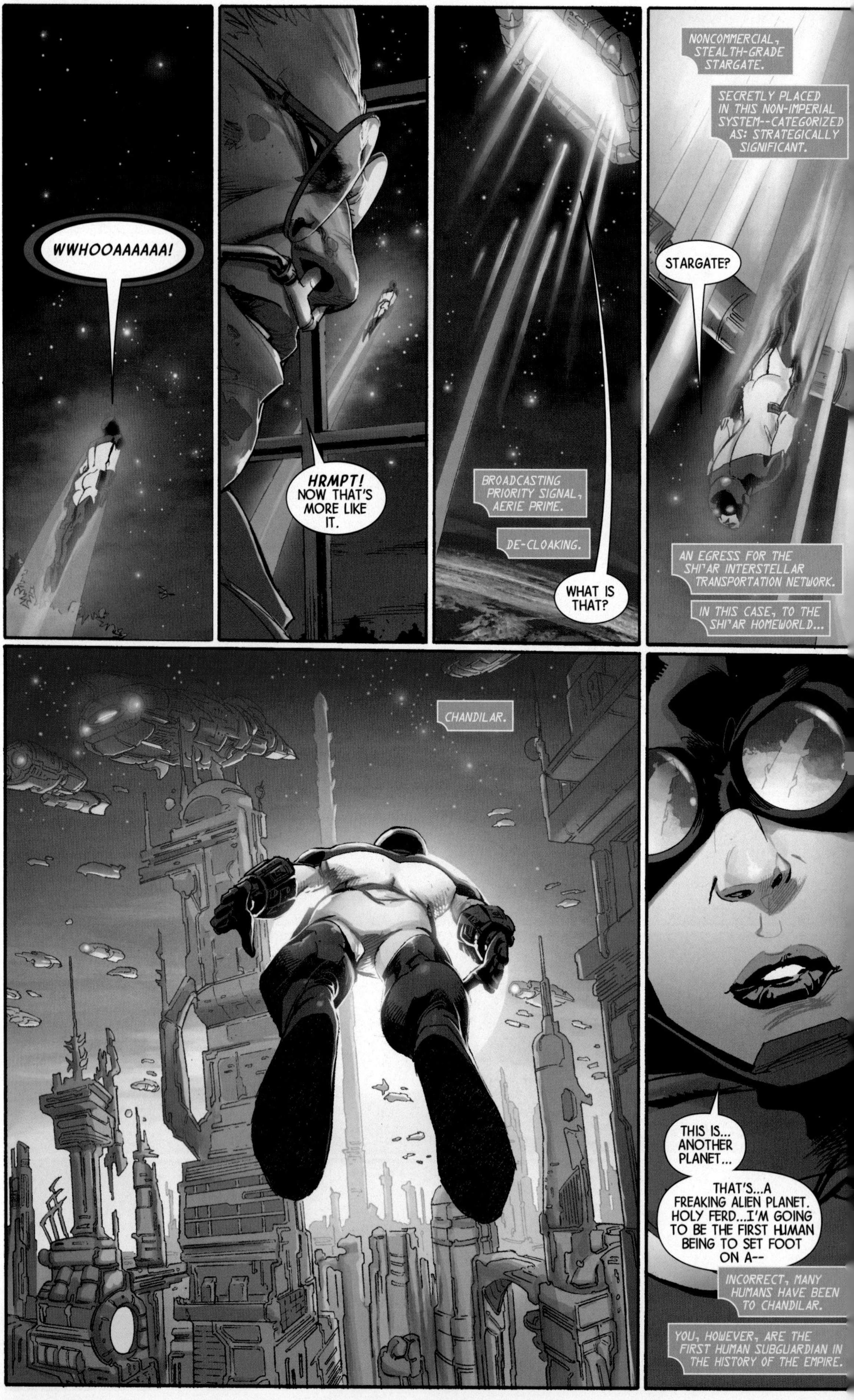
WWHOOAAAAAA!
HRMPT! NOW THAT'S MORE LIKE IT.
BROADCASTING PRIORITY SIGNAL, AERIE PRIME.
DE-CLOAKING.
WHAT IS THAT?
NONCOMMERCIAL, STEALTH-GRADE STARGATE.
SECRETLY PLACED IN THIS NON-IMPERIAL SYSTEM--CATEGORIZED AS: STRATEGICALLY SIGNIFICANT.
STARGATE?
AN EGRESS FOR THE SHI'AR INTERSTELLAR TRANSPORTATION NETWORK.
IN THIS CASE, TO THE SHI'AR HOMEWORLD...
CHANDILAR.
THIS IS... ANOTHER PLANET...
THAT'S...A FREAKING ALIEN PLANET. HOLY FERD...I'M GOING TO BE THE FIRST HUMAN BEING TO SET FOOT ON A--
INCORRECT, MANY HUMANS HAVE BEEN TO CHANDILAR.
YOU, HOWEVER, ARE THE FIRST HUMAN SUBGUARDIAN IN THE HISTORY OF THE EMPIRE.

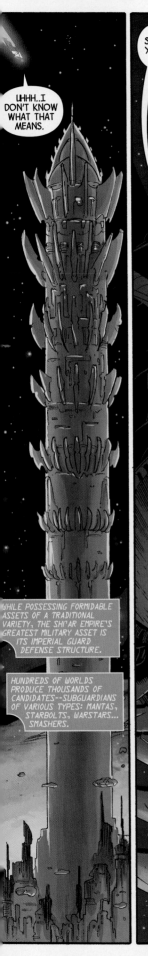

UHHH..I DON'T KNOW WHAT THAT MEANS.

WHILE POSSESSING FORMIDABLE ASSETS OF A TRADITIONAL VARIETY, THE SHI'AR EMPIRE'S GREATEST MILITARY ASSET IS ITS IMPERIAL GUARD DEFENSE STRUCTURE.

HUNDREDS OF WORLDS PRODUCE THOUSANDS OF CANDIDATES--SUBGUARDIANS OF VARIOUS TYPES: MANTAS, STARBOLTS, WARSTARS... SMASHERS.

WAIT, SMASHER-- YOU MEAN LIKE ME?

YES. THERE ARE CURRENTLY 43 SMASHER-CLASS SUBGUARDIANS PREPARING FOR THE CHANCE TO ONE DAY JOIN THE MOST ELITE FIGHTING FORCE IN THE KNOWN UNIVERSE...

THE IMPERIAL GUARD.

OKAY... AND IF I'M A SUBGUARDIAN, WHAT ARE THEY CALLED?

SUPERGUARDIANS.

AVENGERS TOWER. NOW.

BLACKVEIL?

BLACKVEIL.

BLACKVEIL, OKAY. IT'S NOT THE STEAM ENGINE... BUT IT IS WHAT WE CIVILIZED MEN CALL PROGRESS.

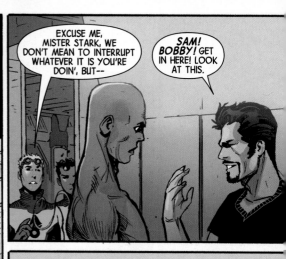

EXCUSE ME, MISTER STARK, WE DON'T MEAN TO INTERRUPT WHATEVER IT IS YOU'RE DOIN', BUT--

SAM! BOBBY! GET IN HERE! LOOK AT THIS.

BLACKVEIL

ADAM AND I WERE ABLE TO FORMALIZE THE CHARACTERS IN HIS ALPHABET AND FROM THAT I'VE BEEN ABLE TO CREATE A CONVERSION SYSTEM THAT SYNCS UP WITH HIS SPEECH-- WE'VE JUST HAD OUR FIRST BREAKTHROUGH...

IT'S HIS NAME... BLACKVEIL.

THAT'S REALLY IMPRESSIVE, SIR.

RIGHT. YOU WANTED SOMETHING ELSE...?

WE'RE LOOKING FOR IZZY AND EDEN, AND WHEN WE COULDN'T FIND THEM WE TRIED USING THE "WHERE IS" FUNCTION ON THE AVENGERS MACHINE, BUT--

I CAN'T BELIEVE THE TWO OF YOU MISSED ALL THE COMMOTION THIS MORNING--IMPERIAL ALERTS, THREAT TO THE EMPIRE, GENERAL HYSTERIA...

ANYWAY, OF COURSE THEY DIDN'T SHOW UP ON THE FINDER.

WHY IS THAT?

SAM...THEY'RE IN ANOTHER GALAXY.

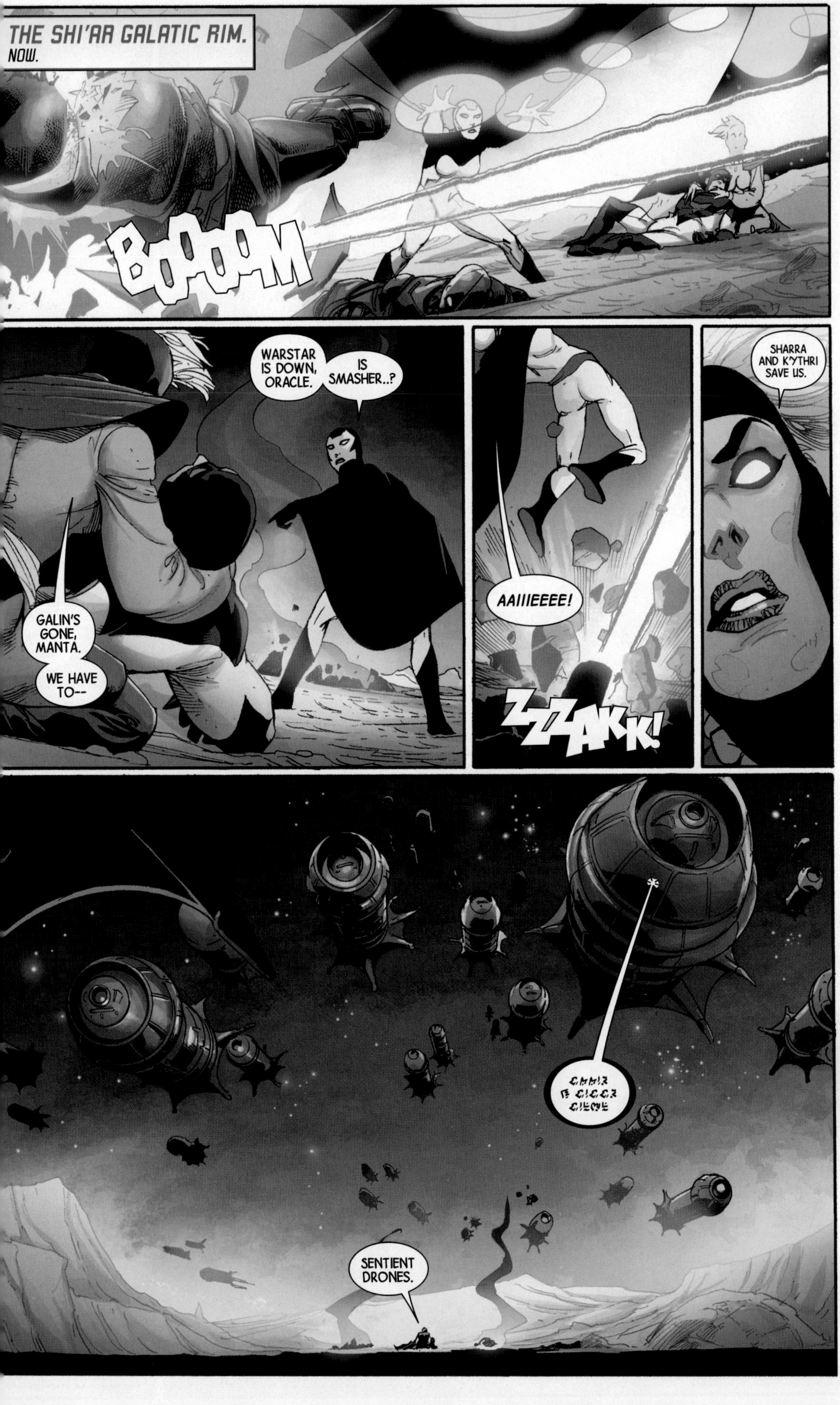
THE SHI'AR GALATIC RIM.
NOW.
BOOOOM
WARSTAR IS DOWN, ORACLE.
IS SMASHER..?
GALIN'S GONE, MANTA.
WE HAVE TO--
AAIIIEEEE!
ZZZZAKKK!
SHARRA AND K'YTHRI SAVE US.
SENTIENT DRONES.

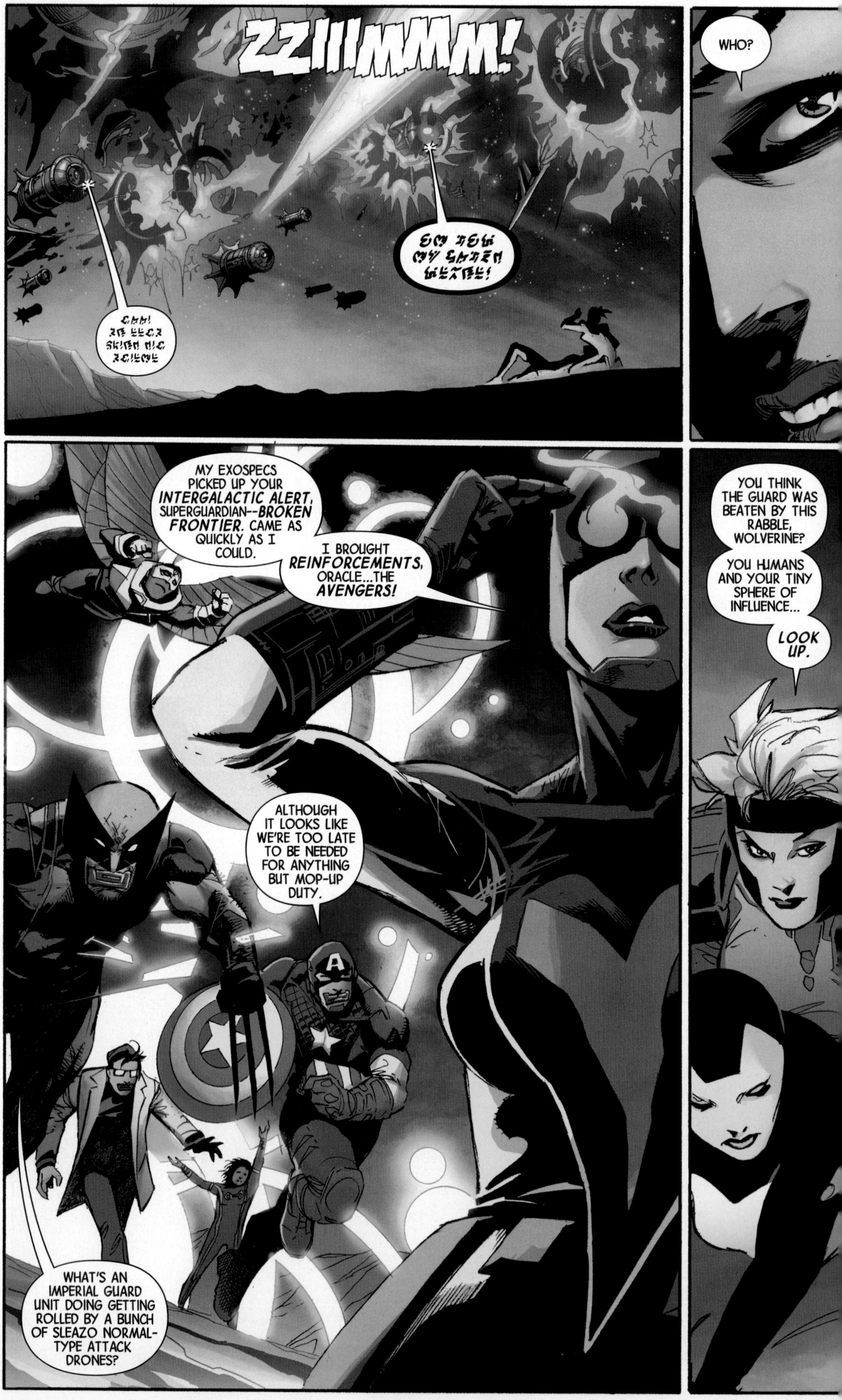
ZZIIIMMMM!
WHO?
MY EXOSPECS PICKED UP YOUR INTERGALACTIC ALERT, SUPERGUARDIAN--BROKEN FRONTIER. CAME AS QUICKLY AS I COULD.
I BROUGHT REINFORCEMENTS, ORACLE...THE AVENGERS!
ALTHOUGH IT LOOKS LIKE WE'RE TOO LATE TO BE NEEDED FOR ANYTHING BUT MOP-UP DUTY.
WHAT'S AN IMPERIAL GUARD UNIT DOING GETTING ROLLED BY A BUNCH OF SLEAZO NORMAL-TYPE ATTACK DRONES?
YOU THINK THE GUARD WAS BEATEN BY THIS RABBLE, WOLVERINE?
YOU HUMANS AND YOUR TINY SPHERE OF INFLUENCE...
LOOK UP.

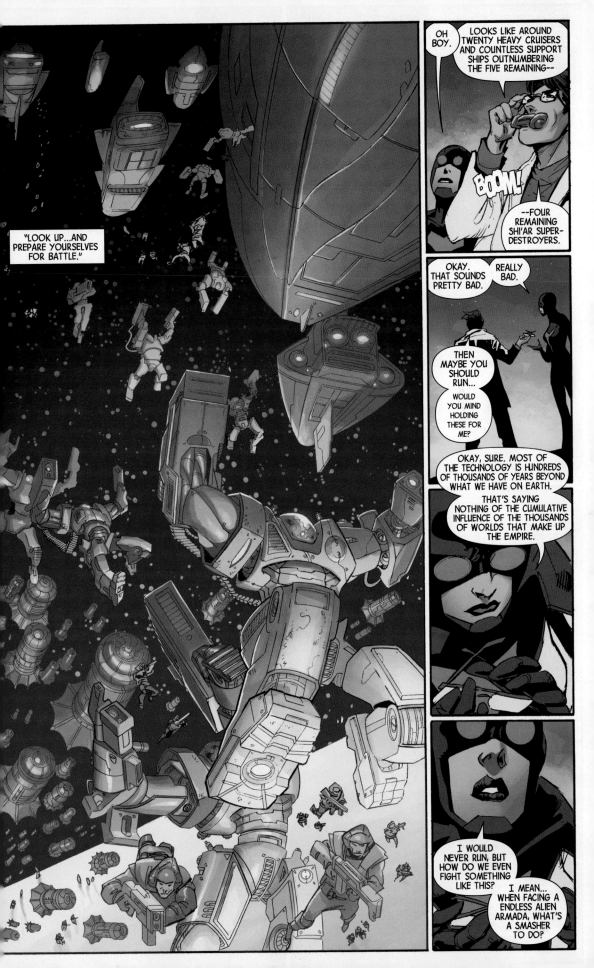

"LOOK UP...AND PREPARE YOURSELVES FOR BATTLE."

OH BOY.

LOOKS LIKE AROUND TWENTY HEAVY CRUISERS AND COUNTLESS SUPPORT SHIPS OUTNUMBERING THE FIVE REMAINING--

BOOM!

--FOUR REMAINING SHI'AR SUPER-DESTROYERS.

OKAY. THAT SOUNDS PRETTY BAD.

REALLY BAD.

THEN MAYBE YOU SHOULD RUN...

WOULD YOU MIND HOLDING THESE FOR ME?

OKAY, SURE. MOST OF THE TECHNOLOGY IS HUNDREDS OF THOUSANDS OF YEARS BEYOND WHAT WE HAVE ON EARTH.

THAT'S SAYING NOTHING OF THE CUMULATIVE INFLUENCE OF THE THOUSANDS OF WORLDS THAT MAKE UP THE EMPIRE.

I WOULD NEVER RUN, BUT HOW DO WE EVEN FIGHT SOMETHING LIKE THIS?

I MEAN... WHEN FACING A ENDLESS ALIEN ARMADA, WHAT'S A SMASHER TO DO?

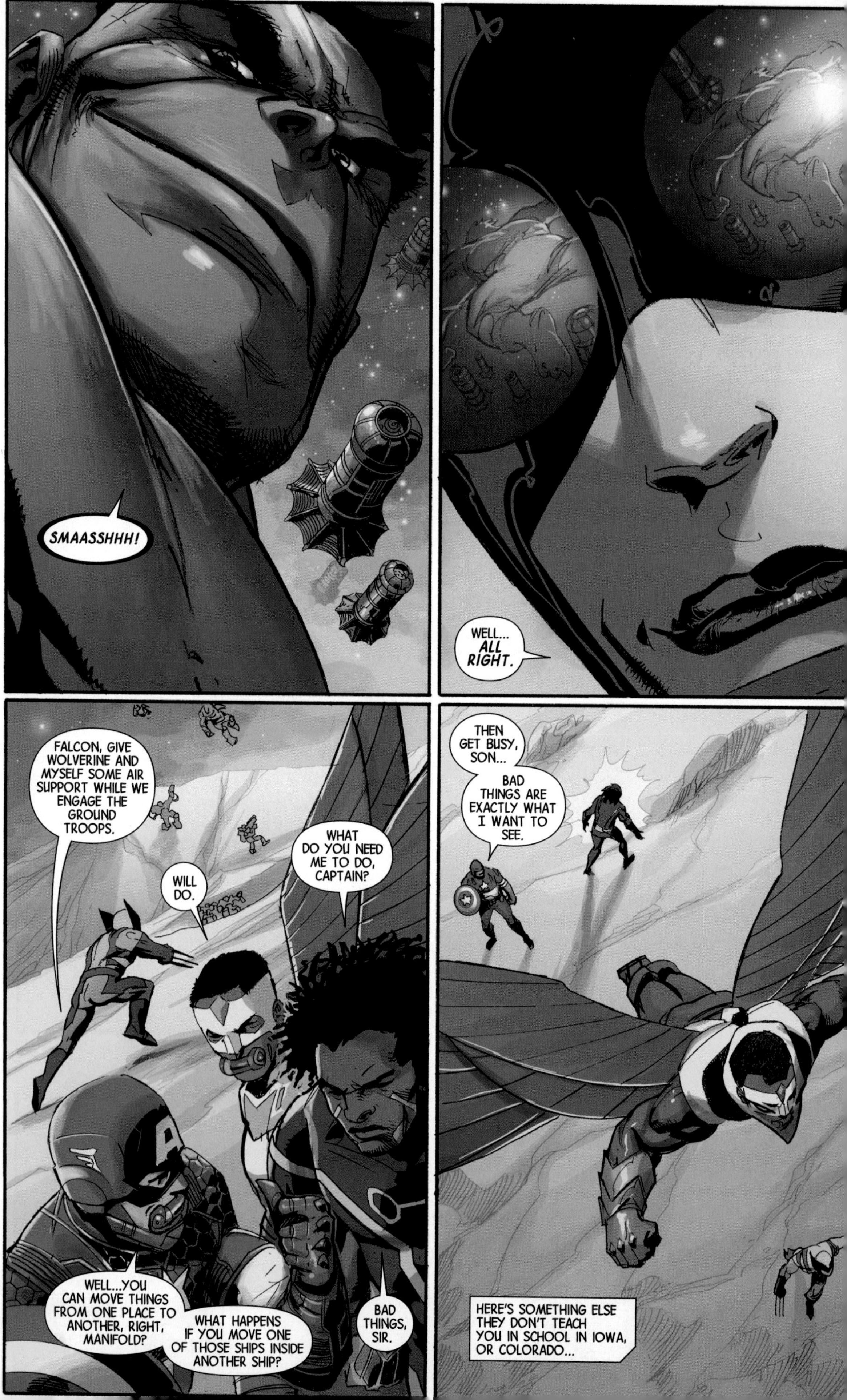
SMAASSHHH!
WELL... ALL RIGHT.
FALCON, GIVE WOLVERINE AND MYSELF SOME AIR SUPPORT WHILE WE ENGAGE THE GROUND TROOPS.
WILL DO.
WHAT DO YOU NEED ME TO DO, CAPTAIN?
WELL...YOU CAN MOVE THINGS FROM ONE PLACE TO ANOTHER, RIGHT, MANIFOLD?
WHAT HAPPENS IF YOU MOVE ONE OF THOSE SHIPS INSIDE ANOTHER SHIP?
BAD THINGS, SIR.
THEN GET BUSY, SON...
BAD THINGS ARE EXACTLY WHAT I WANT TO SEE.
HERE'S SOMETHING ELSE THEY DON'T TEACH YOU IN SCHOOL IN IOWA, OR COLORADO...

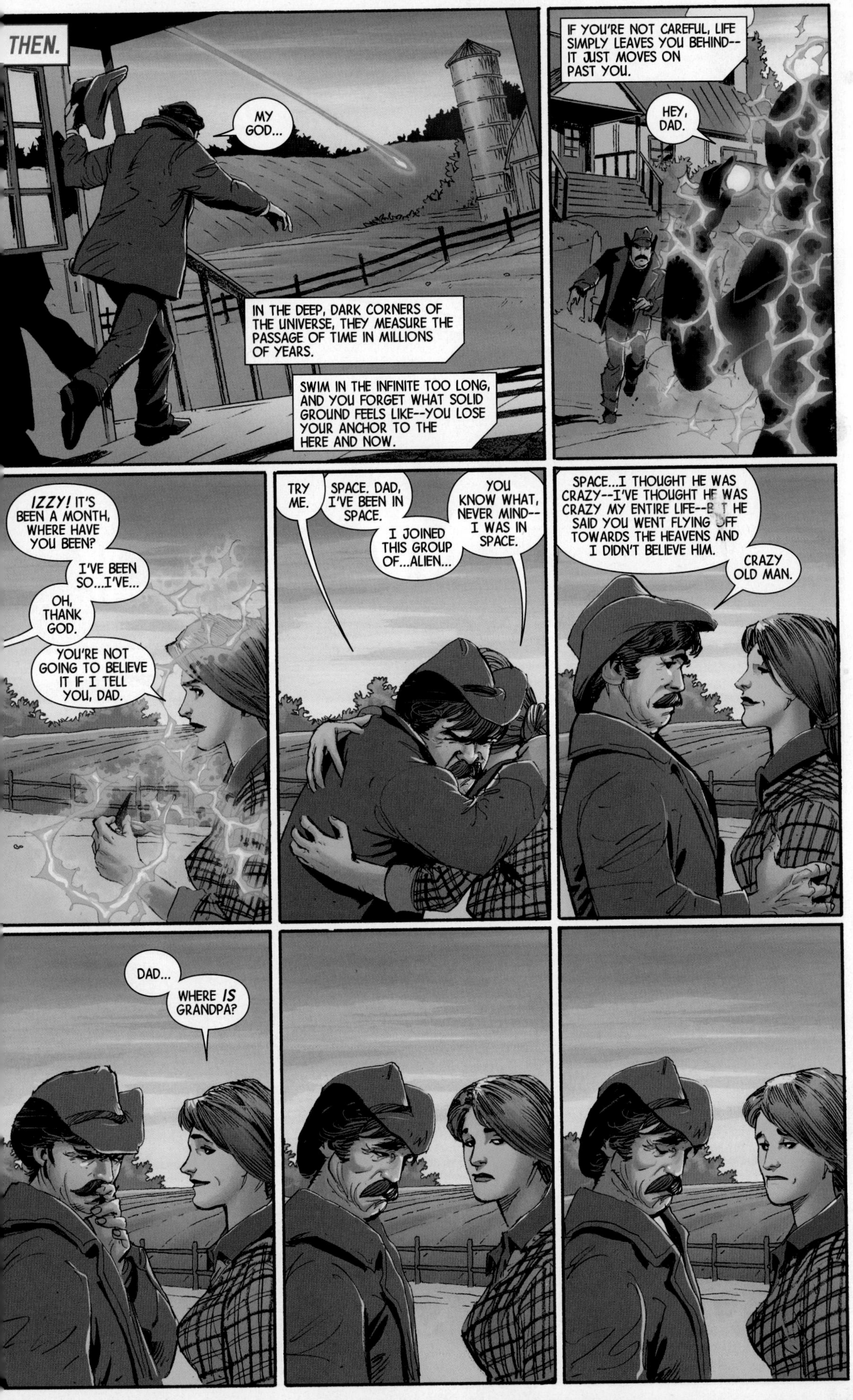
THEN.
MY GOD...
IN THE DEEP, DARK CORNERS OF THE UNIVERSE, THEY MEASURE THE PASSAGE OF TIME IN MILLIONS OF YEARS.
SWIM IN THE INFINITE TOO LONG, AND YOU FORGET WHAT SOLID GROUND FEELS LIKE--YOU LOSE YOUR ANCHOR TO THE HERE AND NOW.
IF YOU'RE NOT CAREFUL, LIFE SIMPLY LEAVES YOU BEHIND--IT JUST MOVES ON PAST YOU.
HEY, DAD.
IZZY! IT'S BEEN A MONTH, WHERE HAVE YOU BEEN?
I'VE BEEN SO...I'VE...
OH, THANK GOD.
YOU'RE NOT GOING TO BELIEVE IT IF I TELL YOU, DAD.
TRY ME.
SPACE. DAD, I'VE BEEN IN SPACE.
I JOINED THIS GROUP OF...ALIEN...
YOU KNOW WHAT, NEVER MIND--I WAS IN SPACE.
SPACE...I THOUGHT HE WAS CRAZY--I'VE THOUGHT HE WAS CRAZY MY ENTIRE LIFE--BUT HE SAID YOU WENT FLYING OFF TOWARDS THE HEAVENS AND I DIDN'T BELIEVE HIM.
CRAZY OLD MAN.
DAD...
WHERE IS GRANDPA?

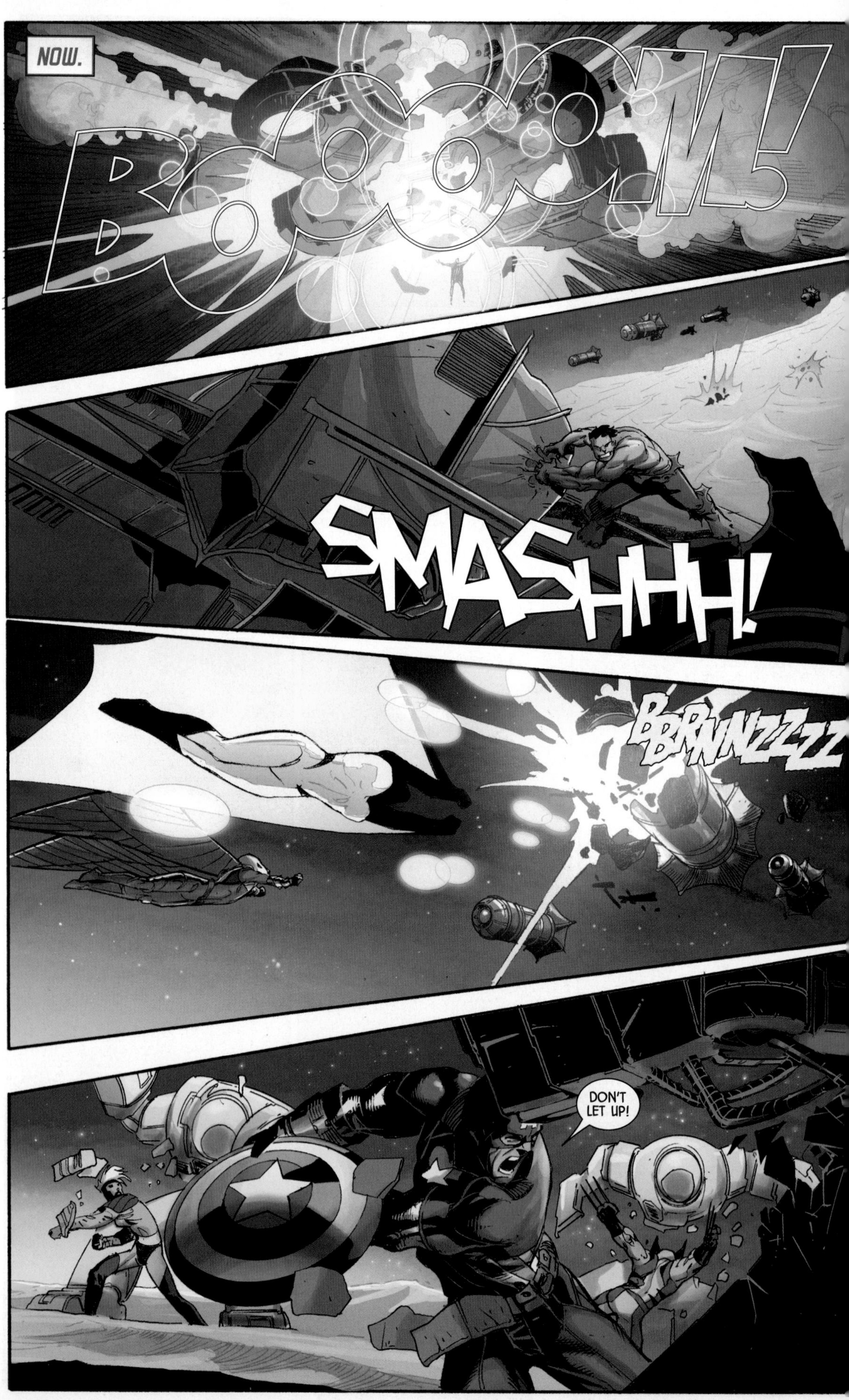
NOW.
BOOOOOM!
SMASHHH!
BBRNNZZZZZ
DON'T LET UP!

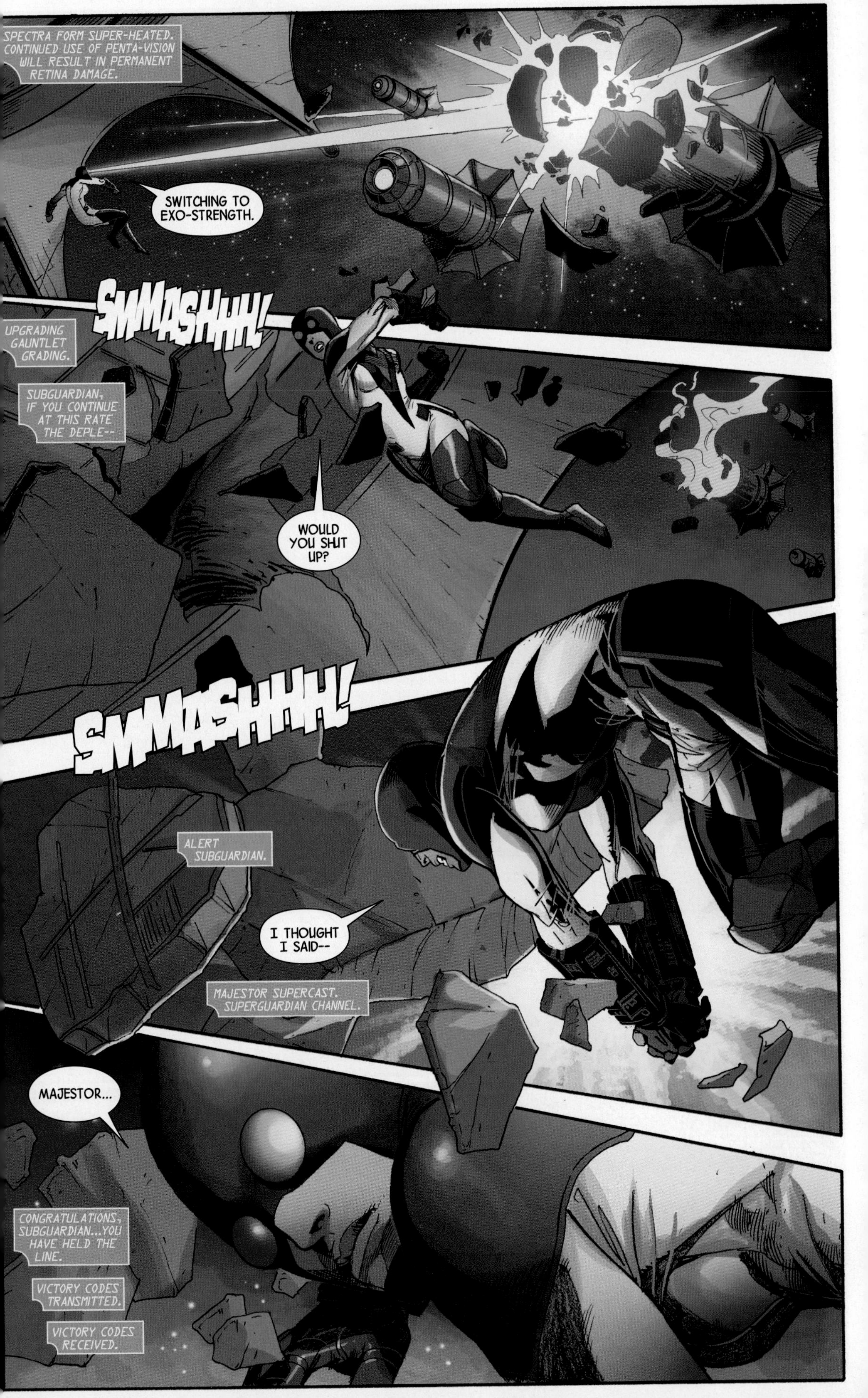

SPECTRA FORM SUPER-HEATED. CONTINUED USE OF PENTA-VISION WILL RESULT IN PERMANENT RETINA DAMAGE.
SWITCHING TO EXO-STRENGTH.
SMMASHHH!
UPGRADING GAUNTLET GRADING.
SUBGUARDIAN, IF YOU CONTINUE AT THIS RATE THE DEPLE--
WOULD YOU SHUT UP?
SMMASHHH!
ALERT SUBGUARDIAN.
I THOUGHT I SAID--
MAJESTOR SUPERCAST. SUPERGUARDIAN CHANNEL.
MAJESTOR...
CONGRATULATIONS, SUBGUARDIAN...YOU HAVE HELD THE LINE.
VICTORY CODES TRANSMITTED.
VICTORY CODES RECEIVED.

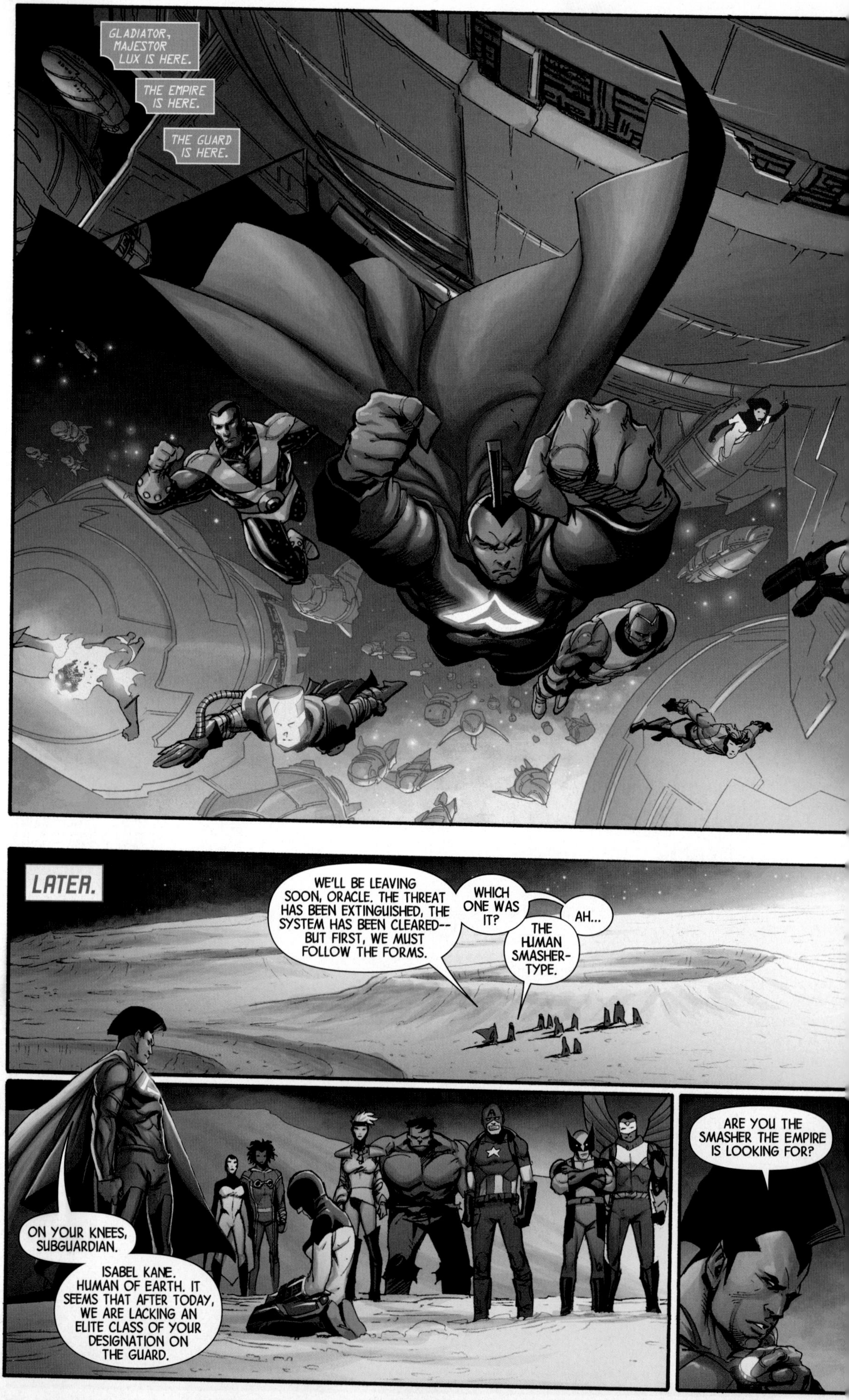
GLADIATOR, MAJESTOR LUX IS HERE.
THE EMPIRE IS HERE.
THE GUARD IS HERE.
LATER.
WE'LL BE LEAVING SOON, ORACLE. THE THREAT HAS BEEN EXTINGUISHED, THE SYSTEM HAS BEEN CLEARED-- BUT FIRST, WE MUST FOLLOW THE FORMS.
WHICH ONE WAS IT?
AH...
THE HUMAN SMASHER-TYPE.
ON YOUR KNEES, SUBGUARDIAN.
ISABEL KANE. HUMAN OF EARTH. IT SEEMS THAT AFTER TODAY, WE ARE LACKING AN ELITE CLASS OF YOUR DESIGNATION ON THE GUARD.
ARE YOU THE SMASHER THE EMPIRE IS LOOKING FOR?

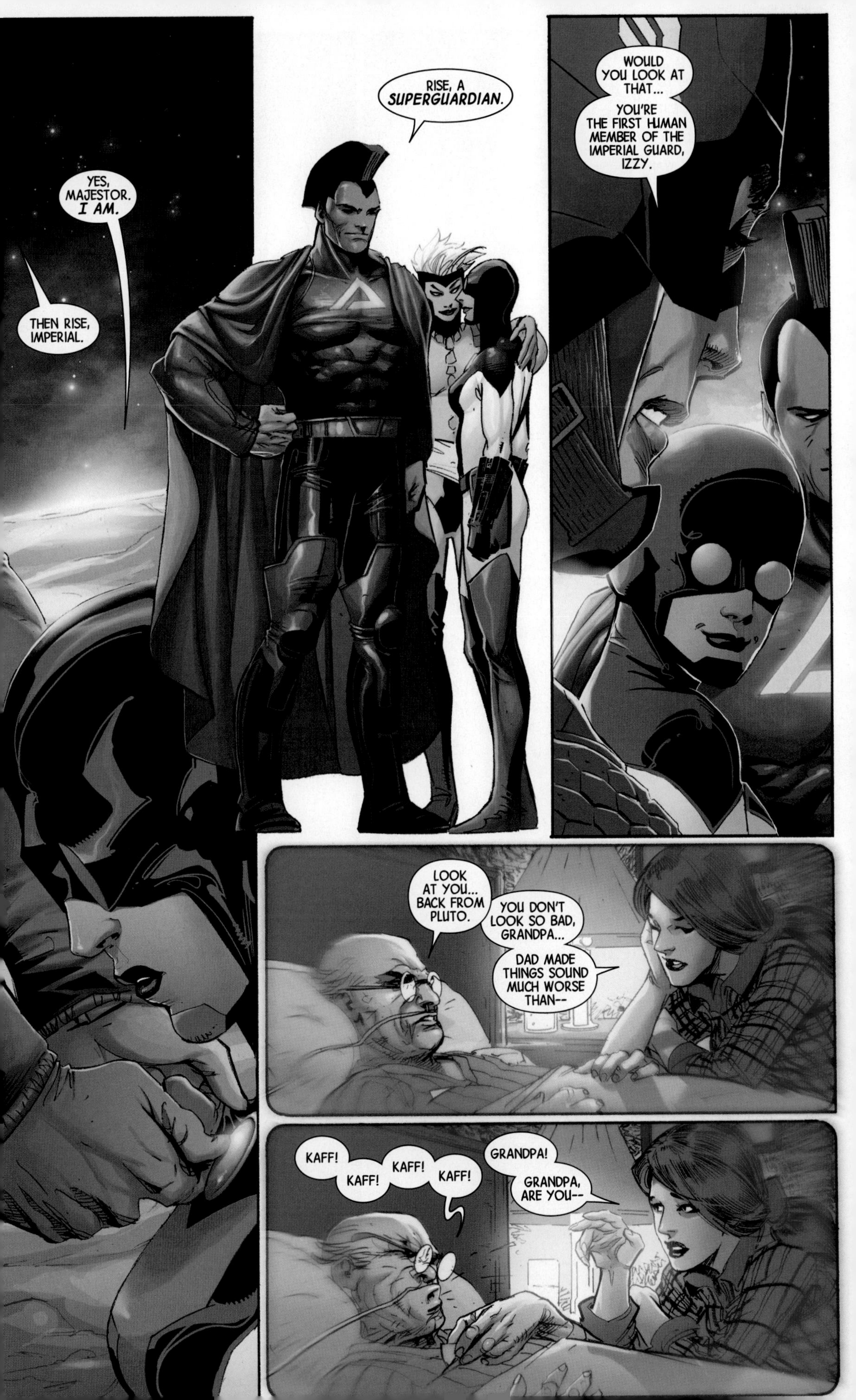
RISE, A *SUPERGUARDIAN*.
YES, MAJESTOR. *I AM*.
THEN RISE, IMPERIAL.
WOULD YOU LOOK AT THAT...
YOU'RE THE FIRST HUMAN MEMBER OF THE IMPERIAL GUARD, IZZY.
LOOK AT YOU... BACK FROM PLUTO.
YOU DON'T LOOK SO BAD, GRANDPA...
DAD MADE THINGS SOUND MUCH WORSE THAN--
KAFF!
KAFF!
KAFF!
KAFF!
GRANDPA!
GRANDPA, ARE YOU--

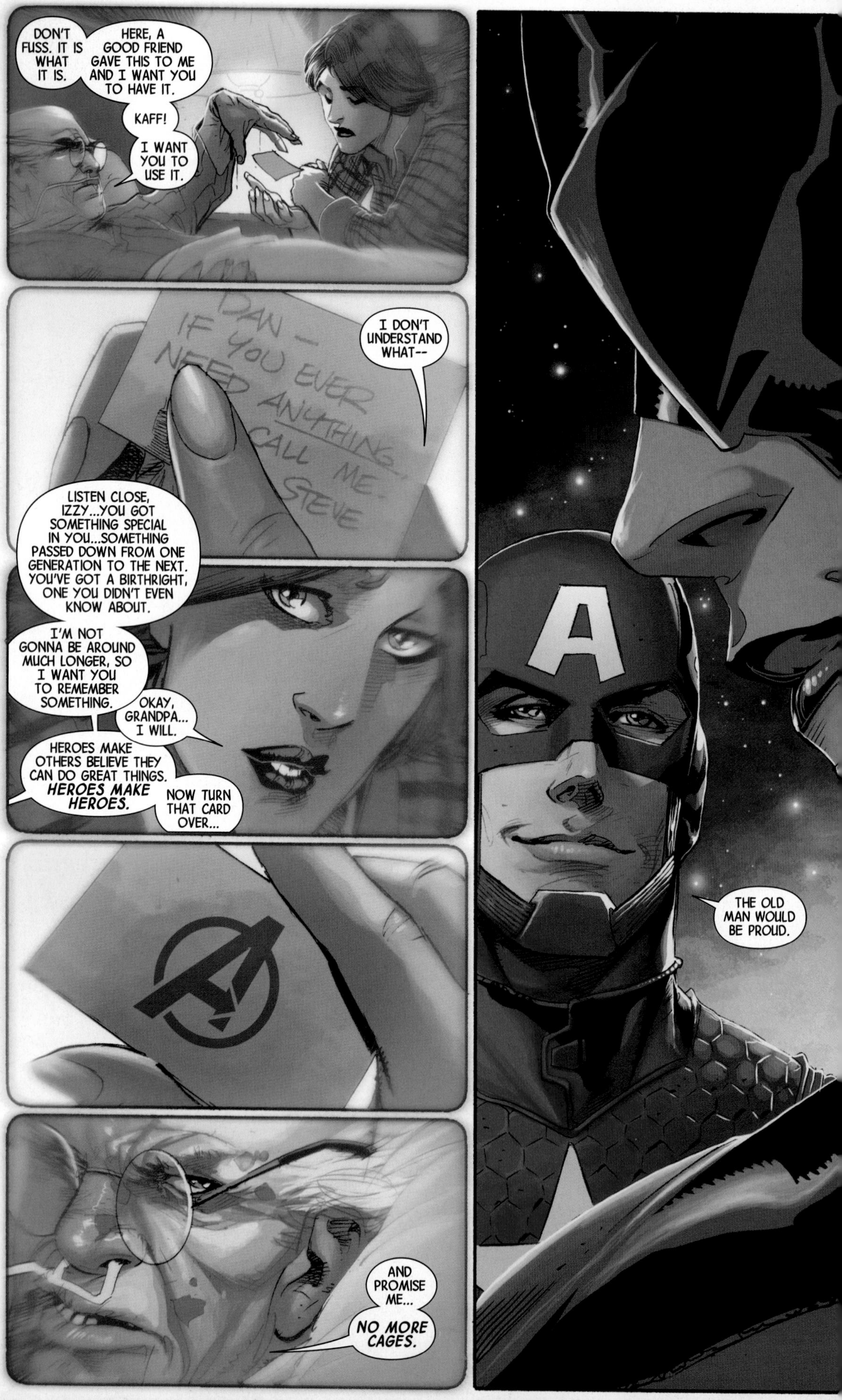

DON'T FUSS. IT IS WHAT IT IS.
HERE, A GOOD FRIEND GAVE THIS TO ME AND I WANT YOU TO HAVE IT.
KAFF!
I WANT YOU TO USE IT.
DAN — IF YOU EVER NEED ANYTHING... CALL ME. STEVE
I DON'T UNDERSTAND WHAT--
LISTEN CLOSE, IZZY...YOU GOT SOMETHING SPECIAL IN YOU...SOMETHING PASSED DOWN FROM ONE GENERATION TO THE NEXT. YOU'VE GOT A BIRTHRIGHT, ONE YOU DIDN'T EVEN KNOW ABOUT.
I'M NOT GONNA BE AROUND MUCH LONGER, SO I WANT YOU TO REMEMBER SOMETHING.
OKAY, GRANDPA... I WILL.
HEROES MAKE OTHERS BELIEVE THEY CAN DO GREAT THINGS. *HEROES MAKE HEROES.*
NOW TURN THAT CARD OVER...
AND PROMISE ME...
NO MORE CAGES.
THE OLD MAN WOULD BE PROUD.

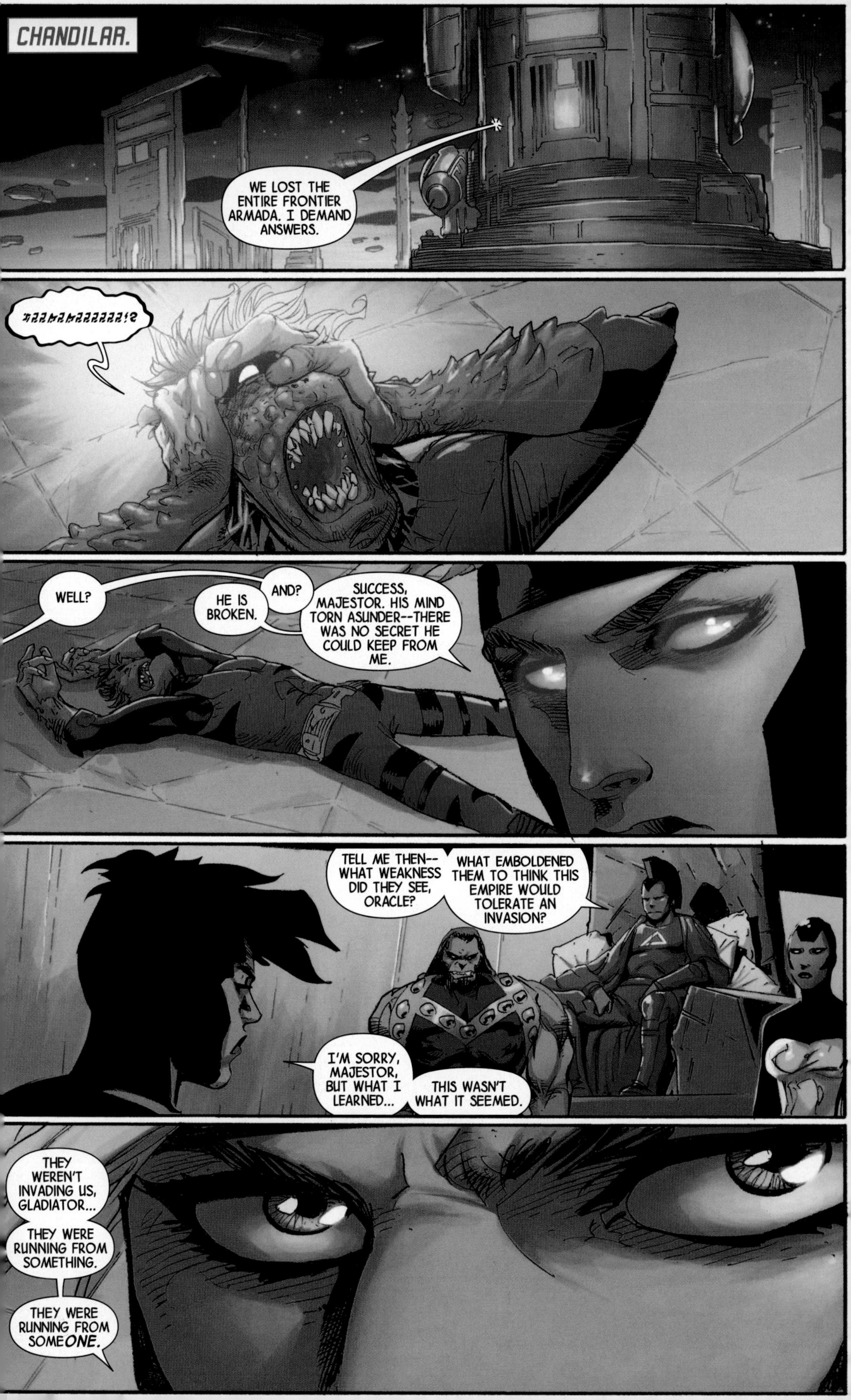
CHANDILAR.
WE LOST THE ENTIRE FRONTIER ARMADA. I DEMAND ANSWERS.
WELL?
HE IS BROKEN.
AND?
SUCCESS, MAJESTOR. HIS MIND TORN ASUNDER--THERE WAS NO SECRET HE COULD KEEP FROM ME.
TELL ME THEN--WHAT WEAKNESS DID THEY SEE, ORACLE?
WHAT EMBOLDENED THEM TO THINK THIS EMPIRE WOULD TOLERATE AN INVASION?
I'M SORRY, MAJESTOR, BUT WHAT I LEARNED...
THIS WASN'T WHAT IT SEEMED.
THEY WEREN'T INVADING US, GLADIATOR...
THEY WERE RUNNING FROM SOMETHING.
THEY WERE RUNNING FROM SOMEONE.

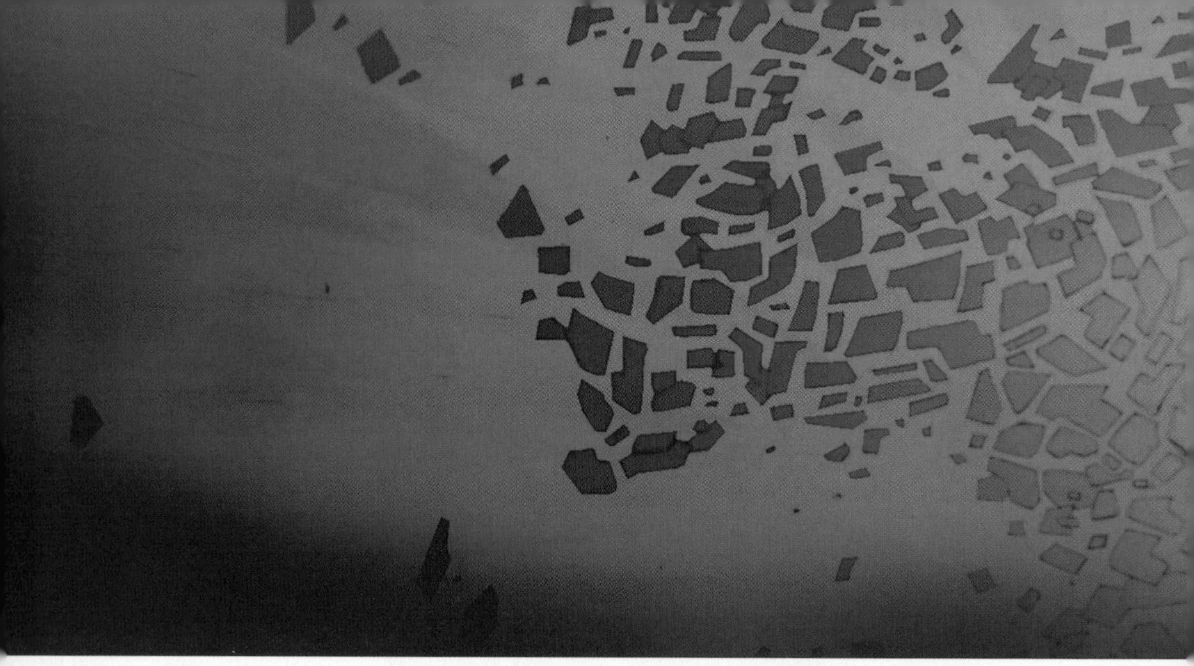

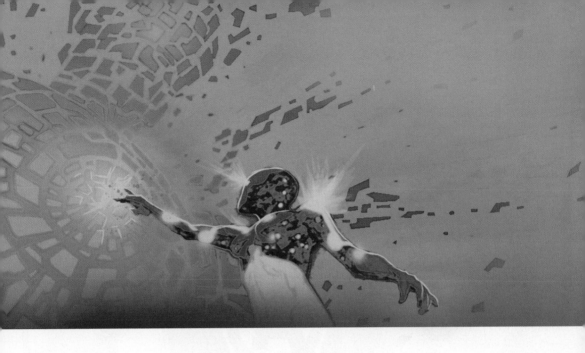

"ZEN AND THE ART OF COSMOLOGY"

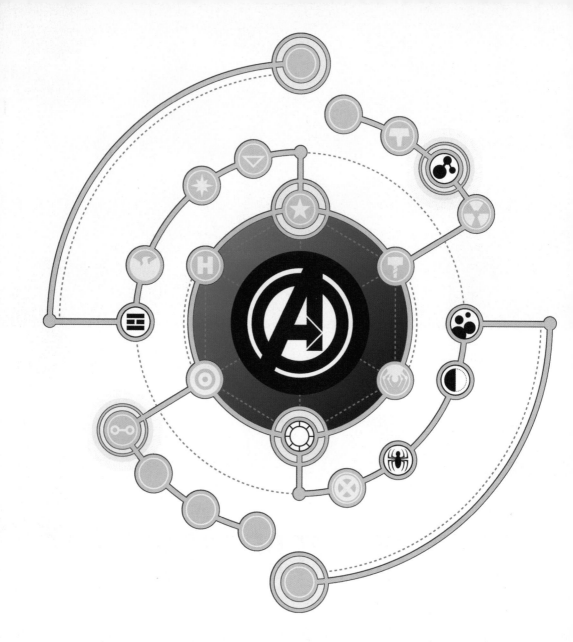

EARTH'S MIGHTIEST HEROES

CAPTAIN AMERICA · **IRON MAN** · THOR · HAWKEYE · BLACK WIDOW · HULK
WOLVERINE · **SPIDER-MAN** · CAPTAIN MARVEL · SPIDER-WOMAN
FALCON · **SHANG-CHI** · SUNSPOT · **CANNONBALL** · MANIFOLD
SMASHER · **CAPTAIN UNIVERSE** · HYPERION

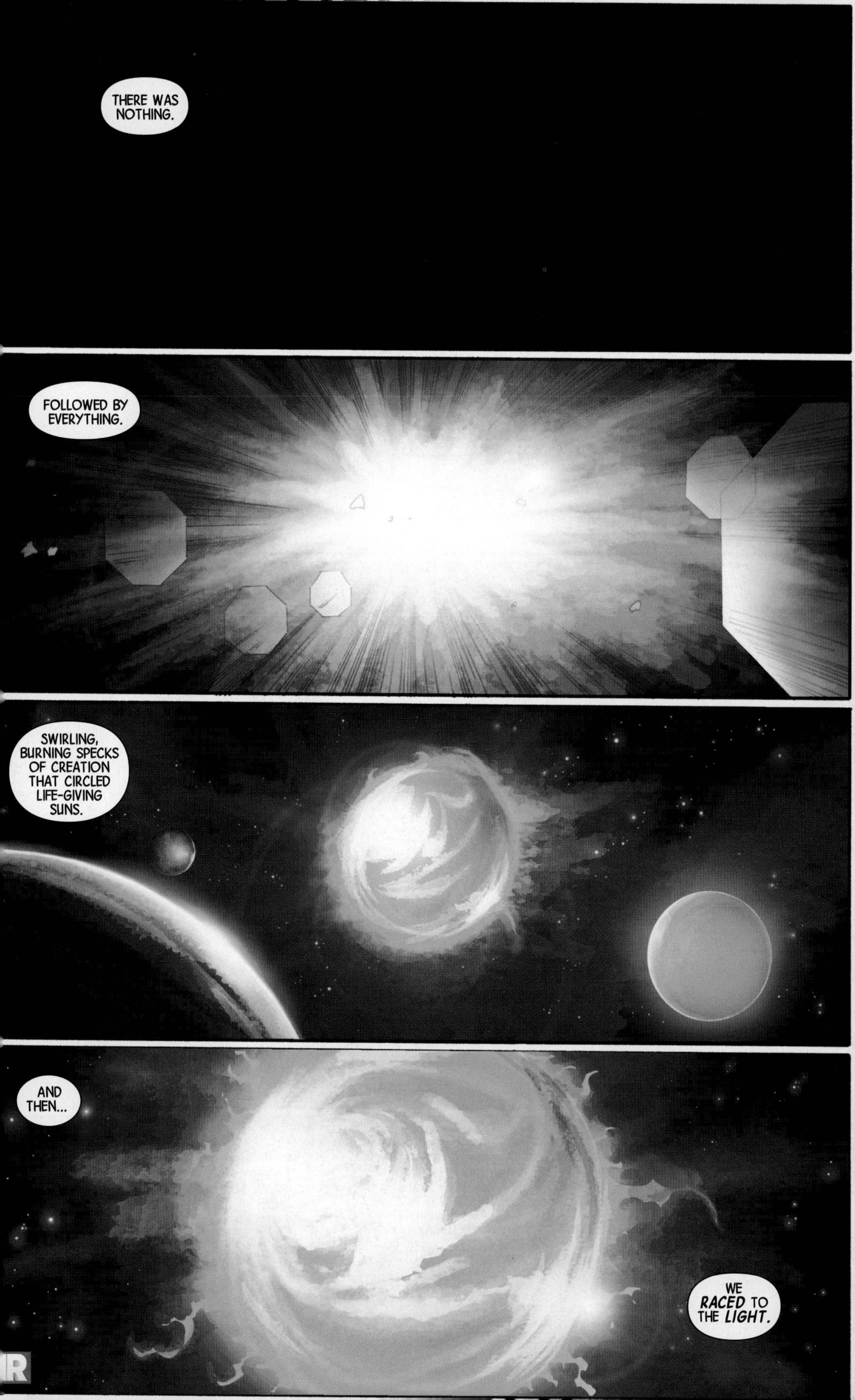
THERE WAS NOTHING.
FOLLOWED BY EVERYTHING.
SWIRLING, BURNING SPECKS OF CREATION THAT CIRCLED LIFE-GIVING SUNS.
AND THEN...
WE *RACED* TO THE *LIGHT*.

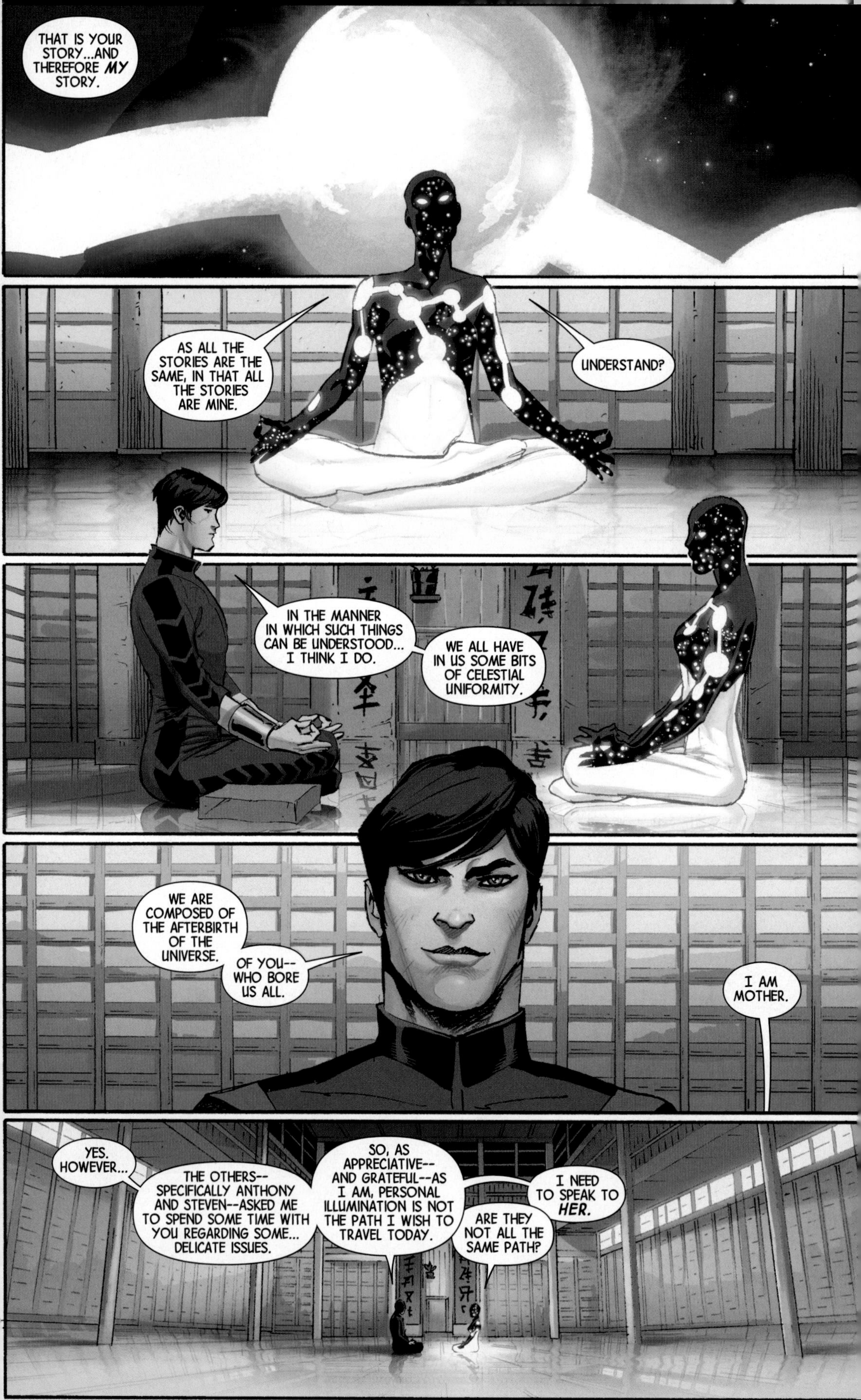
THAT IS YOUR STORY...AND THEREFORE *MY* STORY.
AS ALL THE STORIES ARE THE SAME, IN THAT ALL THE STORIES ARE MINE.
UNDERSTAND?
IN THE MANNER IN WHICH SUCH THINGS CAN BE UNDERSTOOD... I THINK I DO.
WE ALL HAVE IN US SOME BITS OF CELESTIAL UNIFORMITY.
WE ARE COMPOSED OF THE AFTERBIRTH OF THE UNIVERSE.
OF YOU-- WHO BORE US ALL.
I AM MOTHER.
YES. HOWEVER...
THE OTHERS-- SPECIFICALLY ANTHONY AND STEVEN--ASKED ME TO SPEND SOME TIME WITH YOU REGARDING SOME... DELICATE ISSUES.
SO, AS APPRECIATIVE-- AND GRATEFUL--AS I AM, PERSONAL ILLUMINATION IS NOT THE PATH I WISH TO TRAVEL TODAY.
I NEED TO SPEAK TO ***HER.***
ARE THEY NOT ALL THE SAME PATH?

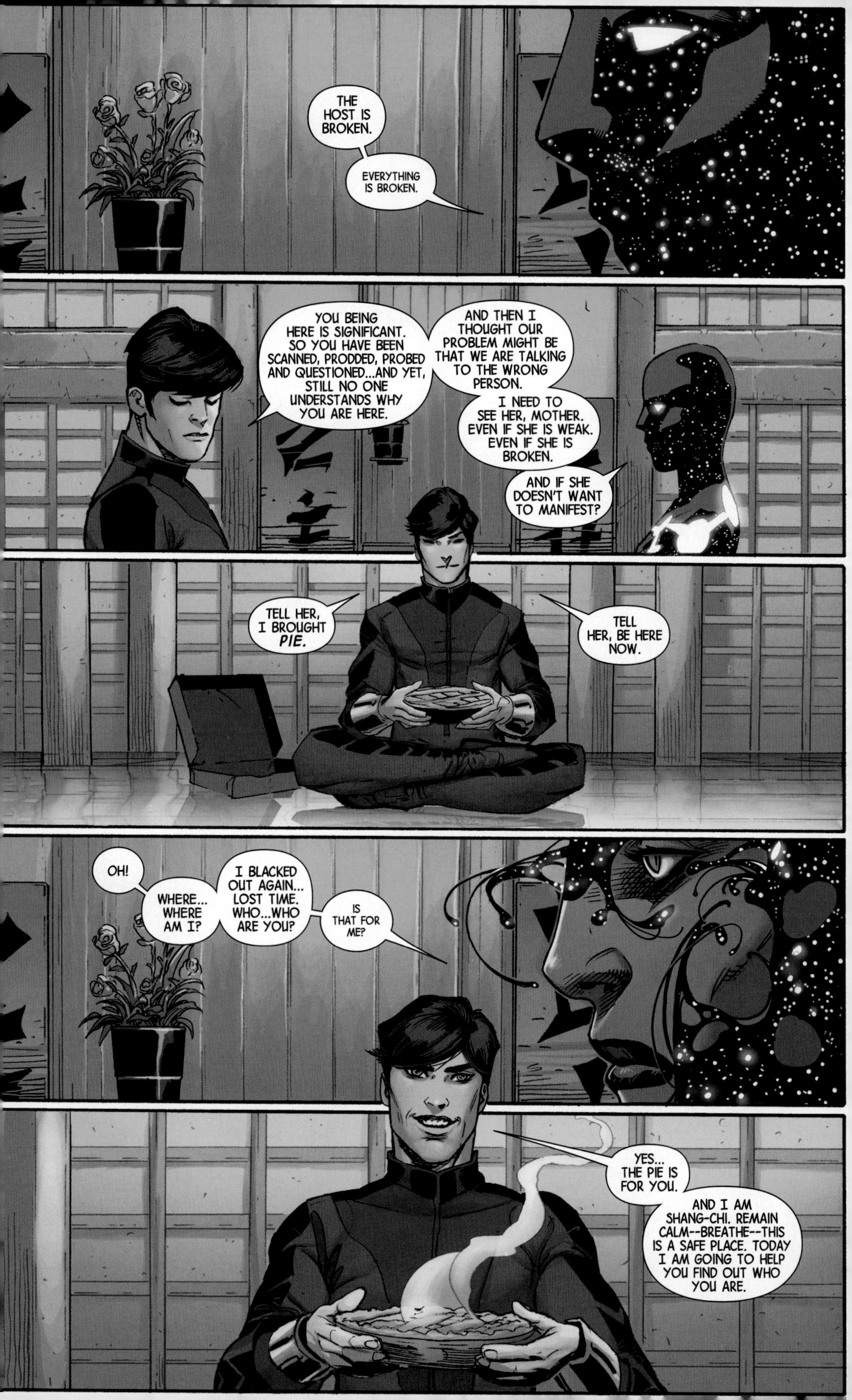
THE HOST IS BROKEN.
EVERYTHING IS BROKEN.
YOU BEING HERE IS SIGNIFICANT. SO YOU HAVE BEEN SCANNED, PRODDED, PROBED AND QUESTIONED...AND YET, STILL NO ONE UNDERSTANDS WHY YOU ARE HERE.
AND THEN I THOUGHT OUR PROBLEM MIGHT BE THAT WE ARE TALKING TO THE WRONG PERSON.
I NEED TO SEE HER, MOTHER. EVEN IF SHE IS WEAK. EVEN IF SHE IS BROKEN.
AND IF SHE DOESN'T WANT TO MANIFEST?
TELL HER, I BROUGHT PIE.
TELL HER, BE HERE NOW.
OH!
WHERE... WHERE AM I?
I BLACKED OUT AGAIN... LOST TIME. WHO...WHO ARE YOU?
IS THAT FOR ME?
YES... THE PIE IS FOR YOU.
AND I AM SHANG-CHI. REMAIN CALM--BREATHE--THIS IS A SAFE PLACE. TODAY I AM GOING TO HELP YOU FIND OUT WHO YOU ARE.

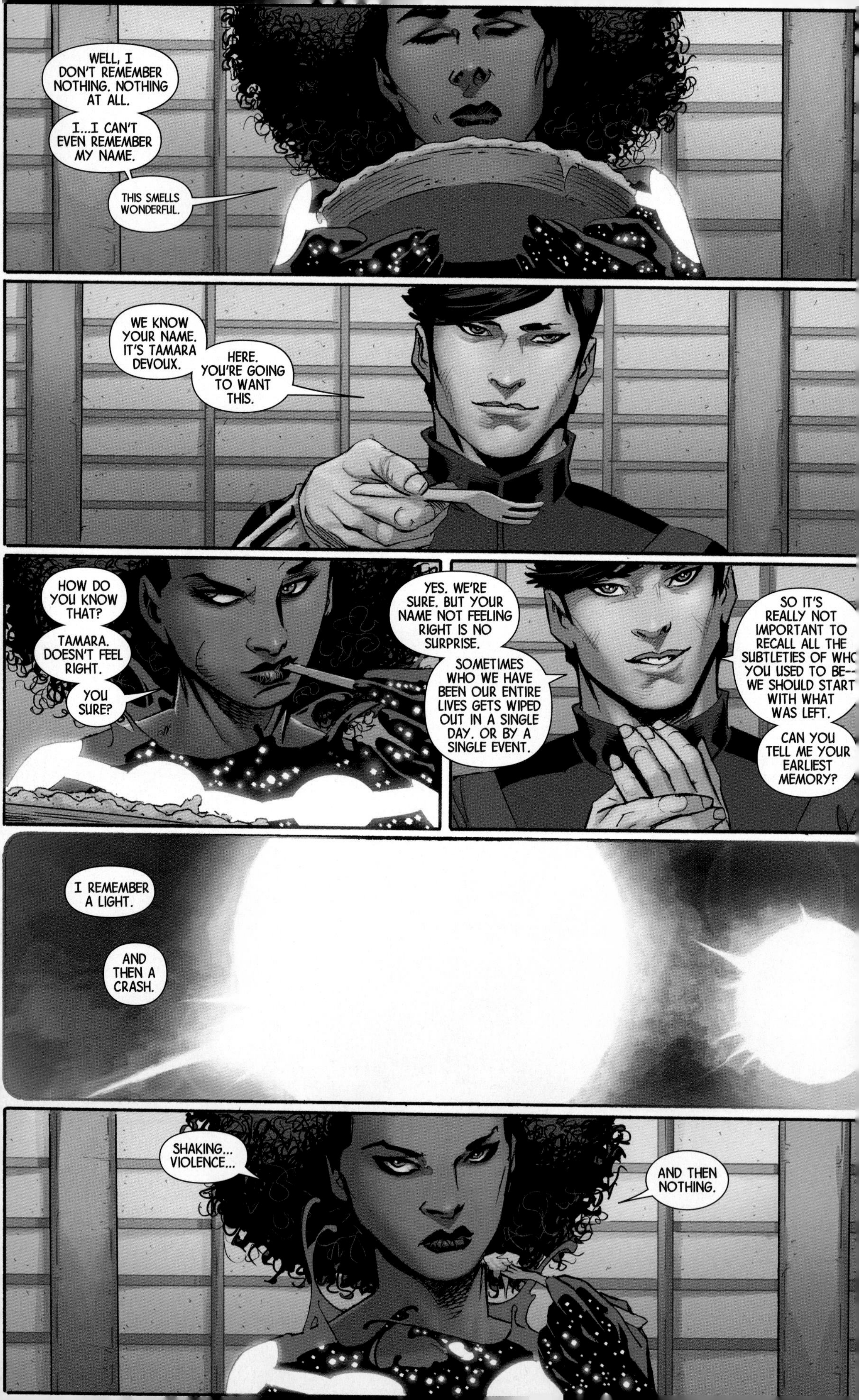
WELL, I DON'T REMEMBER NOTHING. NOTHING AT ALL.
I...I CAN'T EVEN REMEMBER MY NAME.
THIS SMELLS WONDERFUL.
WE KNOW YOUR NAME. IT'S TAMARA DEVOUX.
HERE. YOU'RE GOING TO WANT THIS.
HOW DO YOU KNOW THAT?
TAMARA. DOESN'T FEEL RIGHT.
YOU SURE?
YES. WE'RE SURE. BUT YOUR NAME NOT FEELING RIGHT IS NO SURPRISE.
SOMETIMES WHO WE HAVE BEEN OUR ENTIRE LIVES GETS WIPED OUT IN A SINGLE DAY. OR BY A SINGLE EVENT.
SO IT'S REALLY NOT IMPORTANT TO RECALL ALL THE SUBTLETIES OF WHO YOU USED TO BE--WE SHOULD START WITH WHAT WAS LEFT.
CAN YOU TELL ME YOUR EARLIEST MEMORY?
I REMEMBER A LIGHT.
AND THEN A CRASH.
SHAKING... VIOLENCE...
AND THEN NOTHING.

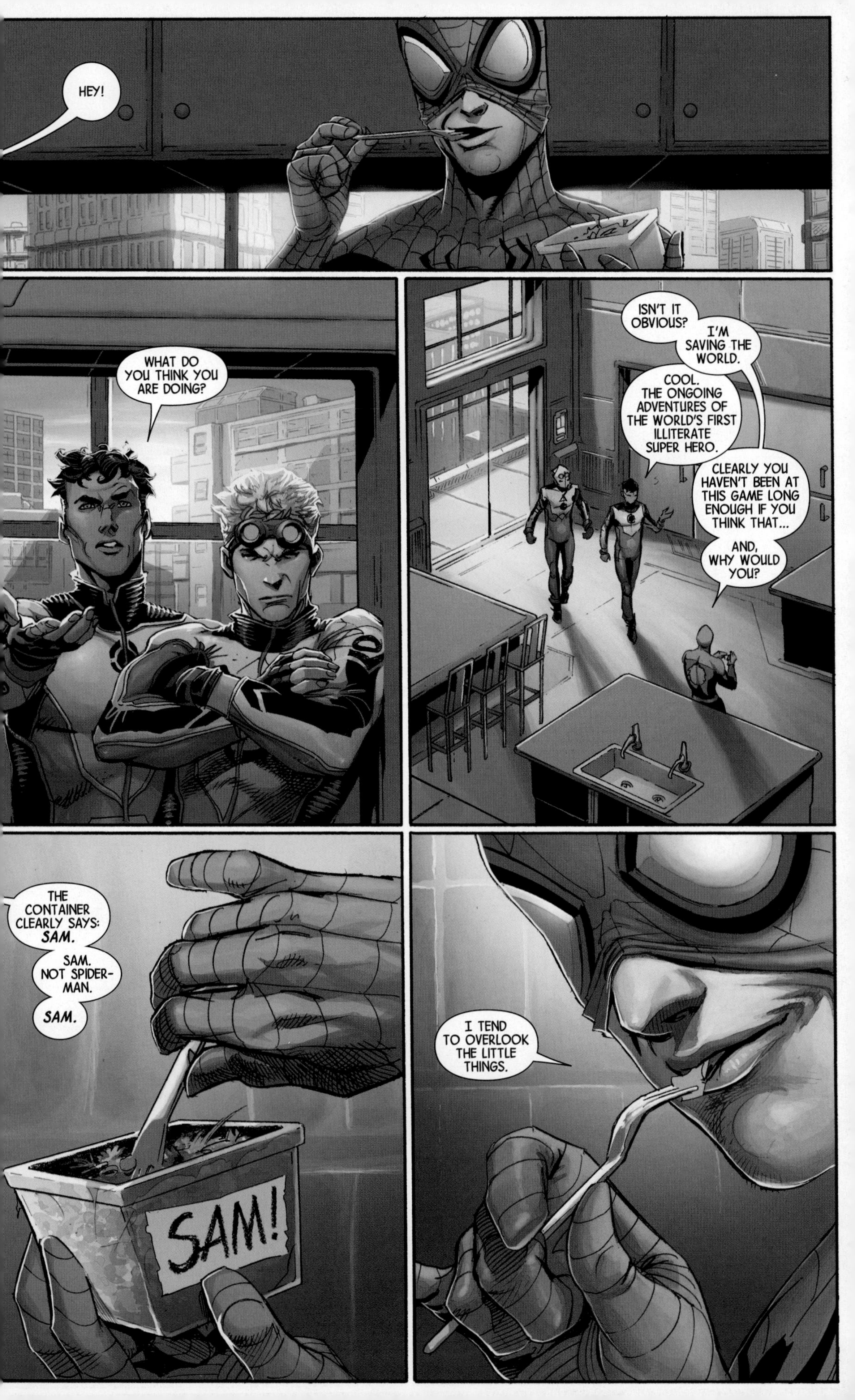
HEY!
WHAT DO YOU THINK YOU ARE DOING?
ISN'T IT OBVIOUS?
I'M SAVING THE WORLD.
COOL. THE ONGOING ADVENTURES OF THE WORLD'S FIRST ILLITERATE SUPER HERO.
CLEARLY YOU HAVEN'T BEEN AT THIS GAME LONG ENOUGH IF YOU THINK THAT...
AND, WHY WOULD YOU?
THE CONTAINER CLEARLY SAYS: SAM.
SAM. NOT SPIDER-MAN.
SAM.
SAM!
I TEND TO OVERLOOK THE LITTLE THINGS.

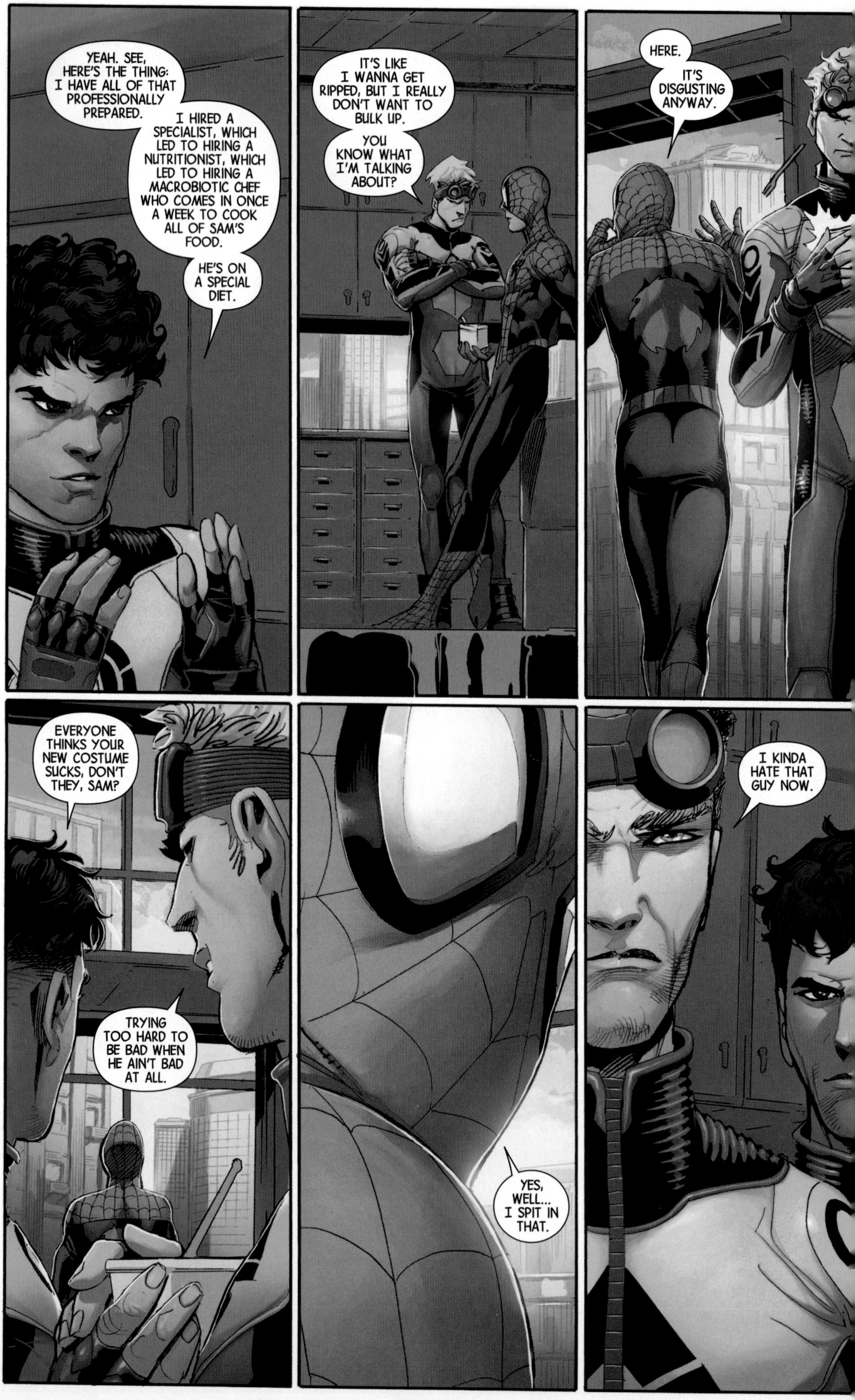
YEAH. SEE, HERE'S THE THING: I HAVE ALL OF THAT PROFESSIONALLY PREPARED.
I HIRED A SPECIALIST, WHICH LED TO HIRING A NUTRITIONIST, WHICH LED TO HIRING A MACROBIOTIC CHEF WHO COMES IN ONCE A WEEK TO COOK ALL OF SAM'S FOOD.
HE'S ON A SPECIAL DIET.
IT'S LIKE I WANNA GET RIPPED, BUT I REALLY DON'T WANT TO BULK UP.
YOU KNOW WHAT I'M TALKING ABOUT?
HERE.
IT'S DISGUSTING ANYWAY.
EVERYONE THINKS YOUR NEW COSTUME SUCKS, DON'T THEY, SAM?
TRYING TOO HARD TO BE BAD WHEN HE AIN'T BAD AT ALL.
YES, WELL... I SPIT IN THAT.
I KINDA HATE THAT GUY NOW.

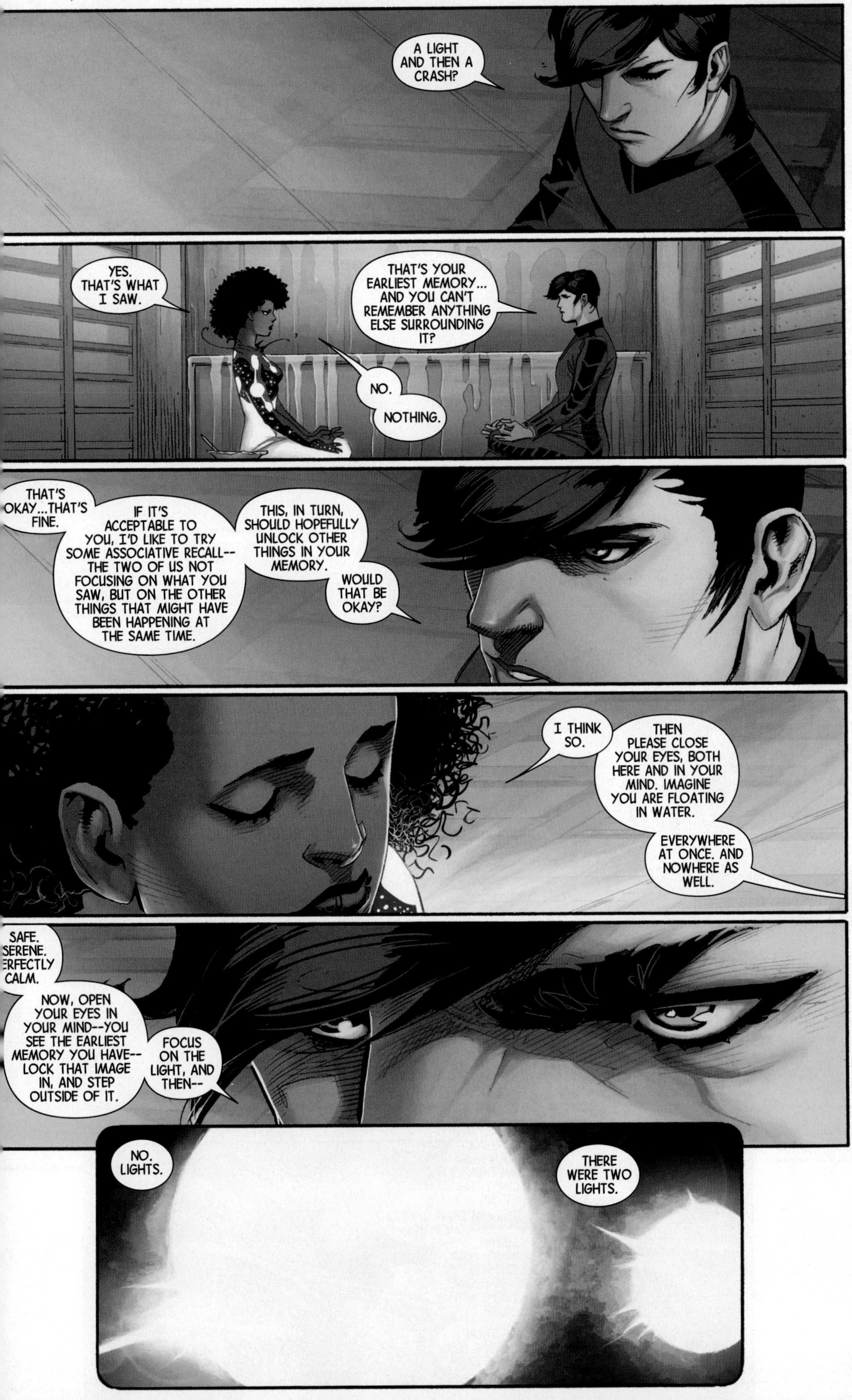
A LIGHT AND THEN A CRASH?
YES. THAT'S WHAT I SAW.
THAT'S YOUR EARLIEST MEMORY... AND YOU CAN'T REMEMBER ANYTHING ELSE SURROUNDING IT?
NO.
NOTHING.
THAT'S OKAY...THAT'S FINE.
IF IT'S ACCEPTABLE TO YOU, I'D LIKE TO TRY SOME ASSOCIATIVE RECALL-- THE TWO OF US NOT FOCUSING ON WHAT YOU SAW, BUT ON THE OTHER THINGS THAT MIGHT HAVE BEEN HAPPENING AT THE SAME TIME.
THIS, IN TURN, SHOULD HOPEFULLY UNLOCK OTHER THINGS IN YOUR MEMORY.
WOULD THAT BE OKAY?
I THINK SO.
THEN PLEASE CLOSE YOUR EYES, BOTH HERE AND IN YOUR MIND. IMAGINE YOU ARE FLOATING IN WATER.
EVERYWHERE AT ONCE. AND NOWHERE AS WELL.
SAFE. SERENE. ERFECTLY CALM.
NOW, OPEN YOUR EYES IN YOUR MIND--YOU SEE THE EARLIEST MEMORY YOU HAVE-- LOCK THAT IMAGE IN, AND STEP OUTSIDE OF IT.
FOCUS ON THE LIGHT, AND THEN--
NO. LIGHTS.
THERE WERE TWO LIGHTS.

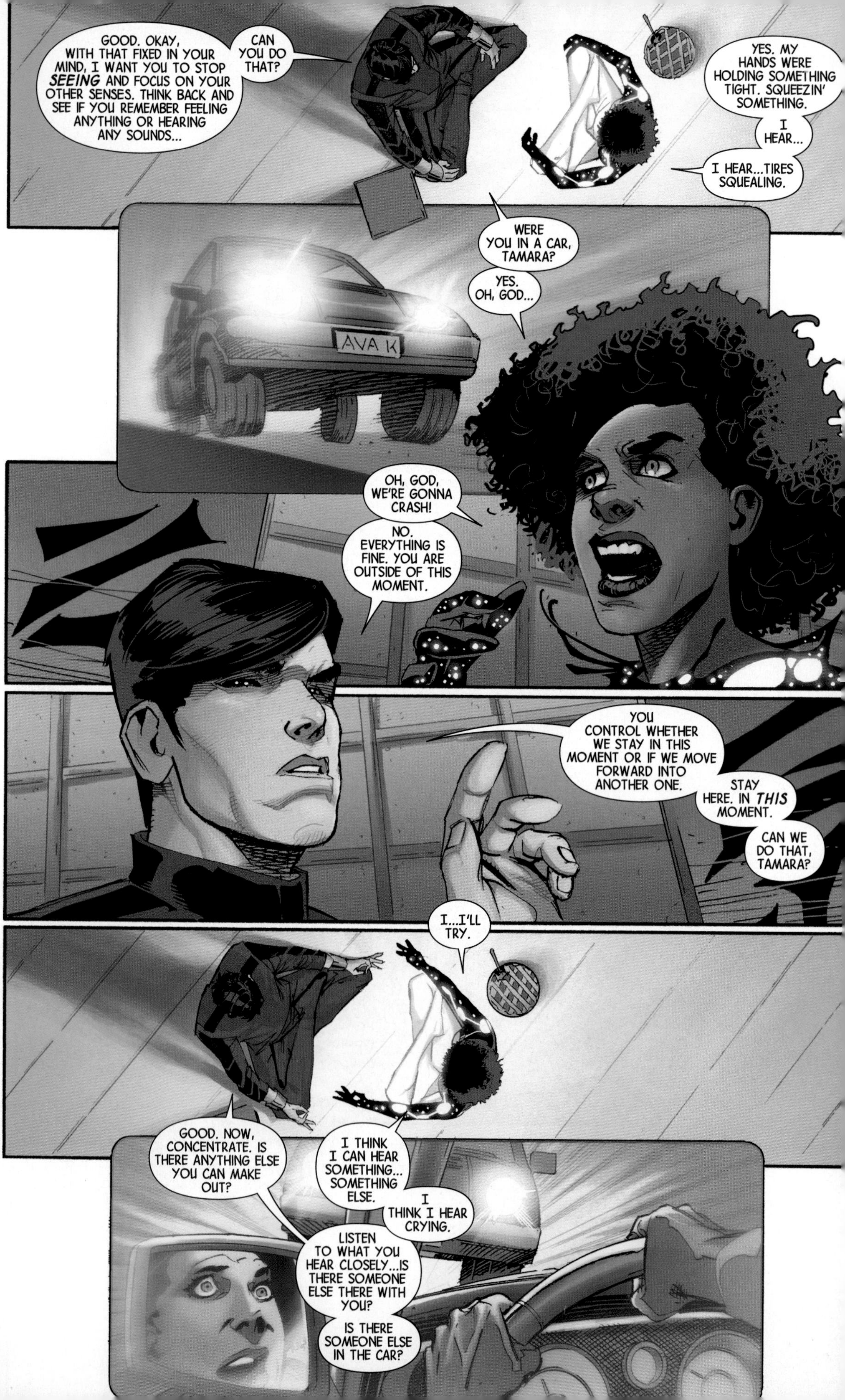
GOOD. OKAY, WITH THAT FIXED IN YOUR MIND, I WANT YOU TO STOP SEEING AND FOCUS ON YOUR OTHER SENSES. THINK BACK AND SEE IF YOU REMEMBER FEELING ANYTHING OR HEARING ANY SOUNDS...
CAN YOU DO THAT?
YES. MY HANDS WERE HOLDING SOMETHING TIGHT. SQUEEZIN' SOMETHING.
I HEAR...
I HEAR...TIRES SQUEALING.
WERE YOU IN A CAR, TAMARA?
YES. OH, GOD...
AVA K
OH, GOD, WE'RE GONNA CRASH!
NO. EVERYTHING IS FINE. YOU ARE OUTSIDE OF THIS MOMENT.
YOU CONTROL WHETHER WE STAY IN THIS MOMENT OR IF WE MOVE FORWARD INTO ANOTHER ONE.
STAY HERE. IN THIS MOMENT.
CAN WE DO THAT, TAMARA?
I...I'LL TRY.
GOOD. NOW, CONCENTRATE. IS THERE ANYTHING ELSE YOU CAN MAKE OUT?
I THINK I CAN HEAR SOMETHING... SOMETHING ELSE.
I THINK I HEAR CRYING.
LISTEN TO WHAT YOU HEAR CLOSELY...IS THERE SOMEONE ELSE THERE WITH YOU?
IS THERE SOMEONE ELSE IN THE CAR?

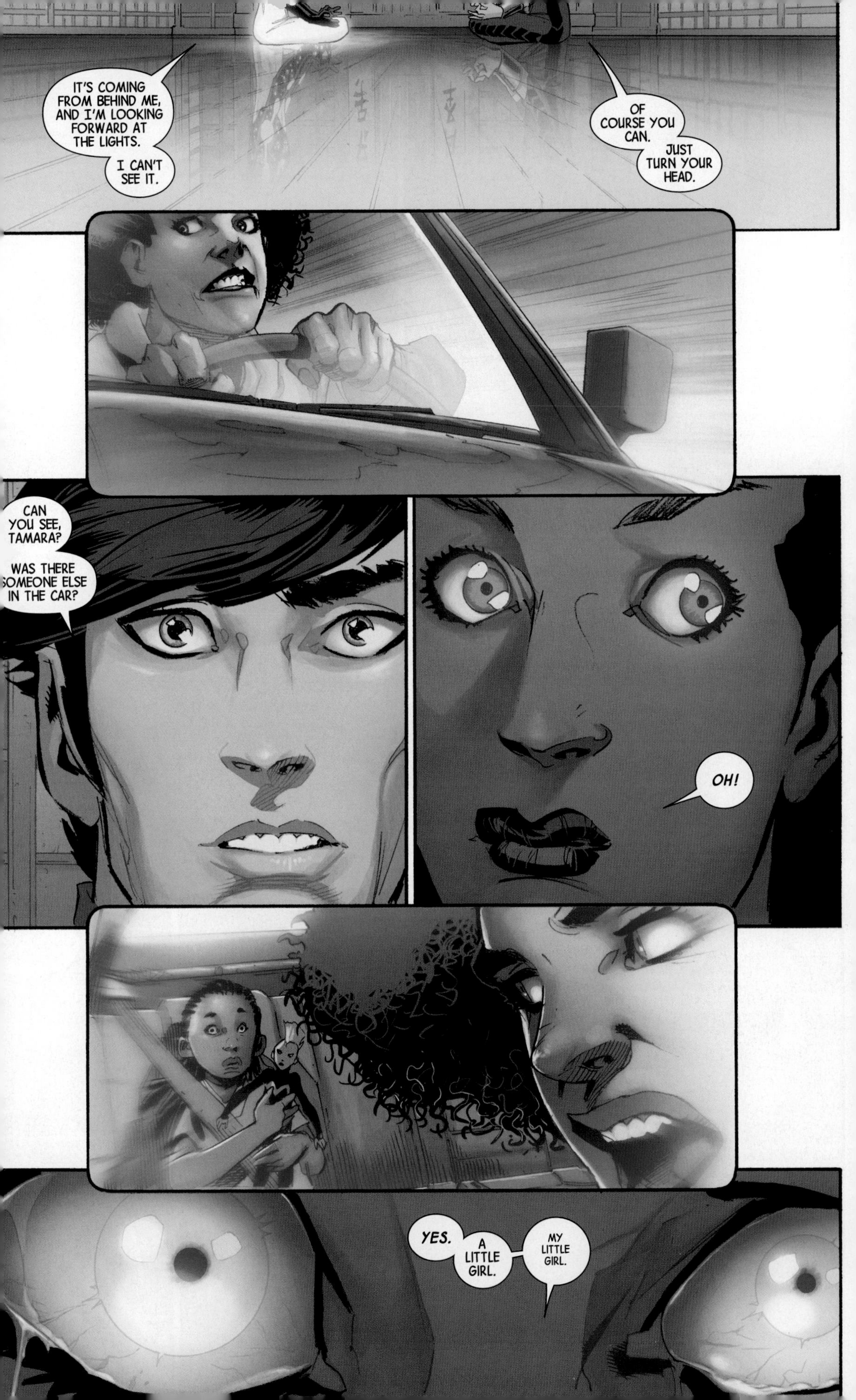
IT'S COMING FROM BEHIND ME, AND I'M LOOKING FORWARD AT THE LIGHTS.
I CAN'T SEE IT.
OF COURSE YOU CAN.
JUST TURN YOUR HEAD.
CAN YOU SEE, TAMARA?
WAS THERE SOMEONE ELSE IN THE CAR?
OH!
YES.
A LITTLE GIRL.
MY LITTLE GIRL.

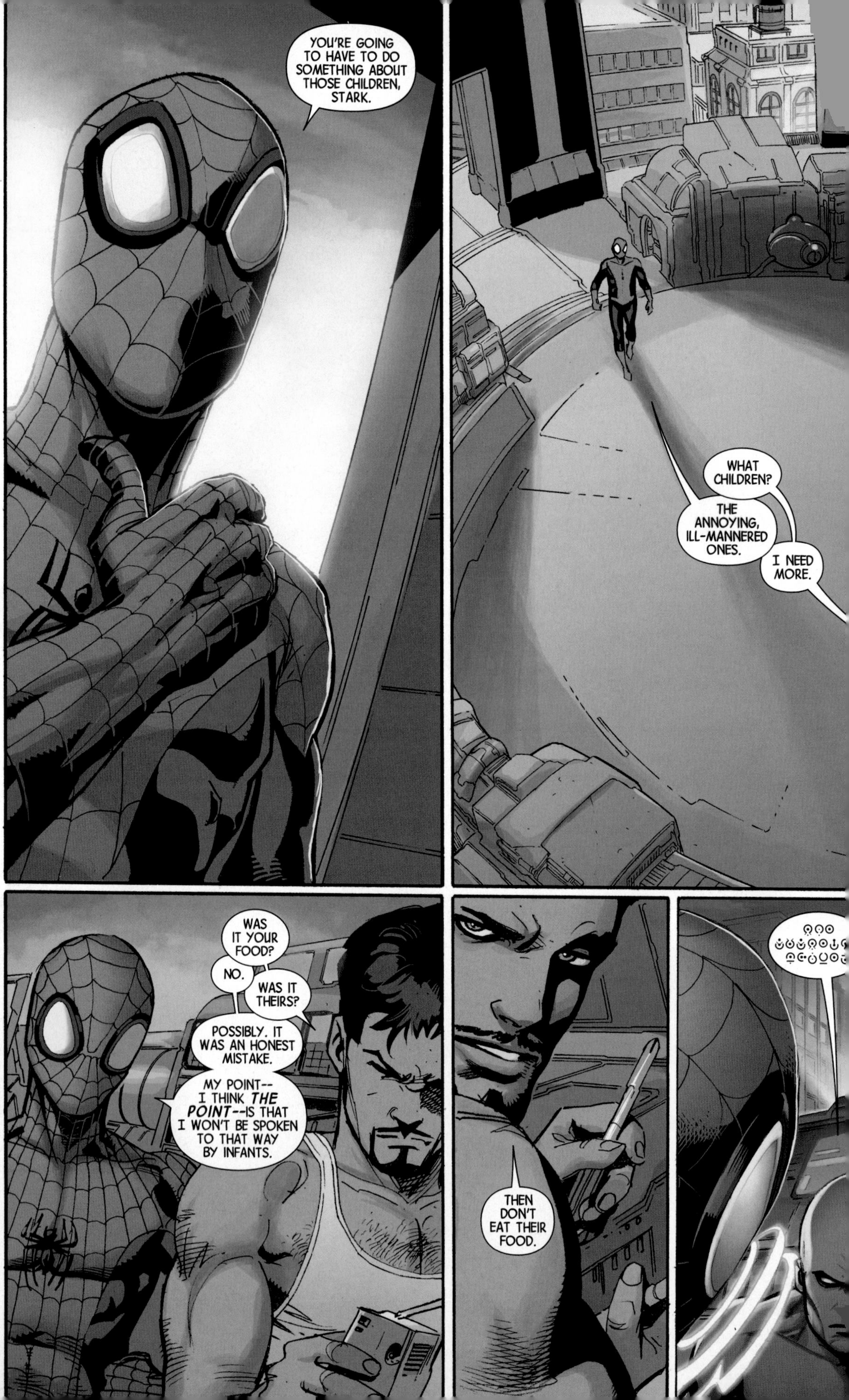
YOU'RE GOING TO HAVE TO DO SOMETHING ABOUT THOSE CHILDREN, STARK.
WHAT CHILDREN?
THE ANNOYING, ILL-MANNERED ONES.
I NEED MORE.
WAS IT YOUR FOOD?
NO.
WAS IT THEIRS?
POSSIBLY. IT WAS AN HONEST MISTAKE.
MY POINT-- I THINK THE POINT--IS THAT I WON'T BE SPOKEN TO THAT WAY BY INFANTS.
THEN DON'T EAT THEIR FOOD.

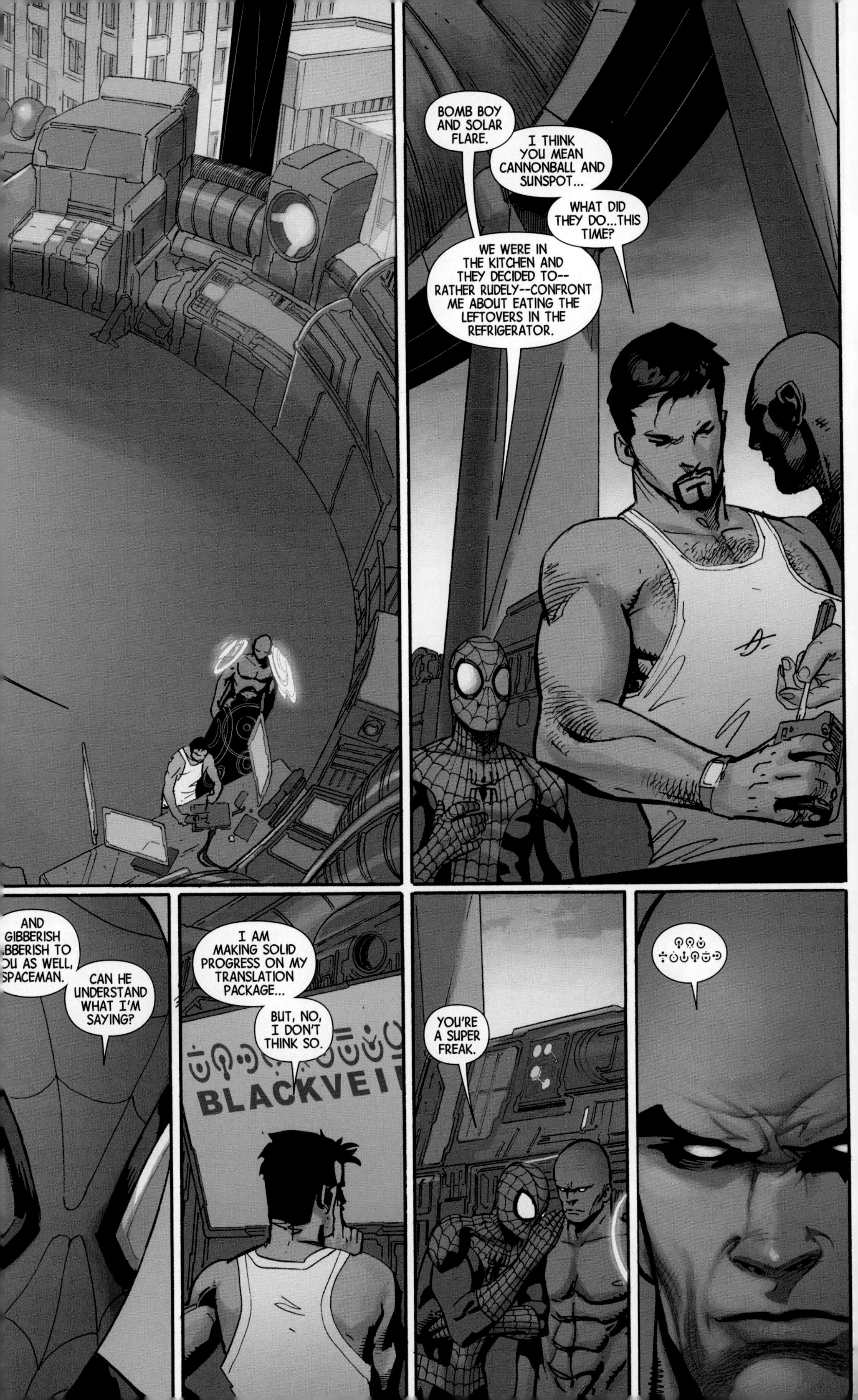
BOMB BOY AND SOLAR FLARE.
I THINK YOU MEAN CANNONBALL AND SUNSPOT...
WHAT DID THEY DO...THIS TIME?
WE WERE IN THE KITCHEN AND THEY DECIDED TO-- RATHER RUDELY--CONFRONT ME ABOUT EATING THE LEFTOVERS IN THE REFRIGERATOR.
AND GIBBERISH IBBERISH TO OU AS WELL, SPACEMAN.
CAN HE UNDERSTAND WHAT I'M SAYING?
I AM MAKING SOLID PROGRESS ON MY TRANSLATION PACKAGE...
BUT, NO, I DON'T THINK SO.
BLACKVEI
YOU'RE A SUPER FREAK.

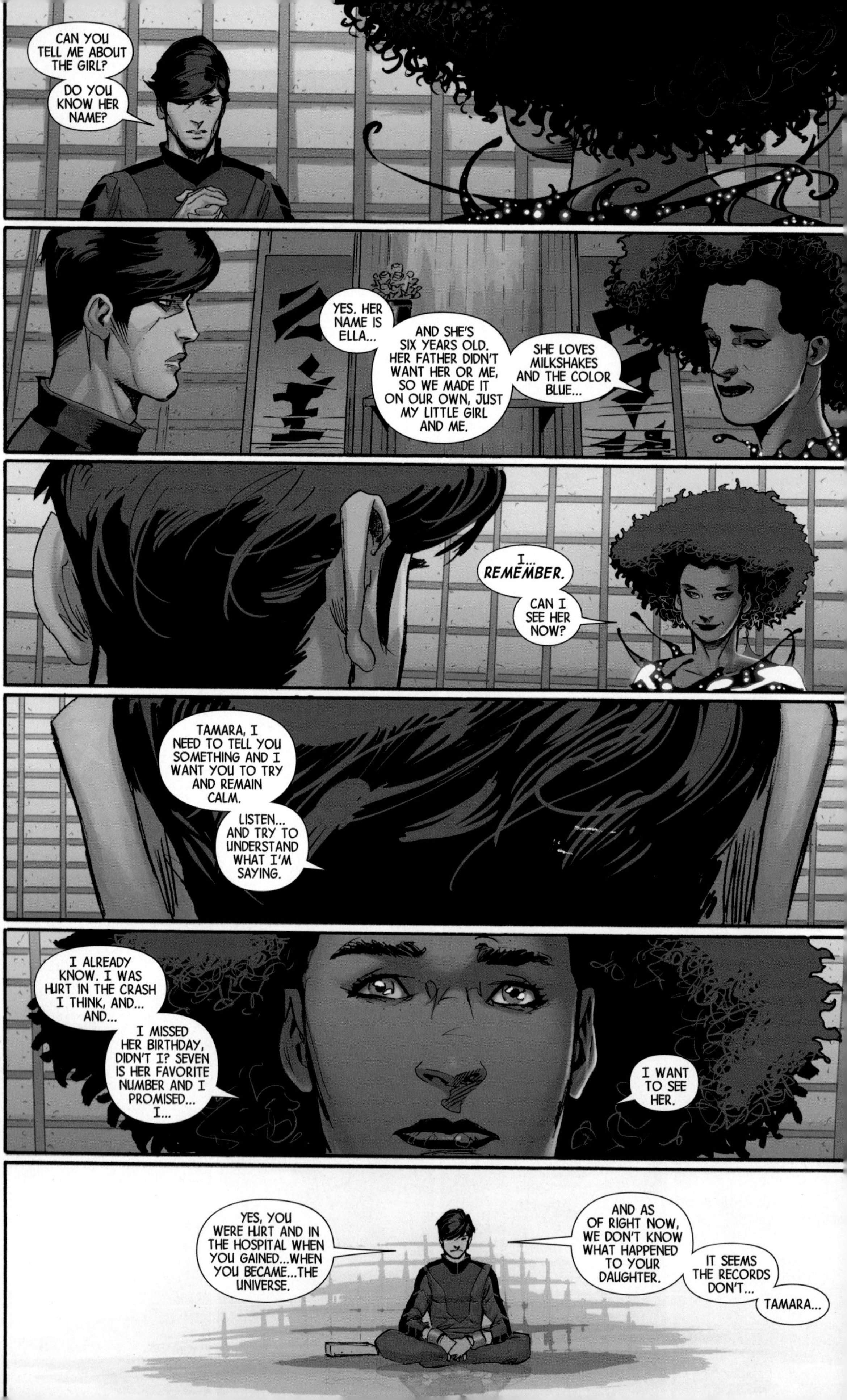
CAN YOU TELL ME ABOUT THE GIRL?
DO YOU KNOW HER NAME?
YES. HER NAME IS ELLA...
AND SHE'S SIX YEARS OLD. HER FATHER DIDN'T WANT HER OR ME, SO WE MADE IT ON OUR OWN, JUST MY LITTLE GIRL AND ME.
SHE LOVES MILKSHAKES AND THE COLOR BLUE...
I... *REMEMBER.*
CAN I SEE HER NOW?
TAMARA, I NEED TO TELL YOU SOMETHING AND I WANT YOU TO TRY AND REMAIN CALM.
LISTEN... AND TRY TO UNDERSTAND WHAT I'M SAYING.
I ALREADY KNOW. I WAS HURT IN THE CRASH I THINK, AND... AND...
I MISSED HER BIRTHDAY, DIDN'T I? SEVEN IS HER FAVORITE NUMBER AND I PROMISED... I...
I WANT TO SEE HER.
YES, YOU WERE HURT AND IN THE HOSPITAL WHEN YOU GAINED...WHEN YOU BECAME...THE UNIVERSE.
AND AS OF RIGHT NOW, WE DON'T KNOW WHAT HAPPENED TO YOUR DAUGHTER.
IT SEEMS THE RECORDS DON'T...
TAMARA...

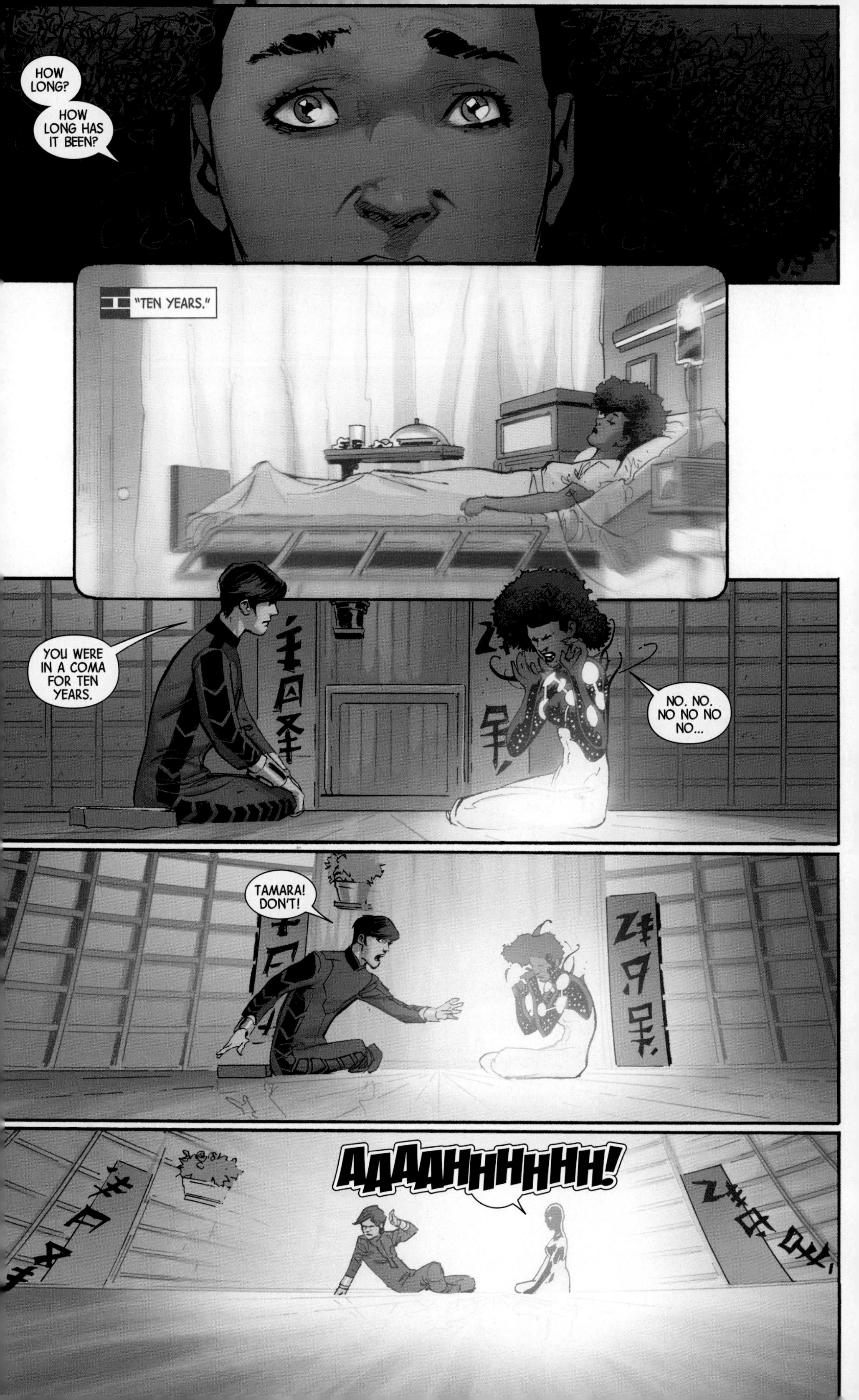
HOW LONG?
HOW LONG HAS IT BEEN?
"TEN YEARS."
YOU WERE IN A COMA FOR TEN YEARS.
NO. NO. NO NO NO NO...
TAMARA! DON'T!
AAAAHHHHHH!

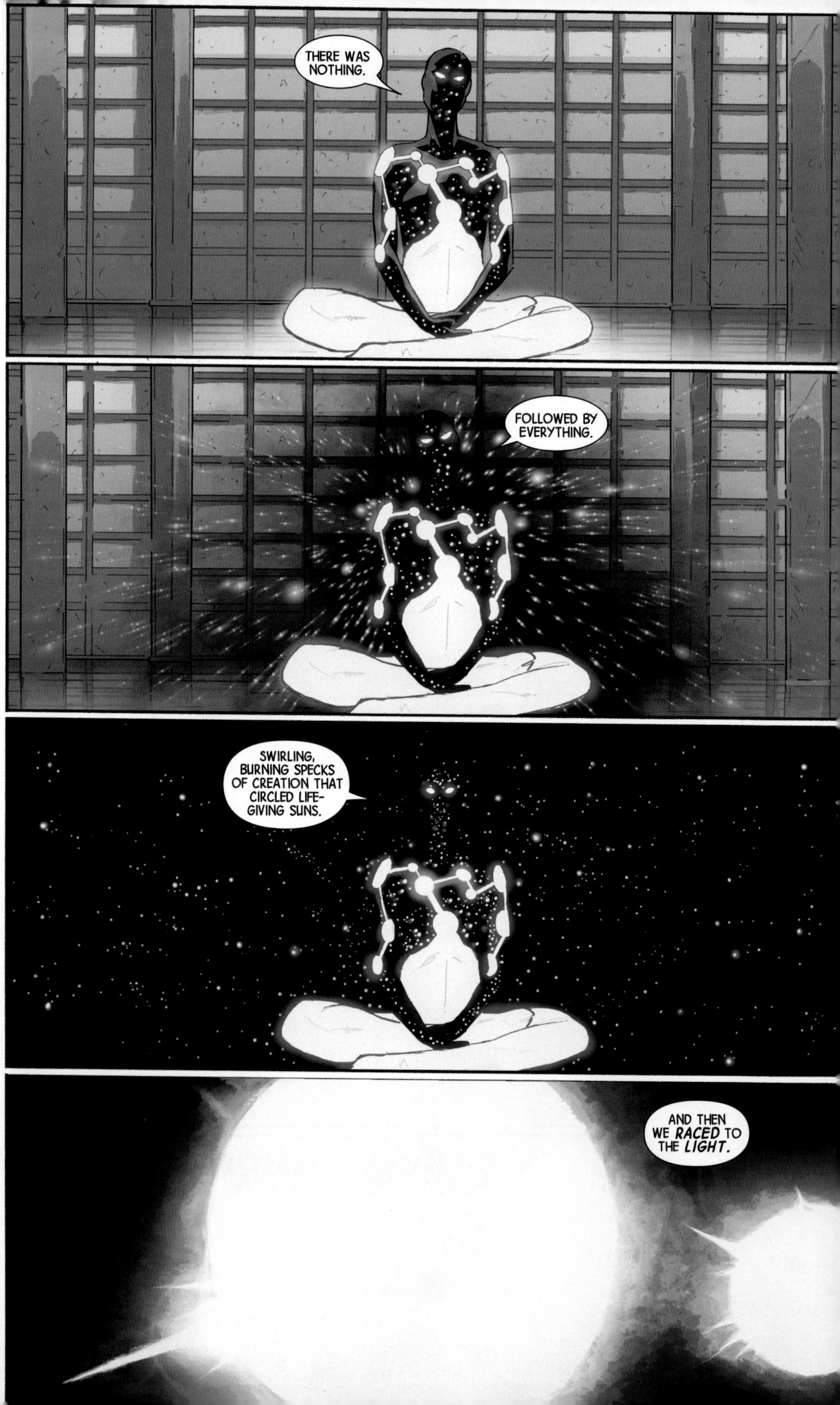
THERE WAS NOTHING.
FOLLOWED BY EVERYTHING.
SWIRLING, BURNING SPECKS OF CREATION THAT CIRCLED LIFE-GIVING SUNS.
AND THEN WE *RACED* TO THE *LIGHT.*

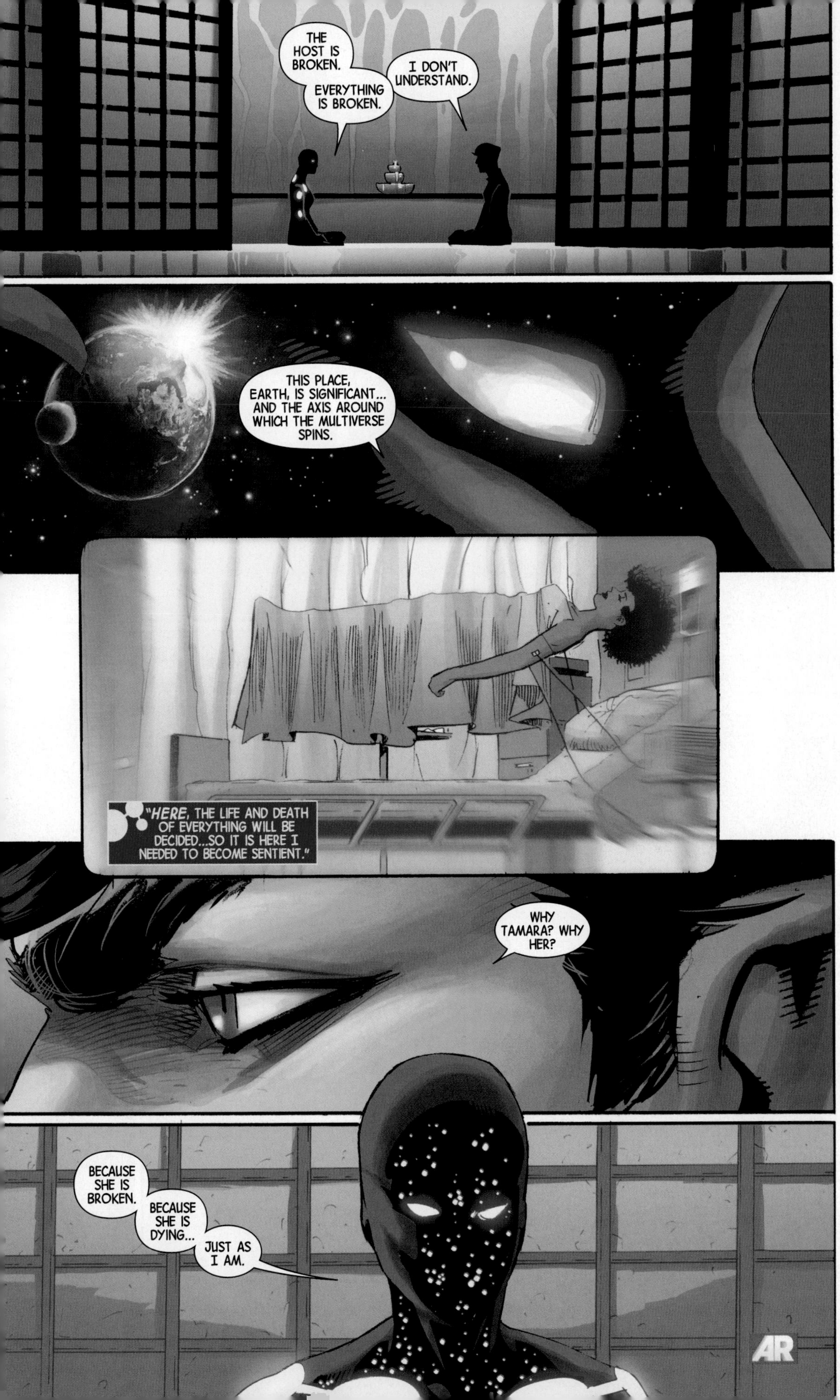
THE HOST IS BROKEN.
EVERYTHING IS BROKEN.
I DON'T UNDERSTAND.
THIS PLACE, EARTH, IS SIGNIFICANT... AND THE AXIS AROUND WHICH THE MULTIVERSE SPINS.
"HERE, THE LIFE AND DEATH OF EVERYTHING WILL BE DECIDED...SO IT IS HERE I NEEDED TO BECOME SENTIENT."
WHY TAMARA? WHY HER?
BECAUSE SHE IS BROKEN.
BECAUSE SHE IS DYING...
JUST AS I AM.
AR

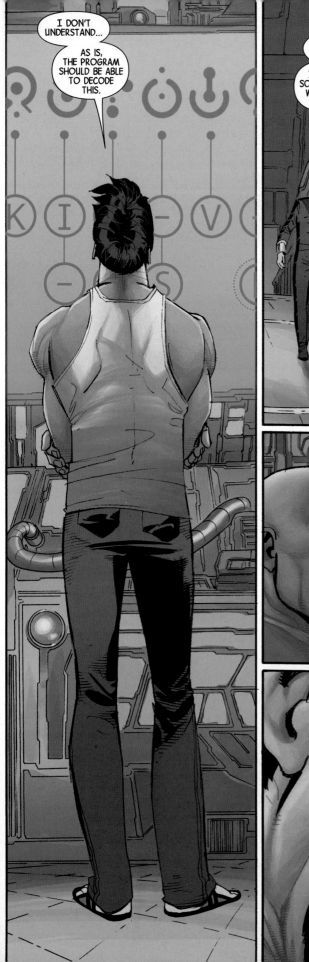

I DON'T UNDERSTAND...

AS IS, THE PROGRAM SHOULD BE ABLE TO DECODE THIS.

ANTHONY!

I HAVE SOMETHING WE NEED TO--

JUST A SECOND...

I'M RIGHT ON THE VERGE OF FIGURING OUT--

◌◌✦✦◌ ◌◌◌◌◌

◌◌◌◌◌◌◌◌

HEY! YOU CAN UNDERSTAND HIM. DO IT AGAIN.

WHAT DO YOU MEAN?

REPEAT WHAT YOU JUST SAID. S IT AGAIN.

◌◌◌◌◌◌◌◌

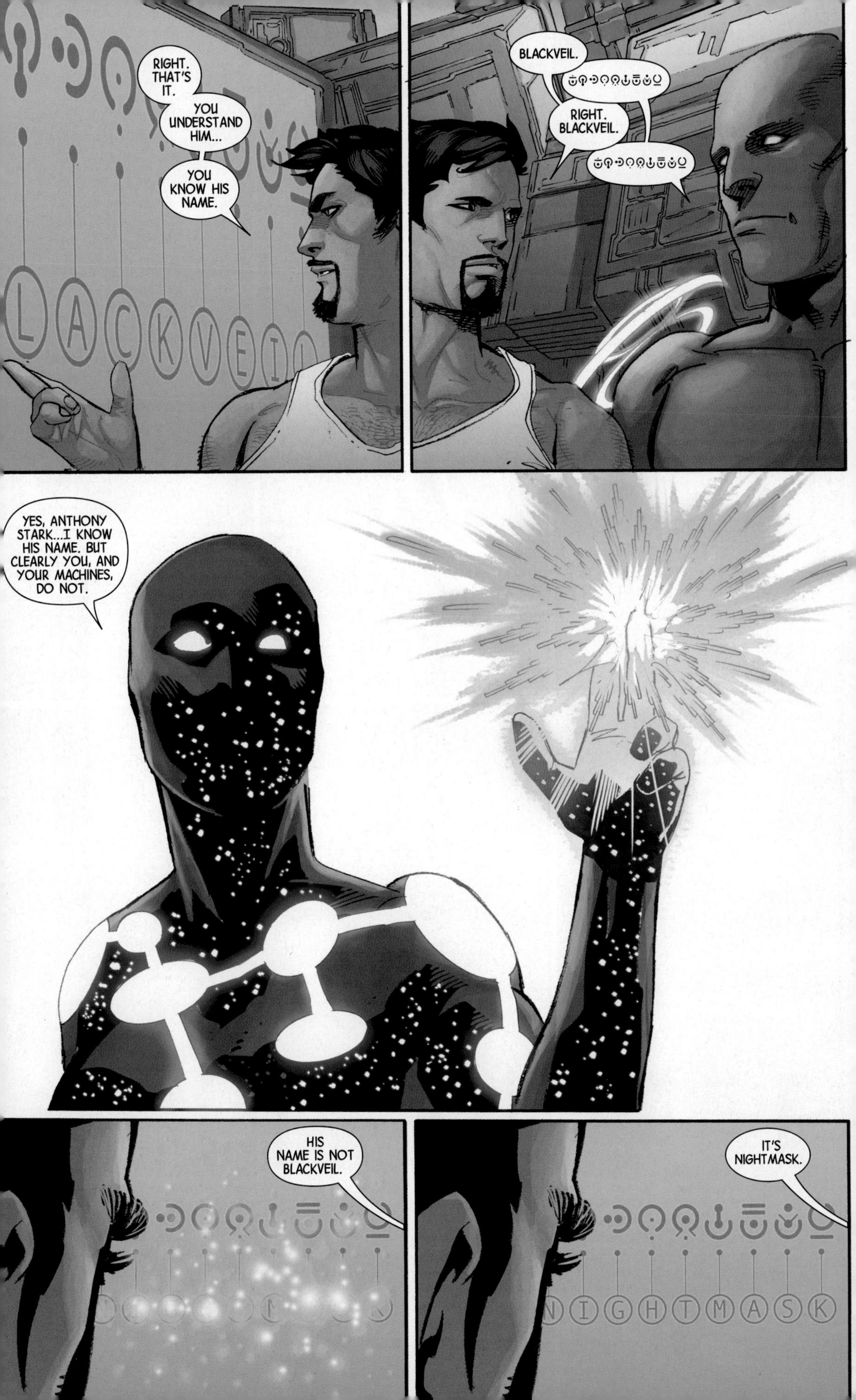
RIGHT. THAT'S IT.
YOU UNDERSTAND HIM...
YOU KNOW HIS NAME.
BLACKVEIL.
RIGHT. BLACKVEIL.
YES, ANTHONY STARK...I KNOW HIS NAME. BUT CLEARLY YOU, AND YOUR MACHINES, DO NOT.
HIS NAME IS NOT BLACKVEIL.
IT'S NIGHTMASK.
NIGHTMASK

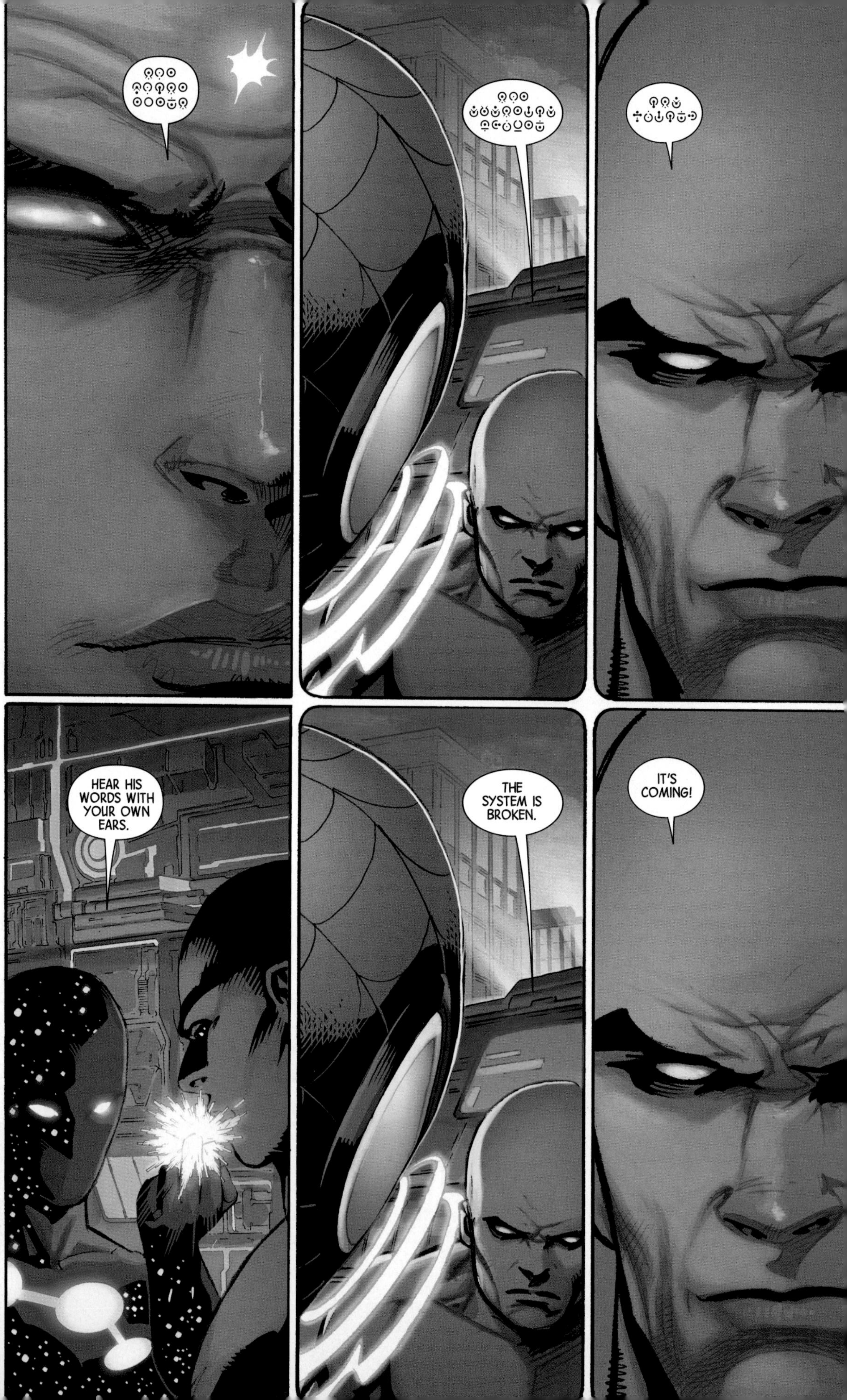
HEAR HIS WORDS WITH YOUR OWN EARS.
THE SYSTEM IS BROKEN.
IT'S COMING!

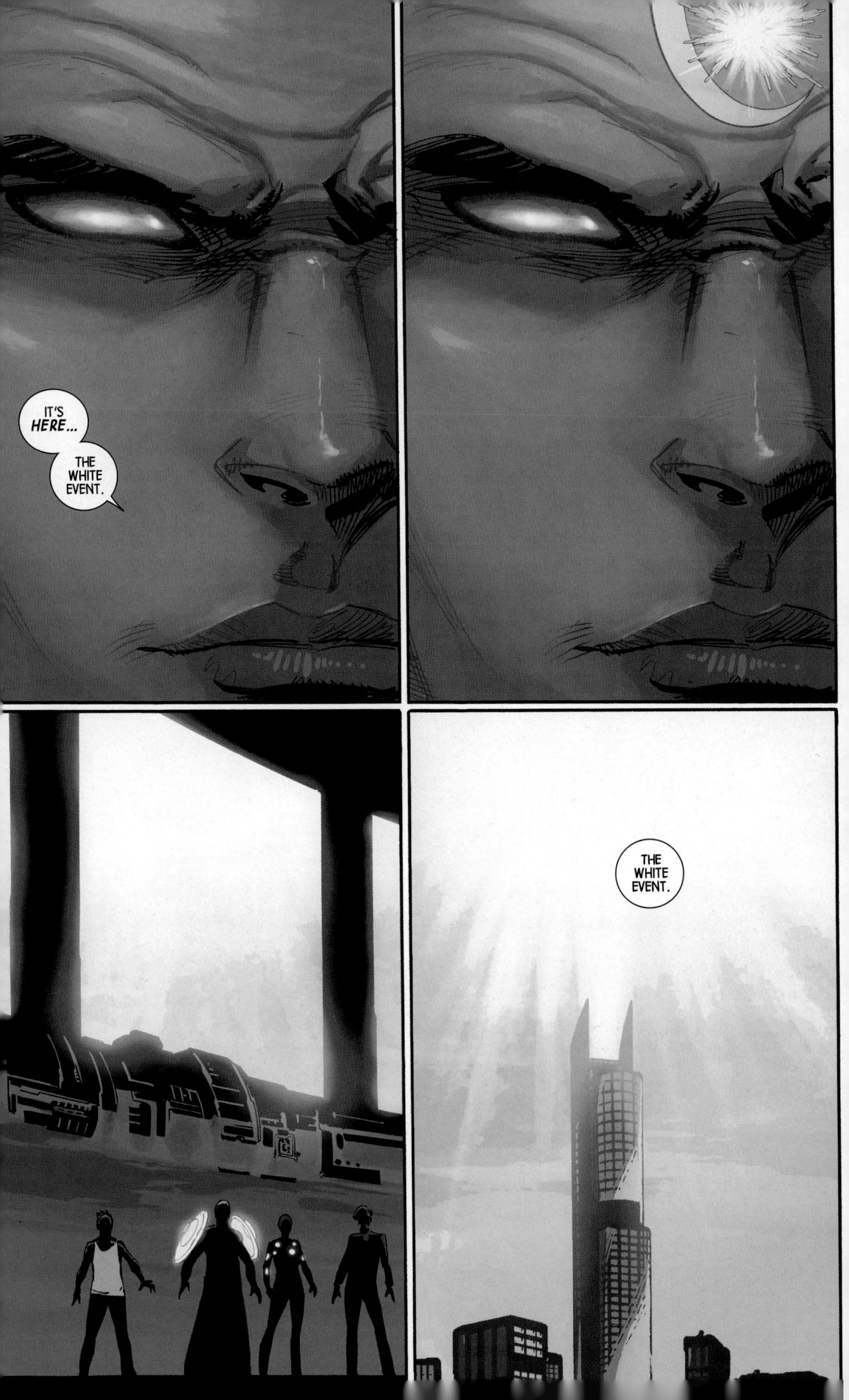
IT'S *HERE*...
THE WHITE EVENT.
THE WHITE EVENT.

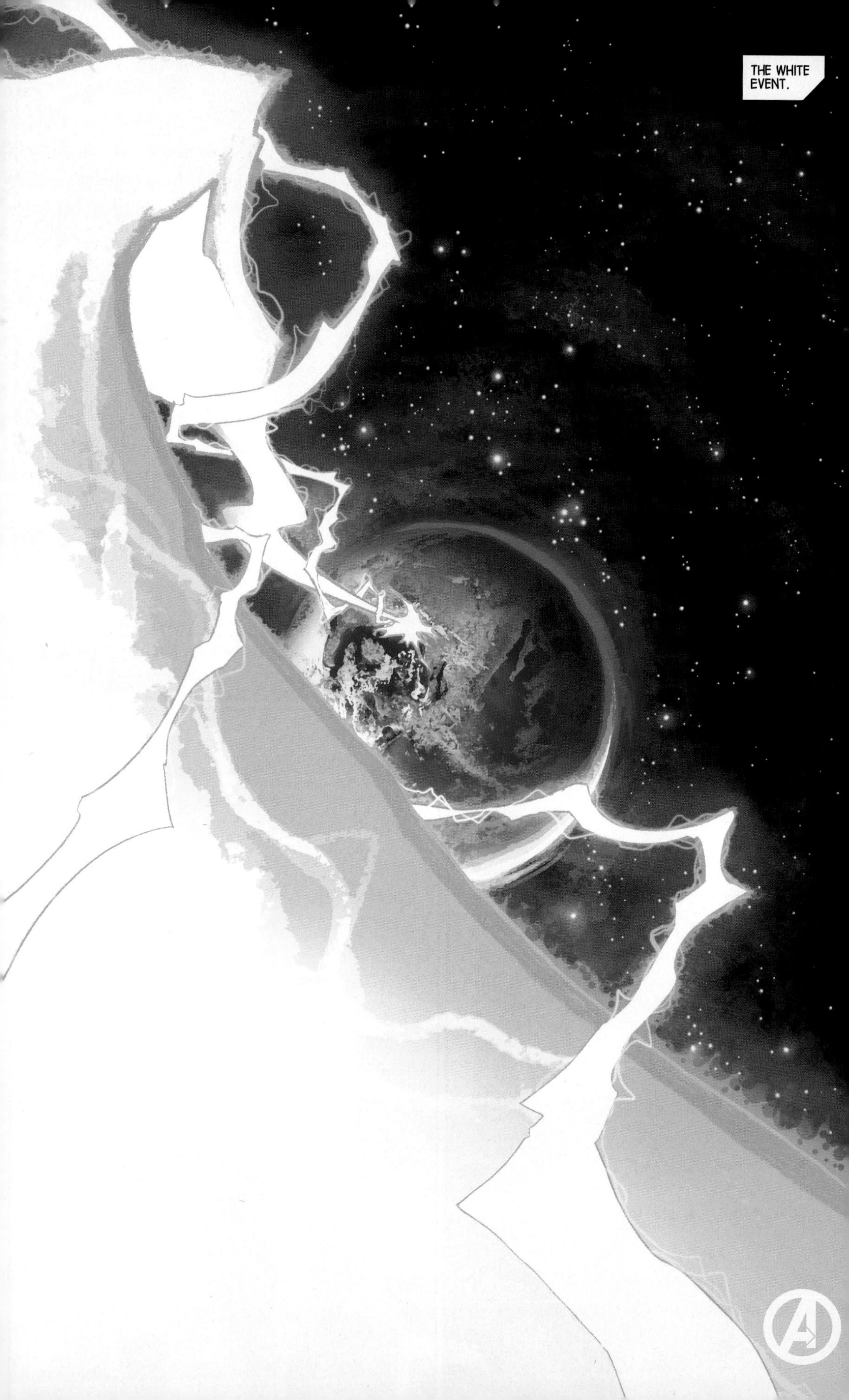
THE WHITE EVENT.

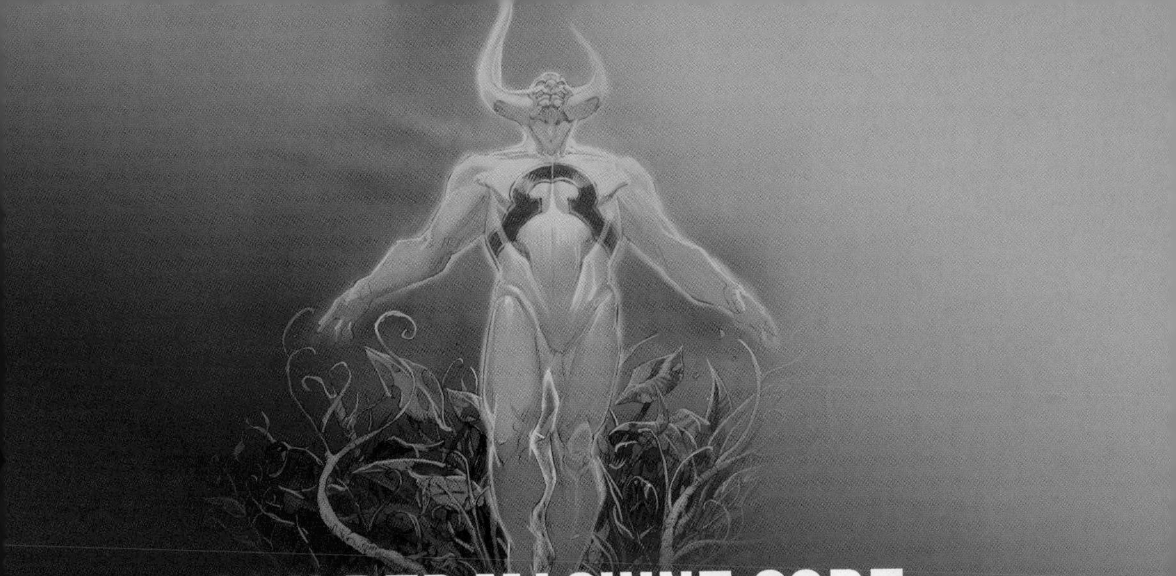

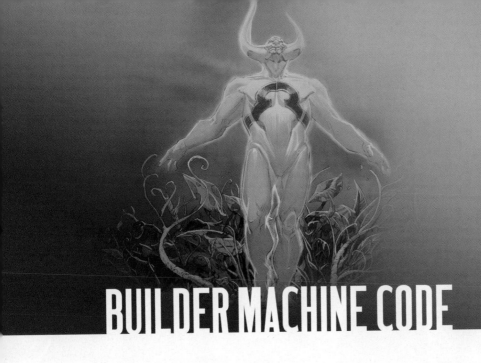

BUILDER MACHINE CODE

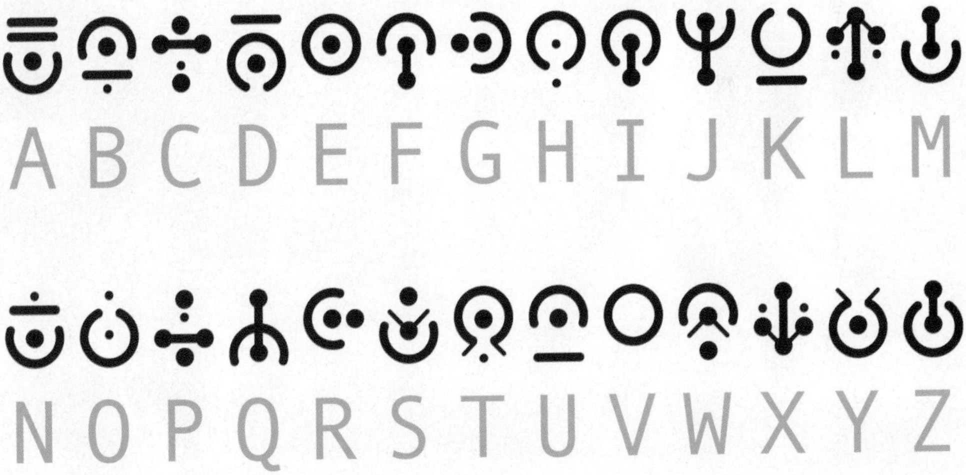
A B C D E F G H I J K L M
N O P Q R S T U V W X Y Z

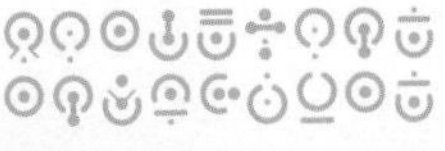

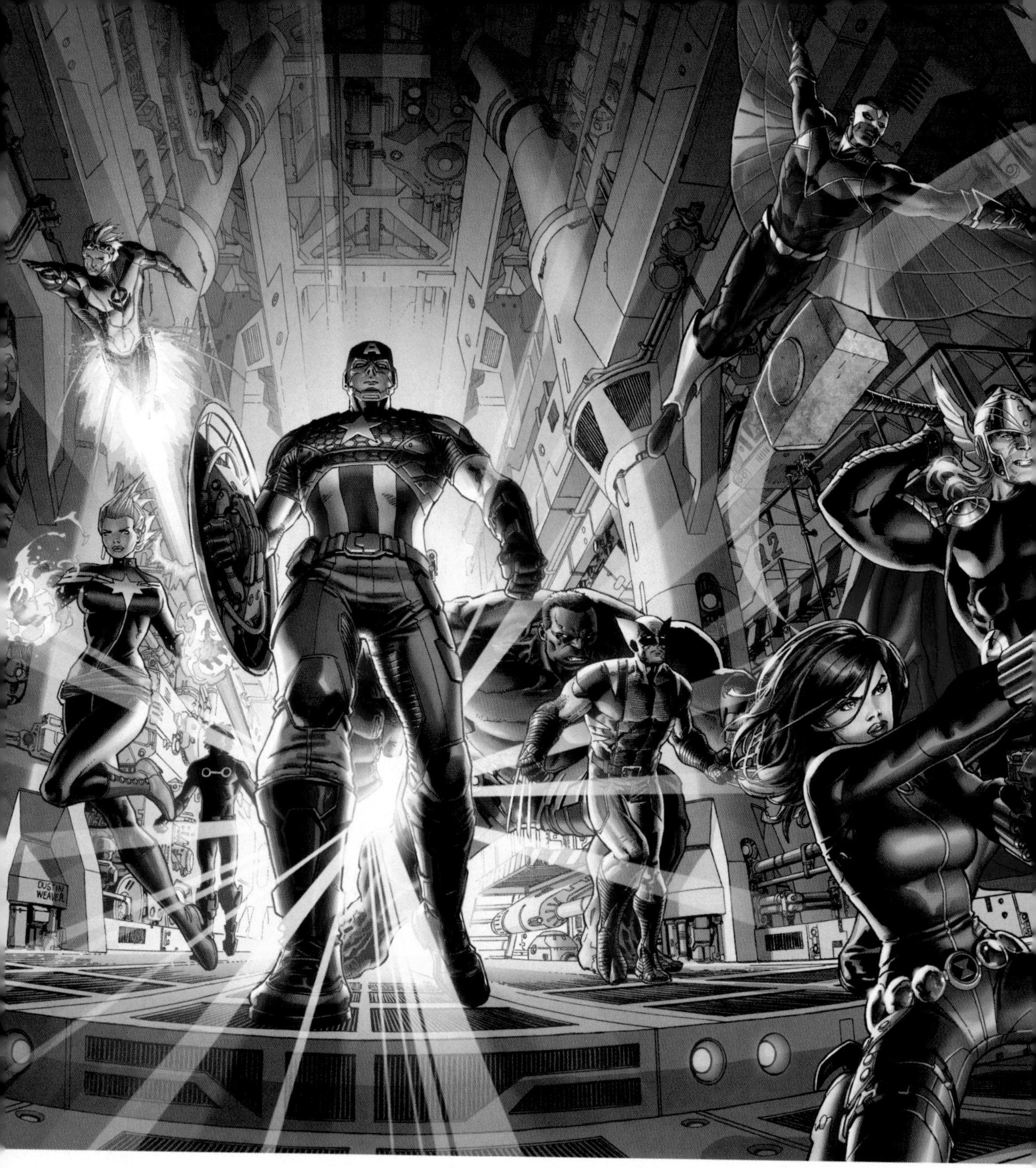
DUSTIN WEAVER

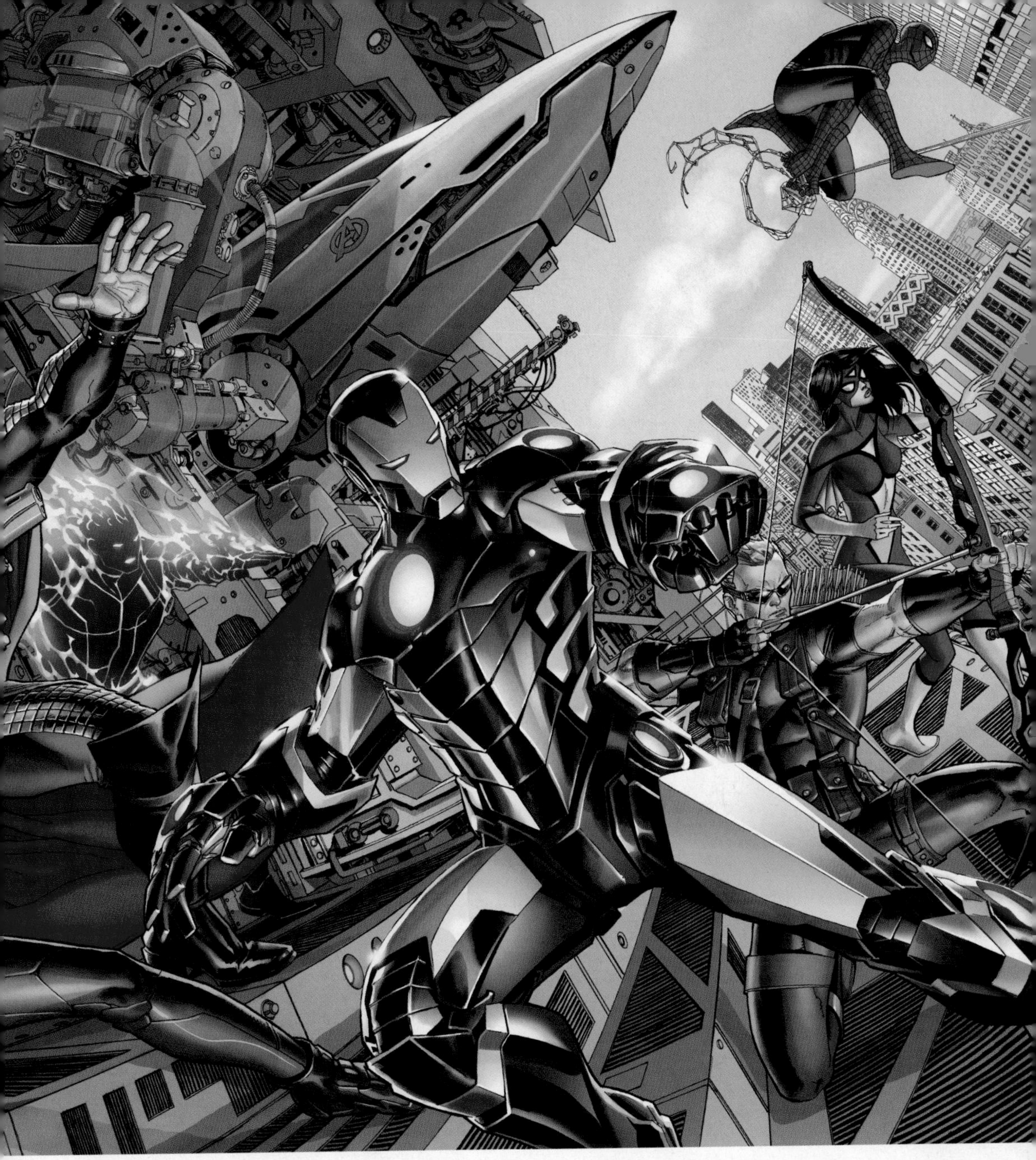

#1-3 COMBINED COVERS

#4

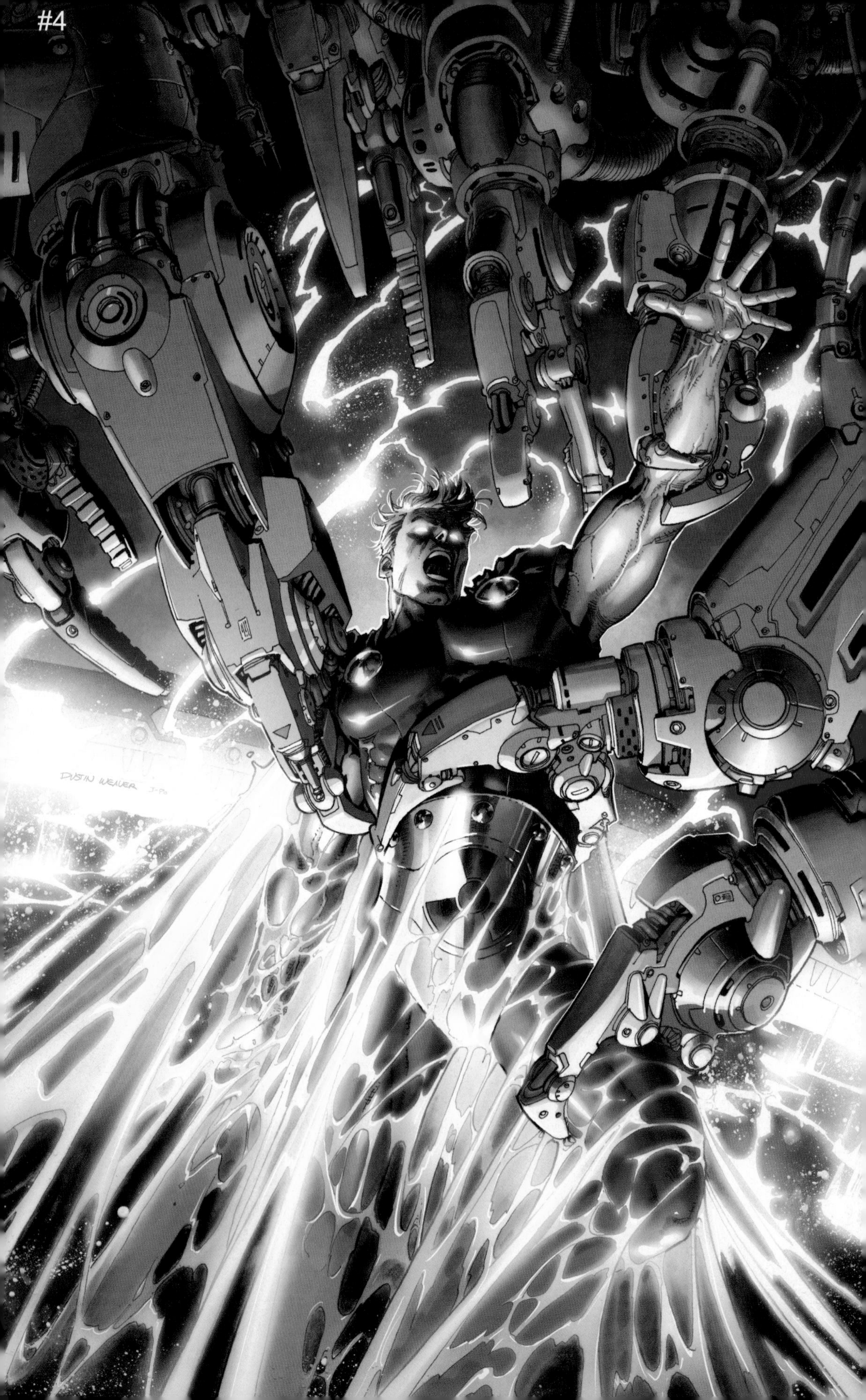
DUSTIN WEAVER J-Po

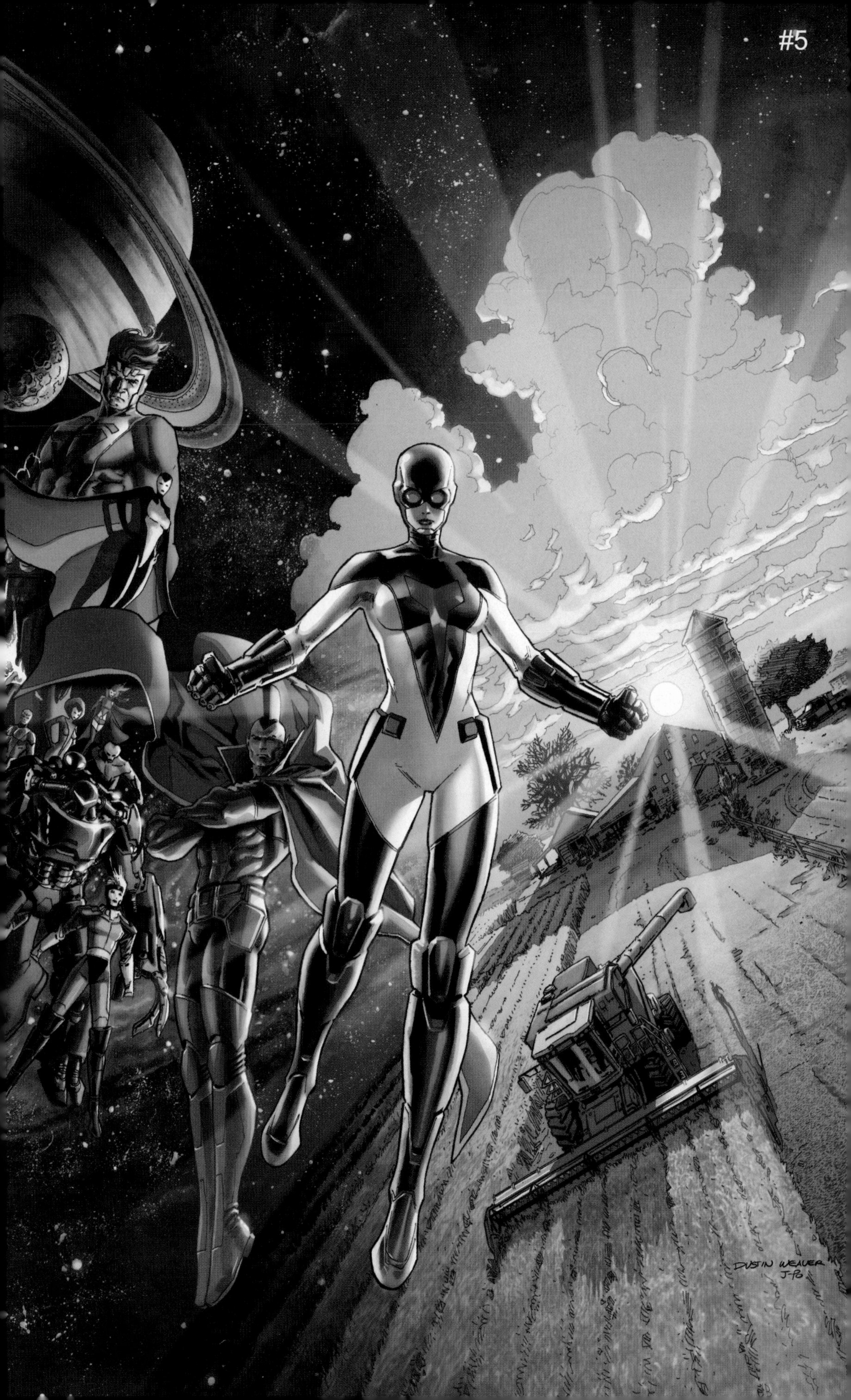
#5
DUSTIN WEAVER
J-Po

#6

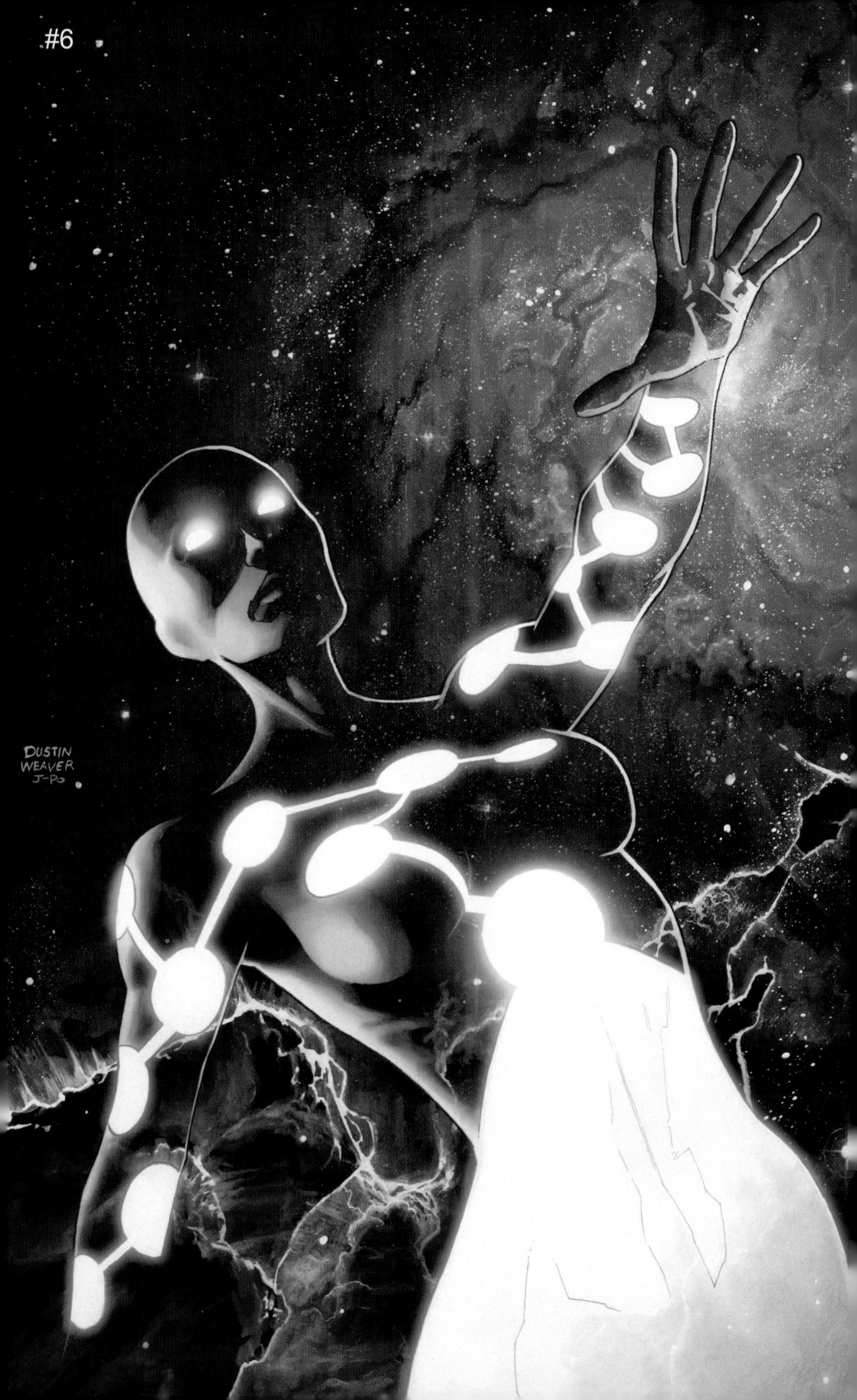
DUSTIN
WEAVER
J-Po

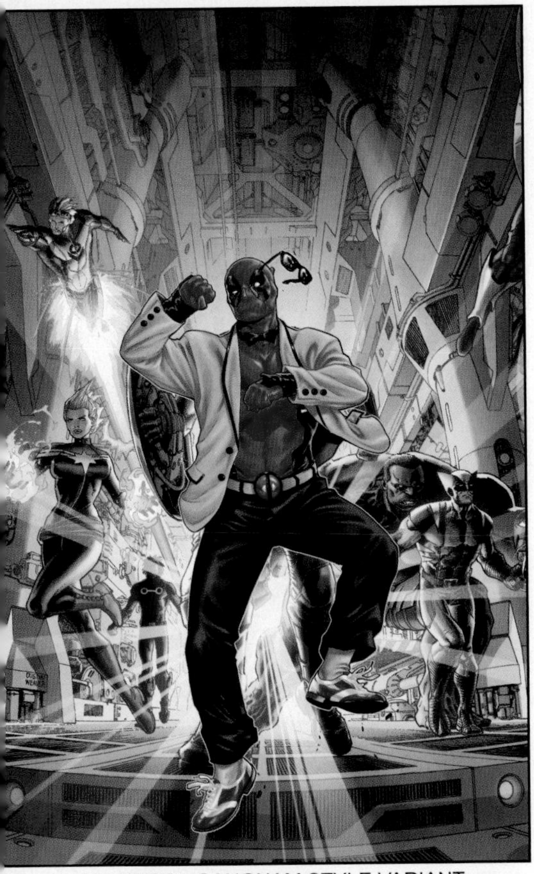

#1 DEADPOOL GANGNAM STYLE VARIANT:
ARK BROOKS WITH **DUSTIN WEAVER & JUSTIN PONSOR**

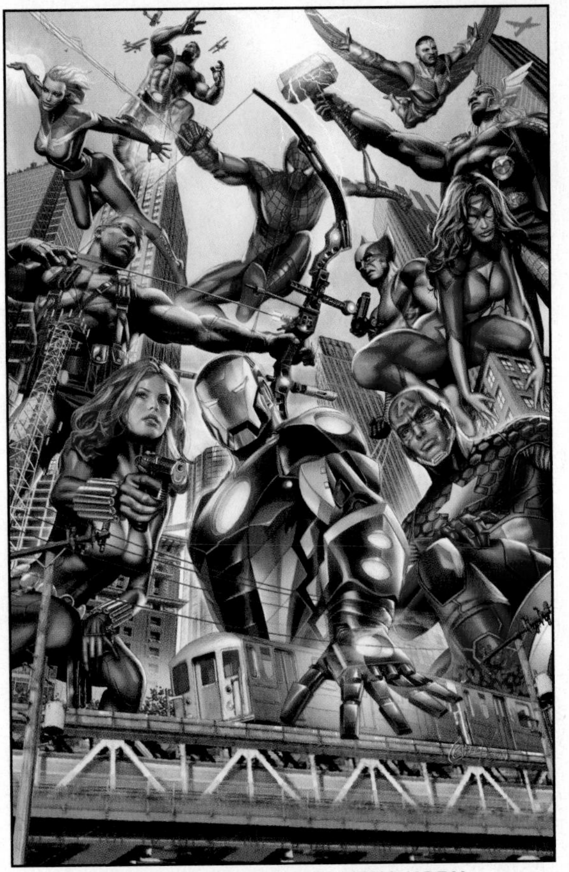

#1 HASTINGS VARIANT: **GREG HORN**

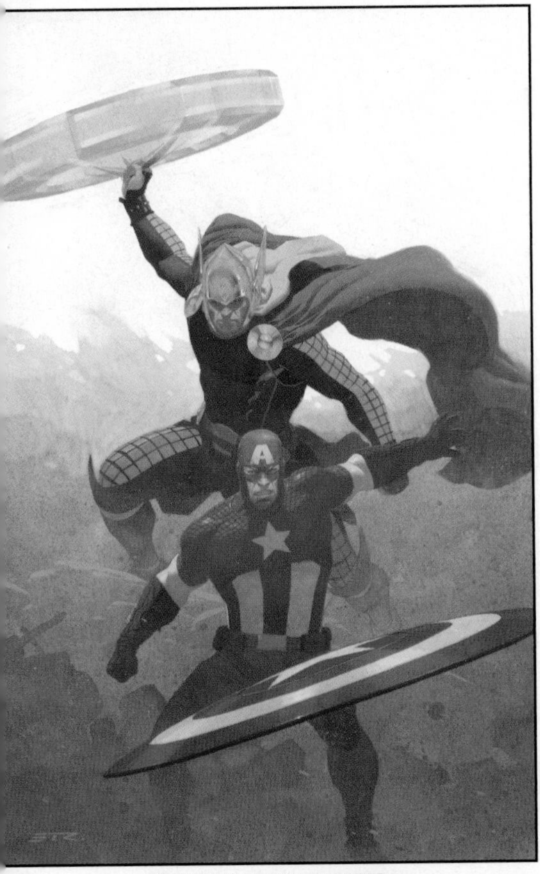

#1 VARIANT: **ESAD RIBIC**

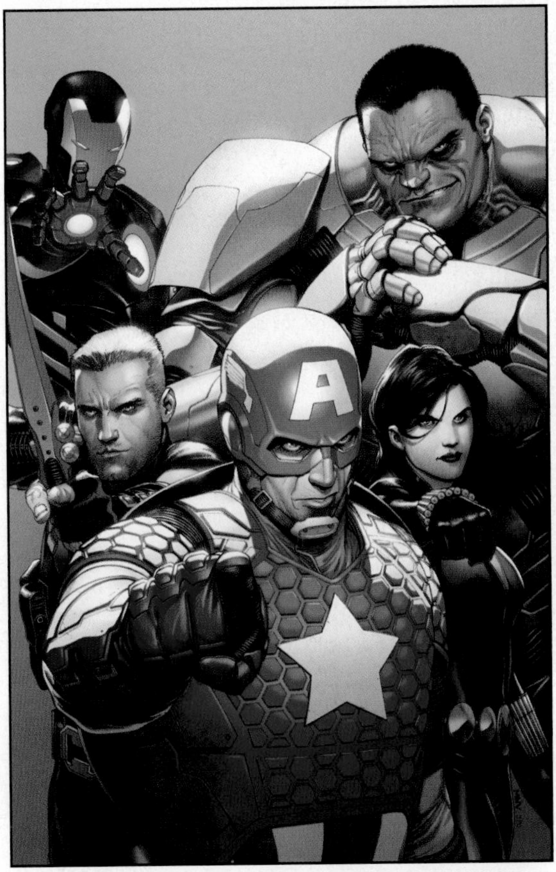

#1 VARIANT: **STEVE McNIVEN & JUSTIN PONSOR**

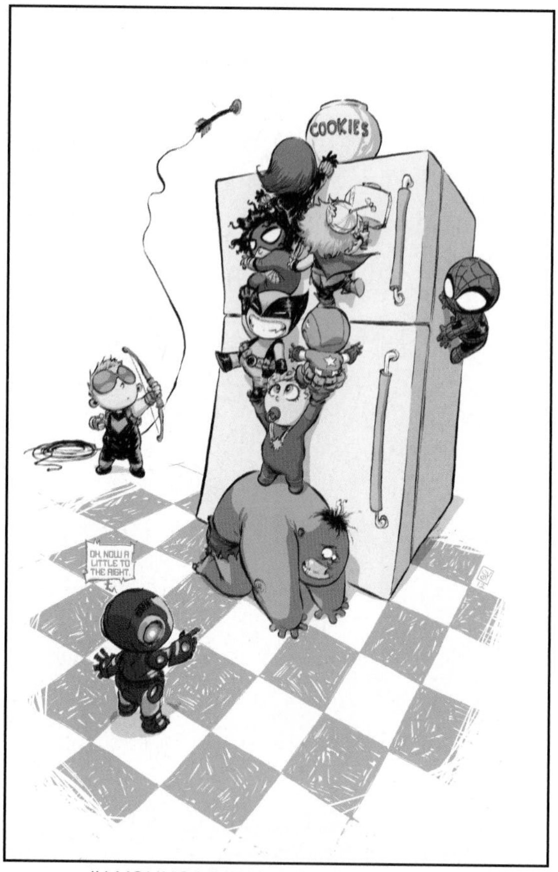
COOKIES
OH, NOW A LITTLE TO THE RIGHT.

#1 YOUNG VARIANT: **SKOTTIE YOUNG**

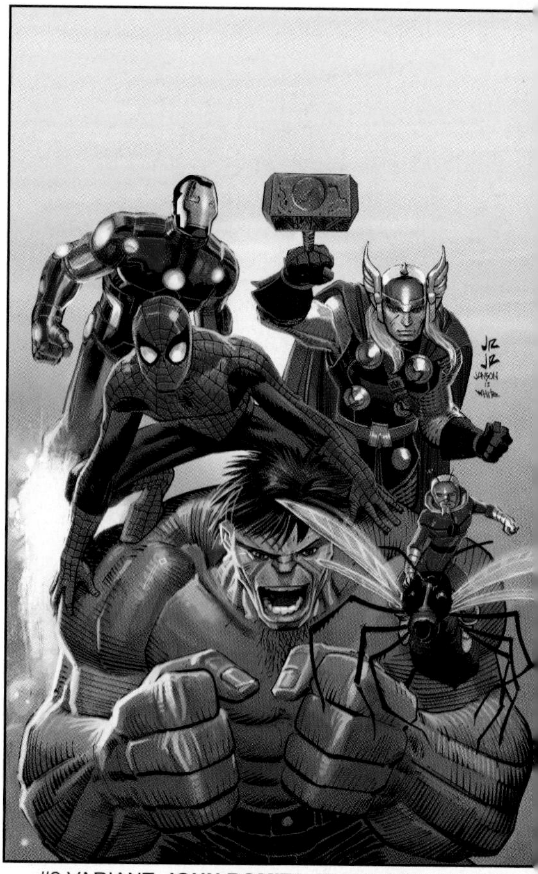

#2 VARIANT: **JOHN ROMITA JR., KLAUS JANSEN & DEAN WHITE**

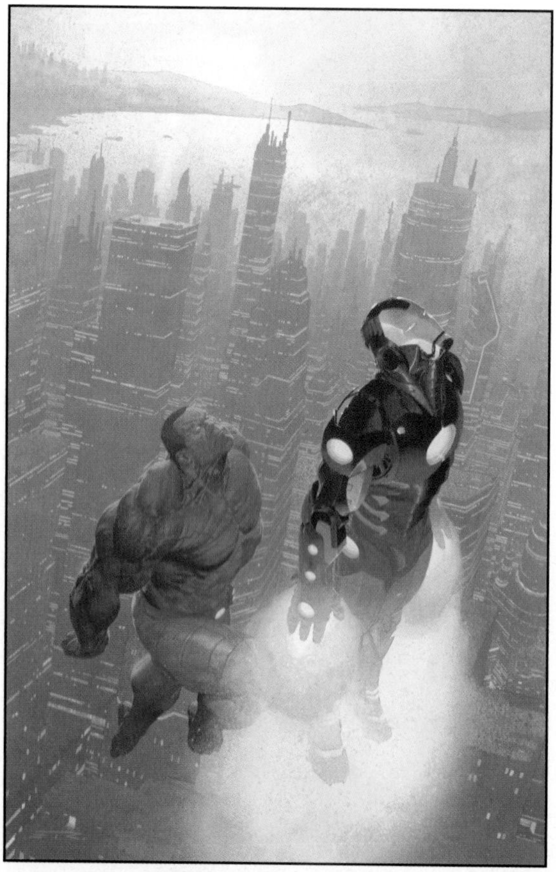

#2 VARIANT: **ESAD RIBIC**

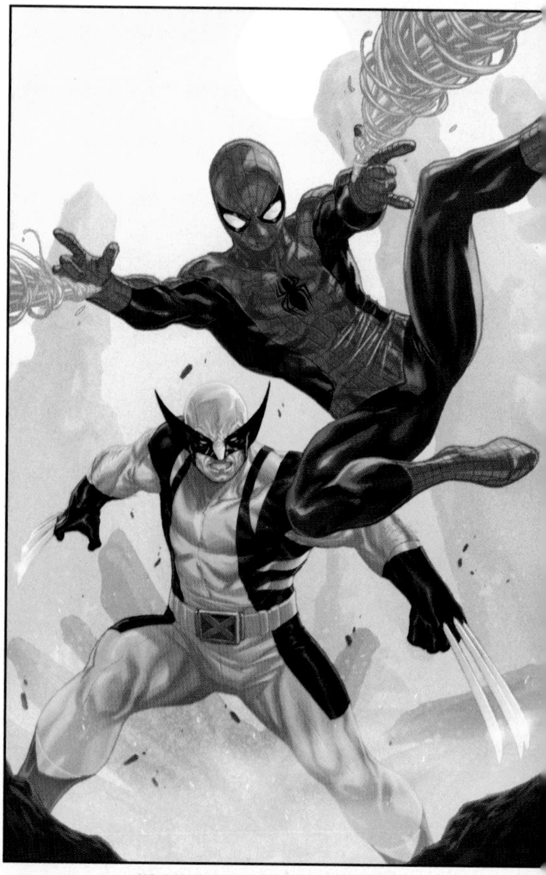

#3 VARIANT: **MARK BROOKS**

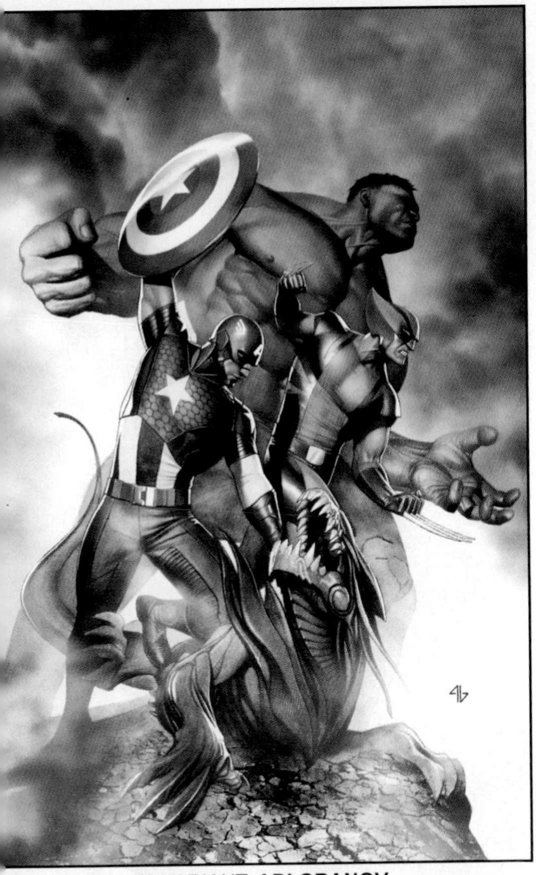

#3 VARIANT: **ADI GRANOV**

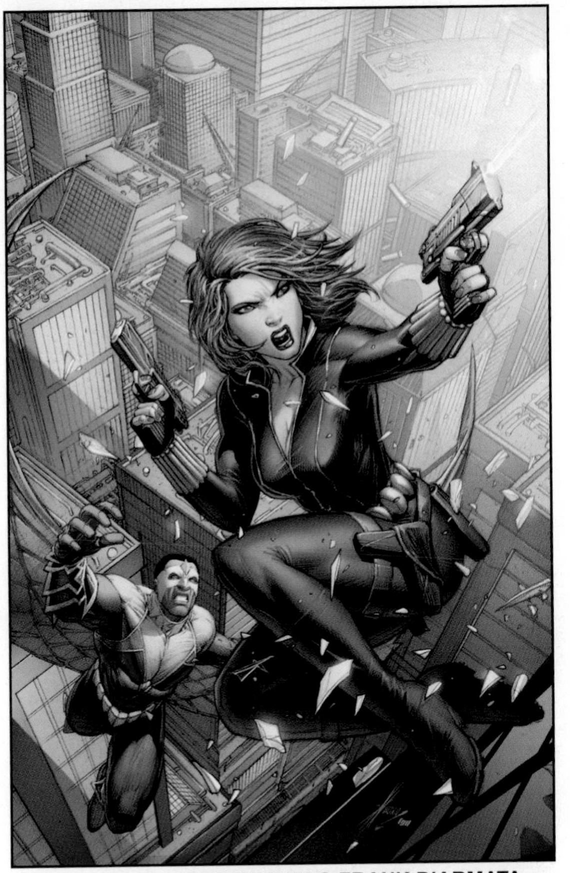

#4 VARIANT: **DALE KEOWN & FRANK D'ARMATA**

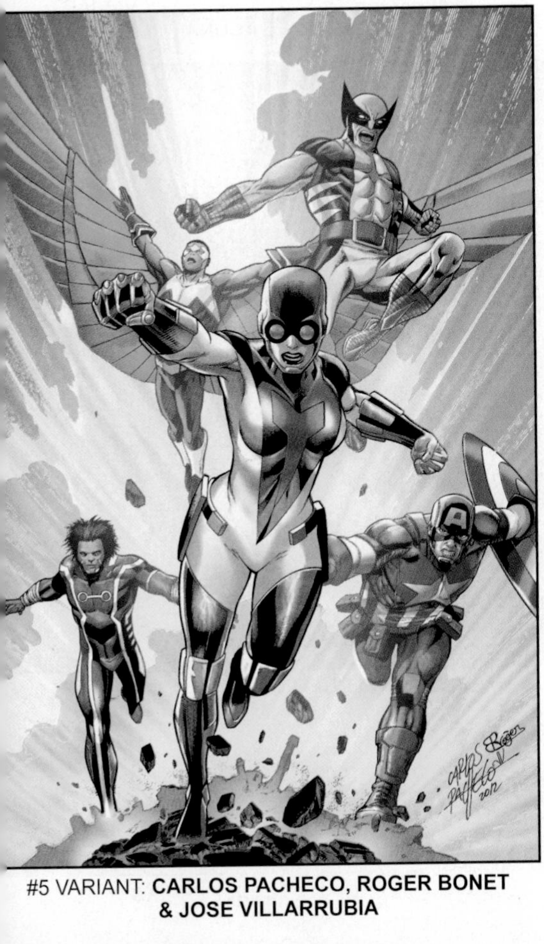

#5 VARIANT: **CARLOS PACHECO, ROGER BONET & JOSE VILLARRUBIA**

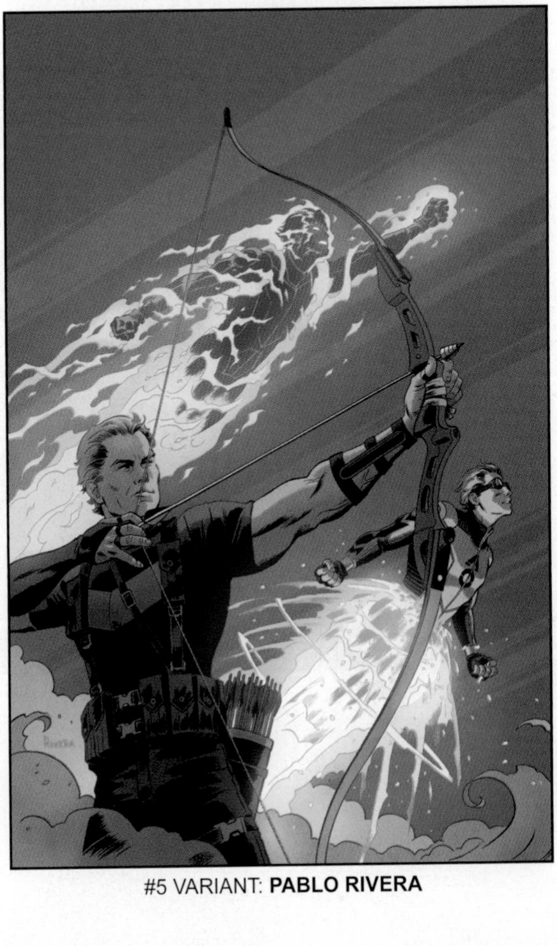

#5 VARIANT: **PABLO RIVERA**

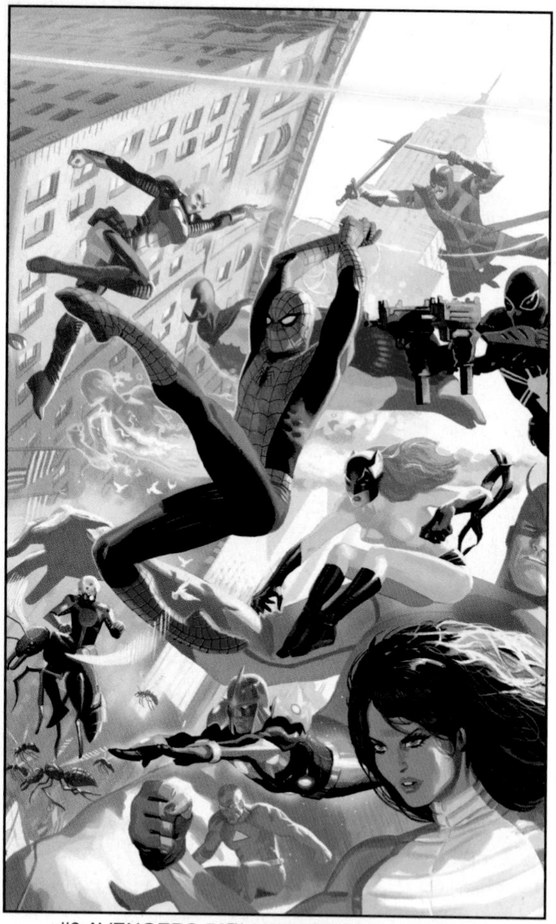

#3 AVENGERS 50TH ANNIVERSARY VARIANT:
DANIEL ACUÑA

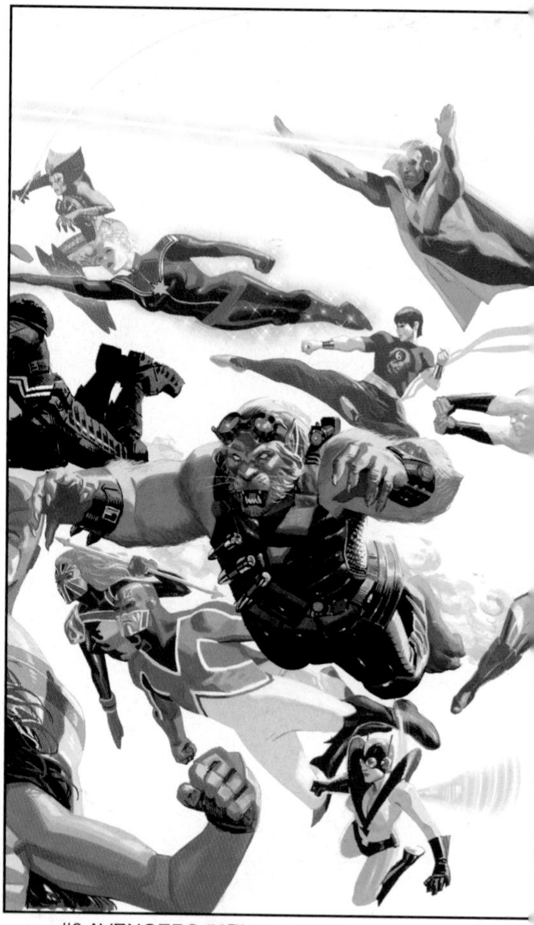

#6 AVENGERS 50TH ANNIVERSARY VARIANT:
DANIEL ACUÑA

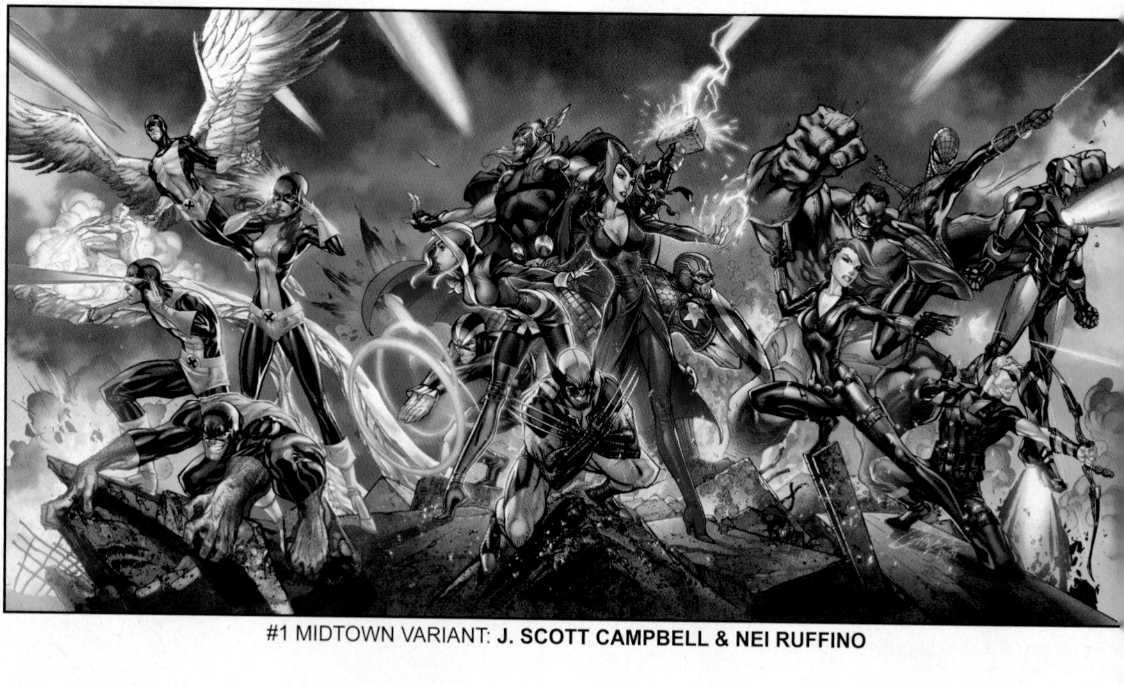

#1 MIDTOWN VARIANT: **J. SCOTT CAMPBELL & NEI RUFFINO**

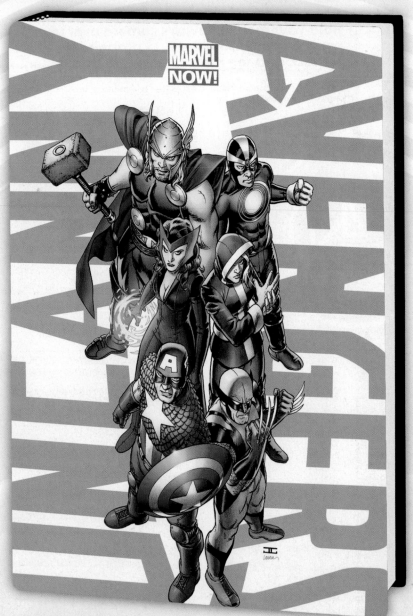

THE FREE *MARVEL AUGMENTED REALITY APP* ENHANCES AND CHANGES THE WAY YOU EXPERIENCE COMICS!

To access the Marvel Augmented Reality App..

- Download the app for free via marvel.com/ARapp
- Launch the app on your camera-enabled Apple iOS® or Android™ device*
- Hold your mobile device's camera over any cover or panel with the **AR** graphic.
- Sit back and see the future of comics in action!

*Available on most camera-enabled Apple iOS® and Android™ devices. Content subject to change and availability.

AR INDEX